Walking, Landscape and Environment

Walking, Landscape and Environment explores walking as a method of research and practice in the humanities and creative arts, emerging from a recent surge of growth in urban and rural walking. This edited collection of essays from leading figures in the field presents an enquiry into, and a critique of, the methods and results of cutting-edge 'walking research'. Walking negotiates the intersections between the human self, place and space, offering a cross-disciplinary collaborative method of research which can be utilised in areas such as ecocriticism, landscape architecture, literature, cultural geography and the visual arts. Bringing together a multitude of perspectives from different disciplines, on topics including health and wellbeing, disability studies, social justice, ecology and gender, this book provides a unique appraisal of the humanist perspective on landscape. In doing so, it challenges Romantic approaches to walking, applying new ideas in contemporary critical thought and alternative perspectives on embodiment and trans-corporeality.

David Borthwick teaches Environmental Humanities at the University of Glasgow's School of Interdisciplinary Studies. Previous publications have centred on ecopoetry, walking and cultural understandings of avian migration. He has also published poetry and non-fiction. His current research uses poetry and non-fiction to examine the depictions of the multivalent nature of place – and the future of place-based thinking.

Pippa Marland is a Leverhulme Early Career Research Fellow based at the University of Leeds, where she is a member of the Environmental Humanities Research Group. Her research project is a study of the representation of farming in modern British nature writing. She has published widely on ecocriticism, ecopoetry and nature writing, and is currently preparing a monograph for publication entitled *Ecocriticism and the Island: Readings from the British-Irish Archipelago* for the Rowman & Littlefield *Rethinking the Island* series.

Anna Stenning is a Wellcome Trust Research Fellow in the Humanities and Social Sciences at Bath Spa University. She has written about nature writing, poetry and disability studies, and she has published both her own poetry and creative non-fiction. Her current research focuses on representations of autistic flourishing, narrativity and eco-anxiety, and she is the author of *Nature, Place and Affect: The Poetic Affinities of Edward Thomas and Robert Frost 1912–1917* for Rowman & Littlefield International. She is also a co-editor, with Nick Chown and Hanna Bertilsdotter-Rosqvist, of Routledge's interdisciplinary collection *Neurodiversity: A New Critical Paradigm*.

Routledge Research in Landscape and Environmental Design
Edited by Terry Clements
Associate Professor, Virginia Tech

Routledge Research in Landscape and Environmental Design is series of academic monographs for scholars working in these disciplines and the overlaps between them. Building on Routledge's history of academic rigour and cutting-edge research, the series contributes to the rapidly expanding literature in all areas of landscape and environmental design.

Walking, Landscape and Environment

Edited by David Borthwick, Pippa Marland and Anna Stenning

Routledge
Taylor & Francis Group

LONDON AND NEW YORK

First published 2020
by Routledge
2 Park Square, Milton Park, Abingdon, Oxon OX14 4RN

and by Routledge
52 Vanderbilt Avenue, New York, NY 10017

Routledge is an imprint of the Taylor & Francis Group, an informa business

British Library Cataloguing in Publication Data
A catalogue record for this book is available from the British Library

Library of Congress Cataloging-in-Publication Data
A catalog record has been requested for this book

ISBN: 9781138630109 (hbk)
ISBN: 9781315209753 (ebk)

Typeset in Sabon
by Swales & Willis, Exeter, Devon, UK

Printed and bound in Great Britain by
TJ International Ltd, Padstow, Cornwall

To the ones who walk with us

Contents

Acknowledgements

We are very grateful to Dr Nick Chown (MSocInd) for his excellent work providing the index for this book. We thank Iain Biggs for his generous willingness to allow us to use his artwork on the cover; Dawn Walton and Testament for agreeing to be interviewed, for their enlightening answers, and for the warm welcome to Sheffield; colleagues who read and commented on this manuscript at various stages; all of the authors of the essays contained in *Walking, Landscape and Environment*, whose exceptional creativity and scholarship have been an inspiration to the editors throughout the process of bringing the collection together; the participants of the walking symposium held by David Borthwick and Anna Stenning at the Solway Centre for Environment and Culture in 2014, which helped to spark some of the thinking behind this volume – these include Linda Cracknell, Jean Langhorne and Margaret Elphinstone, and two of the contributors to this book: Dee Heddon and Gerry Loose; Berghahn Books for their willingness to allow us develop an idea from our special 2017 walking edition of their journal *Critical Survey*, 'One Green Field'; Grace Harrison and her colleagues at Routledge for their ongoing guidance in the preparation of this book; and lastly, our families, friends and animal companions for their love and support, and for 'walking with us' in all of the many ways that phrase might be interpreted.

Contributors

Steve Benford is a Professor in the Mixed Reality Laboratory at the University of Nottingham, where he directs the Horizon Centre or Doctoral Training and the Smart Products research beacon. He has worked in the area of human–computer interaction for over twenty years, collaborating with artists to help create, tour and study interactive artworks. He previously held an EPSRC Dream Fellowship, has been a Visiting Professor at the BBC and was elected to the CHI Academy in 2012.

Mike Collier, University of Sunderland, is a lecturer, writer, curator and artist. He studied Fine Art at Goldsmiths College, London. Much of his work is based around walking – through the city, the countryside and urban edgelands. His work pays close attention to the environment through which he walks and is usually place-specific. He integrates image and text, often drawing on the poetic qualities of colloquial names for places, plants and birds. He has shown in the UK and abroad, and his work is in a number of public and private collections. In 2010 he co-founded WALK (Walking, Art, Landskip and Knowledge), a research centre at the University of Sunderland which looks at the way we creatively engage with the world as we walk through it.

Christos Galanis is a doctoral candidate in Human Geography at the University of Edinburgh. He is the author of the forthcoming book *Mountain Threnody: Walking as Freedom and Belonging among Hillwalkers and Homecomers in the Highlands of Scotland*. He has a Masters in Fine Art in Art and Ecology from the University of New Mexico, where his thesis project *Walking with Donkeys: Rituals of Progress and Domestication* documented inter-species research collaboration and equine–human relations.

Terry Gifford was for 21 years Director of the annual *International Festival of Mountaineering Literature*. A former Chair of the Mountain Heritage Trust, he is the author of *The Joy of Climbing* (2004) and his eighth collection of poetry, *A Feast of Fools* (2018). A second edition of his work *Pastoral* was published in 2019. He is attached to Bath Spa University's Centre for Environmental Humanities.

Amy Hamilton is Professor of English at Northern Michigan University, where she teaches classes on Indigenous American literatures, ecocriticism and environmental literature, and early American literature. She is the author of *Peregrinations: Walking in American Literature* (2018) and co-editor with Tom J. Hillard of *Before the West was West: Critical Essays on Pre-1800 Literature of the American Frontiers* (2014).

Deirdre Heddon holds the James Arnott Chair in Drama at the University of Glasgow. She is the author of many monographs, articles and essays, including *Autobiography and Performance* (2008), and has co-edited a number of collections, including, most recently, *It's All Allowed: The Performances of Adrian Howells* (2016). She is currently working on *Performing Forests*, a monograph for *Performing Landscapes*, a new series for which she is co-editor with Sally Mackey.

Rachel Jacobs is an environmentally engaged digital artist, games designer and Research Associate at the University of Nottingham. Her award-winning work has toured nationally and internationally, and she publishes and presents regularly in academic and non-academic contexts. She co-founded the artist-led collective Active Ingredient in 1996 and the commercial games firm Mudlark Production Company in 2007, and completed a PhD in Computer Science in 2014.

Carl Lavery is Professor of Theatre and Performance at the University of Glasgow. He has authored numerous books and articles on walking, ecology and ruins. He has also made performances from walking. His most recent publication is *What Can Theatre Do? Performance and Ecology* (2018). He is currently working on a special issue of *Performance Research* on an expanded notion of 'drifting'.

Alison Lloyd has documented elements of her life through a passage of movement incorporating walking and dancing since 1976. Recent activity includes a residency at Outlandia in Glen Nevis, Scotland in 2013; a solo exhibition at TG Gallery, Nottingham in 2014 and Winch Gallery, Southend in 2017; and an Instagram Takeover of Edgework in 2018. She is a PhD Research Scholar at Loughborough University, School of the Arts, English and Drama.

Gerry Loose is a poet and artist who works primarily with subjects from the natural world, most specifically with plants, as well as the world of geo-politics. His work is found inscribed and created in parks, botanic gardens and in natural landscapes, as well as in galleries and on the page. His awards include a Robert Louis Stevenson Fellowship, a Creative Scotland Award, a Kone Foundation Award and a Hermann Kesten Fellowship. Walking informs the way he works and is sometimes the subject of his work.

Garry MacKenzie has a PhD in contemporary poetry from the University of St Andrews. He has published a book, *Scotland: A Literary Guide for*

Travellers (2016), and several articles on contemporary literature and the environment. In 2010 he was awarded a Scottish Book Trust New Writer Award, and his poetry has been published in journals including *The Compass Magazine, Dark Mountain, The Scores* and Corbel Stone Press's *Contemporary Poetry Series.*

Misha Myers is a Senior Lecturer and Course Director of Creative Arts at Deakin University, Melbourne, Australia. Her practice-based research is generally collaborative in process, drawing in culturally diverse participants to work together towards social change through located and cross-platform arts-based enquiry, often enabled by digital technologies. She is the author of many articles, chapters and essays on walking aesthetics, locative media and digital performance.

Phil Smith is a performance-maker, writer and academic researcher specialising in making work around walking, site-specificity and 'mythogeographies'. He is a core member of the site-based arts collective Wrights & Sites, which published *The Architect-walker* in 2018. He is presently developing a 'common dance for threatened subjectivities' with choreographer Melanie Kloetzel of Calgary University and working with artist Helen Billinghurst as part of Crab & Bee, recently creating the *Plymouth Labyrinth* exhibition at RAAY Gallery (2019). His publications include *Making Site-specific Theatre and Performance* (2019), *Anywhere* (2017), *Walking's New Movement* (2015), *On Walking* and *Enchanted Things* (2014), *Mythogeography* (2010) and *Guidebook for an Armchair Pilgrimage* (forthcoming) with Tony Whitehead and John Schott. He is an Associate Professor (Reader) at Plymouth University.

Testament is an acclaimed rapper, playwright and world record-holding beatboxer. Born in London to an English father and a Ghanaian mother, his work often deals with identity, community and the search for spirituality. He now resides in West Yorkshire. He is the author of *Black Men Walking* (2018).

Judith Tucker is an artist and academic. Her work explores the meeting of social history, personal memory and geography; it investigates their relationship through drawing, painting and scholarly writing. As well as working in her studio, she is Senior Lecturer in the School of Design at the University of Leeds. She has exhibited widely both in the UK and abroad. Recent exhibition venues include London, Sheffield, Cambridge and many other regional galleries throughout the UK, and further afield in Gdansk, Poland, Brno, Czech Republic, Vienna, Austria, Minneapolis and Virginia in the USA and Yantai, Nanjing and Tianjin in China. In 2018 she will be one of eight UK artists exhibiting in the *Yantai Landscape Biennale* in China. She is Co-convener of the LAND2 and Mapping Spectral Traces networks and is part of Contemporary British Painting, a platform for contemporary painting in the UK. She also writes academic essays which can be found in academic journals and in books published by Rodopi, Macmillan, Manchester University Press, Intellect and Gunter Narr Verlag, Tübingen.

Dawn Walton is founder, former Artistic Director and CEO of Eclipse, the UK's principal Black-led production company. With Eclipse, Dawn developed Revolution Mix, the largest ever delivery of new Black British productions for stage screen and radio, and Slate: Black. Arts. World, which enables Black independent artists based in the North of England develop sustainable models of production. *Black Men Walking* (2018) was the first Revolution Mix production.

Introduction

Anna Stenning and Pippa Marland

I believe that most industrial-zone human beings need to rethink time, space and their own bodies before they will be equipped to be as urbane and as pedestrian (or at least non-motorized) as their predecessors.

(Rebecca Solnit, 'Still walking', *Wanderlust*)

What follows in *Walking, Landscape and Environment* is our first step at mapping an area of enquiry: the relationship between walking and the arts at a particular point in time. We wanted to discover how the field of walking literature and art responds to the contemporary world as the 21st century reaches the end of its second decade. This led us to consider in what way walking can serve as a methodology for creative writing, research and performance in response to the social and natural worlds of the Anthropocene. Finally, we hoped to discover the key questions that currently engage artists, writers and researchers in this field, and to highlight the recent developments in their work that point to new directions in walking studies.

The background to this enquiry is the critical theory known as ecocriticism, which began in earnest in the 1990s, with a focus on 'green' readings of Romanticism and nature writing on both sides of the Atlantic. As an interdisciplinary study of the many ways that culture informs our understanding of, and relationship to, the non-human environment, ecocriticism followed on from other forms of humanistic cultural critique that sought to understand the altered world that we found ourselves in as a result of globalization and new forms of human-produced risk. One of these areas of critique was the humanistic turn in geography which defined place and related ideas as the products of human activities and relations.[1] Practitioners across these fields had one thing in common: a shared interest in walking as both a creative and investigative practice.

These early works across the humanities have subsequently been charged by environmentalists with anthropocentrism and under-theorization, particularly in failing to sufficiently question the basis of the concepts of 'nature' and 'environment' upon which so much of the work was formed. Another perceived weakness of ecocritical treatments of place was their tendency to focus on local places in the West, to the exclusion of the global South and the networks of power that have resulted in an unequal distribution of environmental burden among minority and disenfranchised groups.[2] This critique coincided with literary theorists who sought in anthropology and social justice movements a more encompassing idea of place attachment that accounted for differential experiences according to both geographic location and social status.[3] There has been a similar re-examination of the concept of 'landscape', largely emanating from cultural geography, with a focus on dynamic cultural, ecological and material processes, rather than static features such as artefacts. This parallels the movement within literary criticism towards understanding affective – as opposed to cognitive or picturesque – landscapes. This asks us to consider the ways in which, according to Christine Berberich, Neil Campbell and Robert Hudson, 'we feel, sense, know, cherish, memorise, imagine, dream, desire or even fear landscape'.[4]

Given our expertise and backgrounds as scholars of mainly British and American literature and art, we decided to focus on the ways that walking might serve as a method of approaching questions about landscape and environment. But since we are also ecocritics, and motivated to engage with the broader issues facing environmentally minded writers and artists (and bearing in mind these extensions and politicizations of the concepts of nature, environment, landscape and place), we were motivated by the question, 'Can walking by Western artists, researchers and writers still be a transgressive act?'

According to Rebecca Solnit in her new preface to the influential *Wanderlust: A History of Walking* (2014), walking is more relevant now than ever because it is a means of bringing people together to protest undemocratic institutions, because it provides an alternative to carbon-based modes of transportation, because it is free, because it reminds us of the pleasure we may find (if we are lucky) in our own embodiment, and finally, because it celebrates 'the time inbetween' more economically productive activities which might otherwise be seen as wasted.[5] While the consequences of global networks of power maintained by institutions of finance, governance and industry significantly favour those living in the North and Western Hemisphere, drawing attention to their negative effects, including their uneven distribution along lines of location, age, race, gender, bodily capacity and class, may help to introduce practices that are disruptive of them. Climate change will amplify both the inequalities and the perceived harms of a world that is radically unequal in terms of access to both the material and immaterial benefits of being human. In the months we have been preparing this collection for publication, we have witnessed an extraordinary surge in walking demonstrations in support of the environment, from the UK-focused *Peoples Manifesto for Wildlife*, delivered to Westminster by a band of 10,000 marchers in September 2018, to the ongoing Youth Climate Strikes in which schoolchildren in over 100 countries around the world have been taking to the streets to protest their governments' failure to tackle climate change, to the growing global Extinction Rebellion, which, during

April 2019, staged street-based demonstrations from 'Auckland to Accra, Mexico City to Vancouver'.[6] On 1 May 2019 the UK Government approved a motion to declare an environment and climate emergency, one of the key demands of the Extinction Rebellion, suggesting that Solnit is right about the ongoing potential of walking as an effective mode of protest.[7]

Through its celebration of public spaces, urban and otherwise, peripheral forms of knowledge and imagination, *Wanderlust* serves as a 'polemic against industrialization, privatization of open lands, the oppression and confinement of women, suburbia, the disembodiment of everyday life and a few other such things'.[8] In this way, it chimes with phenomenological ecocriticism, which emphasizes that it is through our senses, rather than our intellects, that we interact with the environment. However, the re-embodiment that Solnit and others invoke is not without critics, particularly those who believe it retains the subject-object dualism of Romantic attitudes to nature, the '"embedded and embodied ideology" [. . .] that we exist in a "lifeworld"' that is somehow apart from us.[9] This ideology causes us to 'falsely hold rationality to be the problem, rather than the social forms in which reason emerged'.[10] According to Timothy Morton and others, ecocritical scholarship should not reject the roles of reason and language, since these are no less 'natural' than intuition or sensory perception: thinking so perpetuates the dualism that places humans in a unique category above all forms of life.

Those who are sympathetic to both Solnit's valuation of walking and Morton's 'ecological thought' can find recourse in deep engagements with materialist philosophy, in which human forms of rationality and subjectivity coexist with a thoroughly materialist cosmology. This is the position of a number of the writers in *Walking, Landscape and Environment*, who show us that in walking we become aware of our complex entanglement with material, social and cultural processes that extend well beyond our awareness and which have altered with the changes brought about by the Great Acceleration (the point at which anthropogenic environmental effects began to grow significantly, often dated as beginning in 1945 at the end of the Second World War).[11] This collection brings together the most diverse forms and strands of research, informed by different perspectives, but converging on related questions and ideas. Many of our authors are motivated by social and environmental issues, all of them are concerned with aesthetics and new ways of thinking about walking. Some are looking to define the development of the walking arts from a much longer temporal and geographic perspective, while others focus on the role that walking has played in a particular moment in space and time.

It is difficult to separate the themes of this book into neat categories relating to the genres and forms it addresses: poetry, nature writing, performance art, digitally mediated walking, pilgrimage, activism, social justice, the visual arts, psychogeography and art walking. Writing about walking, like the act of walking itself, informs new ways of looking at the world, and many of these essays and their originating projects are based on cross-disciplinary partnerships and collaborations between writers and artists with diverse areas of expertise. The collection provides evidence that walking and conversations about walking can create a literal and metaphoric space outside of the most environmentally destructive social forms: the individualism, privatization and hyperspecialism that are perpetuated by corporate academia and dominate contemporary society. Yet, as Phil Smith argues in relation to psychogeography's practice of the *dérive* in Chapter 13 of this collection:

> If there is always a hint of resistance in the anachronism of walking, then, equally, there are also individuals and organisations ready to monetise alternative walking practices. More importantly, the dominance of health recreational walking (often bookended by car rides) almost entirely swamps resistant walking practices in the more general discourses around walking.

This book seeks to intervene in more general discourses around walking, particularly within the humanities. In recognition of the essays' own resistance to division along the lines of discipline, we have instead grouped them together into three broadly themed parts. In the first, entitled 'Walking in: lines, contours, pilgrimages', the authors present engagements with and deviations (or detours) from 'traditional' categories of culture and walking, including poetry, public art and art walking, photography, and pilgrimage memoir. Our second part, 'Walking with: people, places, politics', continues some of the more difficult questions raised in the first part, addressing the neglect of cultural walking practices by particular groups, and walking practices that are themselves problematic within broader and environmental movements. These essays also draw out the unequal sense of freedom to walk – a consideration of the restrictions on walking relating to class, gender, and ethnicity permeates these essays – while at the same time reflecting on the power of collective walking to renegotiate traumatic histories and erasures and to effect forms of renewal and restoration. Finally, the third part, 'Walking on: routes, directions, steps', considers the state of our current knowledge about innovative creative and critical practices that point to the future of the walking arts and related cultural critique, foregrounding new directions in psychogeography and the digital arts, proposing new Anthropocene frames for existing traditions of walking, and challenging ableist notions of walking literature.

Part I begins with Gerry Loose's creative piece 'Walking in (900 questions concerning walking)', which sets the scene perfectly for the book's scope of enquiry and prepares us for the different perspectives that emerge in the chapters that follow. Loose provocatively turns our attention to the 'why's and where's' of walking – 'Are we too busy to walk? If so, why do we teach our children to walk?' He highlights the connection between walking and thinking, and acknowledges the 'unsung walkers' as well as the other-than-on-foot walking of 'those of us who, for whatever reason, cannot walk'. He also delicately reminds us of the non-human world, asking, 'Why does that hare cross my path just here? Why does the purple thistle grow?' In Chapter 2, 'Lines, walks and getting lost: contemporary poetry and walking', Garry MacKenzie considers the 'walk poems' of W.S. Graham, Susan Stewart and Thomas A. Clark. They are poets, MacKenzie suggests, who use walking 'to close the gap between poem and world'. His chapter demonstrates the flexibility of walking as analogue for other processes such as composing and/or reading a poem, all of which resist being pinned to one meaning or one interpretation: 'For individual poems and individual walks,' MacKenzie writes, 'their meaning is their happening.' Alison Lloyd's photo essay 'Contouring alone and with a companion in the Dark Peak, Derbyshire between September 2014 and November 2017' in Chapter 3 draws attention to the 'happening' of her photographs, emphasizing the embodiment of the walker, the paraphernalia of walking equipment and the technological means by which the images are captured. Cumulatively, these features function as a means of productive estrangement that, like the walk poems in Mackenzie's chapter, generate searching questions about the relationship between the walking self and the terrain one walks through. *Walking, Landscape and Environment* has, sometimes by design and sometimes through pure serendipity, become the site of dialogue and cross-referencing between authors; Judith Tucker's Chapter 10 in Part II features an insightful reading of Lloyd's practice.

Carl Lavery's Chapter 4, 'Walking and theatricality: an experiment in weathered thinking (*kairos*)', also revolves around the paradox that while walking produces a privileged intimacy with particular places, that intimacy never resolves into something finished and substantial. He proposes a new ecological theory of walking constructed around a 'percolating constellation of concepts – *kairos*, intimacy, atmosphere, weather and theatricality' – looking especially at moments of revelation experienced through walking. Significantly, Lavery argues that 'theatricality', more than performance *per se*, can be a means of usefully 'undoing' the pedestrian subject and opening them to a series of 'incorporeal thoughts, feelings and becomings'. He then applies these insights in an evocative, peripatetic and longitudinal account of Minty Donald, Nick Millar and Neil McGuire's Glasgow-based public artwork *THEN/NOW*. Part I ends with Chapter 5, Mike Collier's polyvocal essay on the notion of 'conversive pilgrimage', a practice that entails collaborative walking with other humans and a kind of heightened attentiveness to, and honouring of, the non-human world. The latter is expressed through Collier's evocative 'found poems', which consist of lists naming all the flora and fauna seen and heard on the walks. Collier asserts that 'pilgrimage is not about affirmation – that is, confirming long-held imaginings about a place, space or faith. It is about discovery'. This conversive, discovery-oriented approach prepares us very effectively for the move into Part II, with its accounts of group walking.

Though very few of the essays in the collection feature solitary walkers, those in Part II stand out as involving collaborative walking practices. This is not to say, however, that group walking always counts as a form of self-discovery or communal recreation: it can also invoke the history of forced relocations and imperialistic conquest.[12] In Chapter 6, '"This world that walks": cultural destruction, cultural renewal, and social justice on the trails of North American Indigenous removal', Amy Hamilton remembers the thousands of walkers who perished as a result of the 19th-century Indian Removal Act, and describes the series of marches, called *Nihígaal bee Iiná*, undertaken in 2015 by the Diné of the Navajo Nation, commemorating the 150th anniversary of the removal trail their ancestors were forced to walk. For Hamilton, these marches that retrace paths walked in abject circumstances, while acknowledging the historical shattering of communities, can also been seen to effect forms of renewal, providing 'a path back to self-determination and cultural coherence'. Retelling the stories of forced or suppressed movement in poetry and literature by indigenous or marginalized writers can also develop cultural and individual resilience, a process Hamilton brings out in the second part of her essay, which explores work by Diné poet Luci Tapahonso, Chicaza writer Linda Hogan and Cherokee novelist Diane Glancy. In Chapter 7, 'The trouble with Munro bagging: summiting as erasure in the Highlands of Scotland', Christos Galanis draws attention to another form of historical cultural domination: the suppression of indigenous folk walking practices in the Scottish Highlands along with the imperialist connotations and roots of the modern practice of 'Munro bagging'. Drawing on his own original ethnographic research with hill walkers in Scotland, Galanis concludes persuasively that 'this narrow and prescriptive regime of conquering or collecting Highland summits perpetuates a poverty of the imagination and eclipses alternative walking practices that might allow for more reciprocal and mutually nourishing qualities of relationship to be explored and modeled'.

As Hamilton notes in Chapter 6, 'the ability to move is intimately connected to self-determination and cultural autonomy', a particularly relevant insight in relation to the next two essays in this part: the interviews in Chapter 8 with Dawn Walton and Testament (the director and author of the play *Black Men Walking*, respectively), and Deirdre Heddon and Misha Myers's '*The Walking Library for Women Walking*' in Chapter 9. *Black Men Walking* was inspired by the Sheffield Black Men's Walking Group, and Walton and Testament reflect in Chapter 8 on the problems encountered by the Black community when walking in rural areas – the 'different kind of visibility' as Walton puts it – as well as the benefits of such walking: its role in recovering largely hidden Black histories; its physically and emotionally restorative elements; and the way in which group walking forges strong community bonds. For Testament, while 'walking cityscapes is also valuable, . . . there is something special about being close to nature and being exposed to the elements'. He concludes: 'Perhaps it forces us not to walk alone.' Heddon and Myers also explore problems of erasure and different kinds of visibility in Chapter 9, which gives an account of three iterations of *The Walking Library for Women Walking*. Working against a background of walking art in which women have been rendered largely invisible, *The Walking Library* 'seeks to make walking women unavoidably manifest'. Heddon and Myers draw out the masculinist construction of historical accounts of walking as an aesthetic practice, and show how public walking by groups of women can act as a form of restitution, of restoring elided histories, and of asserting the right to 'take up public space'. The walks were enriched by the walkers' practice of reading from books taken from the artists' *Walking Library* (a collection created by inviting people to donate books which were 'good to give to a woman walking'), with the walks cumulatively representing an intervention not only into the histories of walking, but also the canon of walking literature.

Part II concludes with Chapter 10, 'Walking backwards: art between places in twenty-first-century Britain', Judith Tucker's exploration of the work of several contemporary walking artists. She demonstrates how these artists 'complicate the boundaries of document, artefact and performance', deploy approaches inspired by deep mapping and psychogeography, and, at times, comment on the social and ethical implications of the material accoutrements of walking itself. Finally, she suggests that their embodied practices might work towards erasing the barriers between human and non-human, developing 'an understanding of place and subjectivity as fluid and symbiotic'. The chapter effectively draws together several strands of the collection so far: Tucker references Lloyd, Heddon, Myers and Collier, and her discussion of Ingrid Pollard – whose photographs of walkers of Caribbean descent against the background of images of the Lake District interrupt the 'normalized assumptions of who belongs in this freighted British landscape' – chimes powerfully with the interview with Walton and Testament.

The chapters in Part III take up the challenge both of further interrupting normalized assumptions and of addressing walking art and walking studies' next steps. Anna Stenning argues in Chapter 11, 'Autism and cognitive embodiment: steps towards a non-ableist walking literature', that it is possible for individual accounts of 'complex embodiment' to question the rhetoric of individual perfectibility and self-reliance that is at the heart of many of our cultural understandings of walking. In her readings of Temple Grandin's *Animals in Translation* and Chris Packham's *Fingers in the Sparkle Jar*, both of which unsettle the ideology of human exceptionalism by describing their narrators' cognitive embodiment as autistic individuals, she shows how our cultural obsession with individuality and overcoming limits, evident in the ideology of ableism, is detrimental to both the cultural identities of disabled people and our awareness of our dependency on other species.

Equally, walking and other modes of assisted movement by injured and disabled bodies generate new types of knowledge or sharing in non-hierarchical ways: they can recall events that do not conform to narratives of cultural progress, or serve as a means to encounter diverse human and non-human lives. As Rachel Jacobs, Pippa Marland and Steve Benford demonstrate in Chapter 12, 'Walking with the digital: *Heartlands – 'Ere Be Dragons* and *A Conversation Between Trees*', it is not so much the immediacy of the experience that cultural forms invoke that counts, but rather the ways in which they might develop environmental awareness, particularly of issues such as climate breakdown that pose the greatest threats to our collective future. Within the context of affective landscapes, two digital artworks by Active Ingredient show that we may become emotionally engaged with data, and furthermore, that this connection enhances our attachment to nature and our comprehension of environmental change. Jacobs, Marland and Benford's pioneering research demonstrates the need to radically rethink our relationship with technology, to allow us to address both the social and ecological challenges posed by outmoded ideas of 'landscape'.

In Chapter 13, 'The crisis in psychogeographical walking: from paranoia to diversity, ecology and salvage', Phil Smith addresses both the conviviality and experimentalism of contemporary psychogeographic practice. A wide range of work based on radical walking – including 'painting, mapping, installations, sound walks, led, guided and mis-guided walks' – are, he urges, ahead of those that depend on 'nature walks' in their potential for addressing the climate crisis. Smith shows that through their emphases on cooperation, assemblages and contingencies, works such as Jess Allen's performative 'Tracktivism' suggest ways to cope with our collective future vulnerability in the light of increasingly unstable terrain. Smith argues that the Fife Psychogeographical Collective exemplifies this new movement as it suggests that the psychogeographer can 'reverse the panoptical gaze of the modern political machine' and 'landscape as a mirror to reflect back . . .. We can see what you are up to and imagine and enact alternative possibilities.'[13]

Acknowledging the more painful aspects of our experiences of landscape – the melancholy, as much as the awe that belongs to the experience of the sublime – is a thread that runs throughout the chapters in this collection. Terry Gifford's Chapter 14, 'Mountaineering literature as dark pastoral', begins with a poem that considers the felt tensions between beauty and risk in judging conditions on the mountain before assessing a series of five recent works of mountaineering literature within the context of the amplified risks of the Anthropocene. Following on from his *Reconnecting with John Muir*, and in the form of narrative scholarship, Gifford addresses the question of whether the alternative frames of 'dark pastoral' or the 'post-pastoral' might better serve the dual impulses to anxiety and hope that are evident in the modern mountaineers' accounts.[14] While apparently ending on this more theoretical note, Gifford makes a plea for new forms of environmental literature that do not perpetuate either fatalism or escapism. The collection ends, as it began, with the prose-poetry of

Gerry Loose. In a continuation of Chapter 1, 'Walking in (900 questions concerning walking)', in Chapter 15 Loose encourages us to 'Walk on' into the world as it is, mindful of the body, mindful of others, human and non-human, mindful of both memory and the gaps in memory, and mindful of the landscape's entanglements with power. Above all, he enjoins us to understand that 'there is no dichotomy between where we walk and how and on what we walk. No culture, no nature.'

While this is mainly a book about the aesthetic aspects of walking and writing, it is hoped that it will facilitate theoretical negotiations of landscape, space, place and pastoral traditions. At the same time, it directly engages with the politics of walking in many different contexts: privacy and ownership versus freedom and openness; consolidations of power versus distributions of power; violence versus peaceful protest; coexistence, collaboration and empathy versus individualism, profit and extinctions. It seeks to contribute to the ecocritical project of overcoming the Enlightenment hyper-separation of mind and body, spiritual and material, animal and human, male and female. While there is nothing that specifically addresses the 'obesity epidemic' for which walking is often prescribed as the perfect antidote, it considers the ways that walking allows us to overcome bodily and mental passivity while acknowledging our vulnerability and dependence on other lives. Active Ingredient's digital game *Heartlands – 'Ere Be Dragons*, discussed in Chapter 12, with its focus on the physiological impacts of both exertion and the affective properties of a particular environment, playfully draws attention to the intersections of walking and health, and the interviews with Dawn Walton and Testament in Chapter 8 bring out both the physical and emotional benefits of walking and the ways in which it fosters and strengthens community.

Like writing, and unlike many contemporary practices, walking can be linear and unidirectional, or repetitive, irregular, and even circular. In this way, it is more akin to the movements of thought, and therefore has a unique potential to create paths into individual or collective memory. This book has been compiled in a collaboration between editors, and the path hasn't always been easy. In this, it shows the many challenges we face as walkers, writers and thinkers in an age when we are defined by our commercial outputs rather than our ability to see the 'bigger picture'. In walking, there will always be conflicts between developing individual agency and the need to coexist with the others we meet on the way. Given these difficulties, one of the greatest joys of editing this collection has been witnessing the way in which the essays, drawn from such a diverse range of practices and perspectives, chime with one another, making the volume truly 'conversive', to use Mike Collier's term. We believe that the work contained here will continue to resonate with its readers as new connections emerge and new directions are cumulatively revealed. We also hope that the conversation will cross many geographical boundaries, including those we have not been able to breach with the contents of this particular collection. While Amy

Hamilton's Chapter 6 focuses specifically on Indigenous walking and writing practices in the USA, the collection as a whole relates predominantly to the UK scene. But while some essays retain a local orientation, others feature research and iterations of artworks that have crossed continents, bringing perspectives from, for example, the Mata Atlântica forest in Brazil, in the case of Active Ingredient's *A Conversation Between Trees*, and Geelong, Australia in *The Walking Library for Women Walking*. There is a powerful sense throughout the volume that these times require us to think beyond social, cultural, political and geographical limits. As an always unfinished mode of enquiry, the parameters of walking continue to expand, as does its relevance to environmentalist thinking. It is for this reason that the trope of walking is likely to remain powerful as long as literature and art exist on the earth and we continue to seek a means of articulating our dwelling therein. As Gerry Loose concludes at the very end of this collection: 'With our feet we activate the verbs of the earth.'

Notes

1 Y. Tuan, 'Humanistic Geography', *Annals of the Association of American Geographers* 6(2) (1976): 266–276.
2 See, for example, T.V. Reed, 'Toward an Environmental Justice Ecocriticism', in *The Environmental Justice Reader*, edited by Joni Adamson, Mei Mei Evans and Rachel Stein (Tucson, AZ: University of Arizona Press, 2002).
3 See U. Heise, *Sense of Place and Sense of Planet* (Oxford, UK: Oxford University Press, 2008) and D. Massey, *Space, Place and Gender* (Minneapolis, MN: University of Minnesota Press, 1994).
4 C. Berberich, N. Campbell and R. Hudson, 'Affective Landscapes: An Introduction', *Cultural Politics* 9(3) (2013): 313–322.
5 R. Solnit, *Wanderlust* (London: Granta, 2014), vii.
6 www.chrispackham.co.uk/a-peoples-manifesto-for-wildlife; www.theguardian.com/education/2019/mar/14/youth-climate-strikes-to-take-place-in-almost-100-countries-greta-thunberg; https://rebellion.earth/2019/04/16/international-rebellion-update-1-the-rebellion-begins/.
7 www.bbc.co.uk/news/uk-politics-48126677.
8 Solnit, *Wanderlust*, viii.
9 T. Morton, *The Ecological Thought* (Cambridge, MA: Harvard University Press 2012), 218.
10 Ibid.
11 J. Davies, *The Birth of the Anthropocene* (Oakland, CA: University of California Press, 2016), 45.
12 Solnit, *Wanderlust*, 5.
13 Fife Psychogeographical Collective, *From Hill To Sea* (London: Bread and Circuses, 2015), 33.
14 See H.I. Sullivan, 'The Dark Pastoral: Goethe and Atwood', *Green Letters* 20(1) (2016): 47–59, and T. Gifford, *Pastoral* (London: Routledge, 2nd edition, 2019).

Part I
Walking in
Lines, contours, pilgrimages

1 Walking in
(900 questions concerning walking)

Gerry Loose

It's quite clear, axiomatic almost, that to walk in different landscapes is to think different thoughts and thus in different vocabularies and thus also languages. Conasg or conaisg is not the same as whin or furze or gorse, nor yet the same as *Ulex europaeus*. On the strand, I have no, or few, names for the sea plants that I come across in their reds, ochres, browns and livid greens.

When walking, does one follow a train of thought or a path? Or a Way? Or can it be both?

Is it to follow one's nose or one's feet?

Do we walk the same paths day after day, coming to know the hidden bends, the wayside dockens? Or are they the paths of tradition, those of our forebears, the familiar headlands; Gallows Rock; the wee field known to grandparents as Johnny Mara's? Do we nod in recognition as we pass?

Are we in place?

And what do our bodies tell us? Are we tired after the first mile? After ten miles? And when do we relax into time and place?

And those of us who, for whatever reason, cannot walk, do we walk in our memories or our imaginations?

And when we walk in new places as we sometimes must, do we see the familiar or the novel?

What are our waymarkers: shepherd's purse at our feet or the view between hills?

If we set off at sunrise, do we walk until sunset?

When we walk at night, do we wear dark glasses? Walking nights, do we wear owls?

Is it wet underfoot, or dry, or are we joyous, walking on air? Where is the black dog of despair?

When I walk with another, does my pace quicken or slow?

Do we walk on geology or pavement? Are those the same thing?

Why does that hare cross my path just here? Why does the purple thistle grow?

Why are the greenblue mountains constantly walking?

What are the numbers and names of the bones of the foot?

Is walking a science or an art? Or an alchemy?

Are there walking styles; walking rules?

What are walking aids?

When we walk, do we ride clouds? Are we still when we walk?

Are we walking toward a home we never find? A home we never had?

Is it toes in or toes out?

Is going for a walk the same as walking and if so how?

Sleep walking?

I was out for a walk when I met the shepherd at the top of Carrauntoohill, the highest mountain in Ireland.

Is there walking with purpose? Is it marching? Or is it when I walk to the foreshore to gather kelp or in the woods to gather mushrooms? Is the goose-step fascist walking?

Is marching on a protest demonstration liberal walking? Are dance steps ritualized walking?

When I tore my Achilles tendon in two, I limped for two years. Was I still walking?

Why did Dorothy Wordsworth walk in Scotland? Was it in pursuit of the Romantic or to stretch her legs?

Maighister Alasdair, the father of the great Gaelic poet, a Minister, walked a sixty-mile round trip on Sundays from his home in Dalilea to preach in Kilchoan church. Thoreau had political feet. Flâneurs may be true Buddhists.

Who are the unsung of walking? Is it quadrupeds or the folk who deliver our post?

Is there such a thing as wild walking, and what would be tamed walking and guerrilla walking?

When the great stag comes down to the glen, is that walking?

When a sign reads Private: No Admittance, do we walk on anyway? Why are certain streets barred to us with large iron gates? Are politicians afraid of walking?

Are we too busy to walk? If so, why do we teach our children to walk?

Why do wood ants walk in single file?

2 Lines, walks and getting lost

Contemporary poetry and walking

Garry MacKenzie

What exactly does walking have in common with writing and reading poems? How do modern poets bring some of the attributes of walking – pace, linearity, unfolding sensory experiences – into their work? What happens when a poem doesn't simply comprise a lyric account of a speaker walking through a landscape, but instead implies multiple, perhaps imaginary, walks through places? In this chapter I examine how three modern poets – W.S. Graham, Susan Stewart and Thomas A. Clark – bring together poetry and walking. The walks in Graham's and Stewart's poems aren't grounded in their own subjective experiences of travelling on foot, but use hypothetical walks in order to explore the relationships between movement, imagination and poetic creativity. In Clark's poetry, walking is presented as a means of closing the distance between self and world. His prose-poetic aphorisms, *In Praise of Walking*, address the question of what walking means, and his accumulation of lines treading and re-treading this intellectual path is a form of answer. Graham, Stewart and Clark take walking as their subject in the poems I discuss, but their work also shares with walking aspects such as movement, contingency and doubling back.

In his 1967 lecture 'A Poem Is a Walk', A.R. Ammons makes a comparison between walking and poetry that goes some way towards the elision of physical and mental movement found in Graham's, Stewart's and Clark's poems. For Ammons there are four ways in which poems resemble walks. Firstly, 'each makes use of the whole body [. . .] as with a walk, a poem is not simply a mental activity; it has body, rhythm, feeling, sound, and mind'.[1] Negotiating its spatial, aural and other formal qualities is akin to bodily movement. Secondly, both are 'unreproducible': just as you can never take the same walk twice, you can never write the same poem twice.[2] Thirdly, both poems and walks involve 'turns' and 'returns', sequential movement through lines comprised of thoughts, images and tones.[3] Finally, poems and walks share a motion that 'may be lumbering, clipped, wavering, tripping, mechanical' and so on. This motion can only be apprehended by entering into the process – by writing a poem or by going on a walk.[4]

Ammons's argument is not about walking *per se*. His analogy of poetry and walking functions as a way to introduce elements of poetics, mapping these on to recognisable attributes of a familiar activity. For the four points I've highlighted above, a similar analogy could conceivably be made with knitting, furniture making or shipbuilding. However, Ammons concludes his lecture with a point that doesn't readily apply to these creative activities: a poem, like a walk, is 'useless, meaningless, and non-rational'.[5] A poem can't be boiled down to a single paraphrasable meaning that replaces the original work. Likewise, there's no definitive reason for taking a walk, and no universal meaning that can be applied to every stroll, hike or march. For individual poems and individual walks, their meaning is their happening.

Ammons's subject is poetry in general, and he says little in detail about poems which are concerned with actual walks. Neither does he fully examine the question of why poets are drawn to walking. In *Walks in the World*, Roger Gilbert examines numerous manifestations of what he terms 'the walk poem'. For Gilbert, a walk has something of the 'formal unity and lyric concentration' of an artwork, and therefore poets can bring intensity, 'closure' and 'the contingent blend of thought, perception and encounter' to their work by choosing to write about excursions on foot.[6] A walk poem tends to close the space between experience and poem, with an occasion enacted and re-enacted as it's written and read about.[7] For Gilbert there are three kinds of walk poem: those which start with a walk and use it as a means of approaching an underlying truth; those which emphasise how the meandering process of thought is like a walk; and those which focus on the sensory experience of walking.[8] The ultimate aim of all three kinds of walk poem is to give particular attention to the world, by which he means not an individual place, but the world as 'the very horizon of experience'.[9]

For all that the genre attempts to close the distance between poem and experience, Gilbert's walk poem might nevertheless imply another distance: between people and nature. His 'world' is a reality seemingly external to the poet and accessed through walking. As Timothy Morton argues in *Ecology without Nature*, such differentiation perpetuates the idea of 'nature' as distinct from humanity, rather than as a series of ecological, cultural and geological systems of which we are a part; it also tends to homogenise all 'natural' things – landscapes, animals, clouds – into one ontological category.[10] This tension between distance and contiguity is inherent in much landscape poetry, but for Gilbert walk poems have the advantage that their subject is an unfolding experience rather than a static scene. The speaker moves through a landscape and encounters a succession of shifting phenomena, and so nature is less likely to be regarded as a distant totality.[11]

Both Ammons and Gilbert suggest that poems and walks resemble each other in that they unfold in a defined space and time. The poet, and then the reader, move through the lines of thought and image that constitute the poem, and this movement may be like walking. Gilbert, to a greater extent than Ammons, is interested in how poets might exploit the overlap between poetry and walking. The work of W.S. Graham offers an example of the interactions between a journey on foot and a journey on the page, although, as we shall see, this doesn't necessarily involve closure of the space between the poem and the world.

W.S. Graham: lines printed in the snow

In the title poem of Graham's *Malcolm Mooney's Land*, published in 1970, walking is analogous to the act of writing a poem. An expedition on foot provides the poem's overarching structure: it serves as a means of interweaving phenomenological apprehension of an environment with a sequence of thoughts, memories and references. The poem takes the form of a diary by an unnamed explorer, lost and alone in the Arctic and struggling against the conditions and his own isolation. Although 'Malcolm Mooney's Land' was mostly written in 1965, Graham had read Fridtjof Nansen's written accounts of his expedition across Greenland at least as early as 1955,[12] and Tony Lopez has shown that 'Malcolm Mooney's Land' adapts passages from Nansen's *Farthest North*.[13] This grounds the poem in recorded detail. Nansen is mentioned as a third person by the speaker, so this is not a dramatic monologue in the voice of the Norwegian explorer. But neither is this a walk poem establishing its origins in first-hand experience. Rather than simply bolstering the poem's realism, the accumulation of information about the cold, 'my breath a ruff of crystals',[14] and evidence of fauna, 'A fox was here last night [. . .] the prints / All round the tent',[15] also serve to elucidate the abstract world of the poem, in which walking in the snow is akin to printing on a white page.

Instead of closing the gap between poem and experience, the grounding of 'Malcolm Mooney's Land' in Nansen's observations exposes its artificiality, the sense that the Arctic expedition stands for something other than itself. In the opening lines, the speaker recalls friends he has buried 'under the printed snow', and the dazzling light is a visual corollary of an empty page's 'silence'.[16] The speaker proceeds 'Footprint on foot / Print, word on word', eliding the textual progression of the poem and the physical progression of the walk whose trace is left as footprints in the snow.[17]

The first of the poem's five sections establishes its diaristic structure, beginning 'Today, Tuesday', and references to 'Wednesday' and 'Friday' are made in subsequent sections.[18] The movement of the poem is the passage of time and also the stages of the speaker's walk across the snow, yet it's unclear if the speaker is any further along by the poem's end. The defined duration of poem and walk implied in Ammons's and Gilbert's arguments is unsettled in 'Malcolm Mooney's Land', in which the walk is of an unfixed length, becoming a surreal, almost purgatorial experience. Days pass, but are unmoored from their dates, and in the 'white-out in this tent of a place' there is no visual or cartographic confirmation that progress is being made.[19] The poem ends with 'Words drifting on words. / The real unabstract snow.'[20] There is disorientation and silence: in the poem, words, as Ralph Pite has argued, 'do not construct a space between people that can be crossed, they drift on top of each other, an empty obstacle.'[21] The snow is 'unabstract', and any attempt to bring it conclusively into language will fail. The world, rather than being accessed by the walking poet, as in Gilbert's model of the walk poem, is obscured by language, which gets in the way.

Graham claimed that 'a poem is made of words and not of the expanding heart, the overflowing soul or the sensitive observer' – that the poet's self-expression and opinions are not essential to a poem.[22] The results of this process for Graham are poems that are 'objects', a word he repeatedly uses to refer to the cohesion of a poem or sequence.[23] But the object-ness of each individual word is also foregrounded in Graham's poetry, and in doing this Graham takes Ammons's analogy of poems comprising of walk-like, bodily movement as far as it can go: to the level of single steps. In breaking a line at 'foot / Print', as quoted above, Graham delays the expected repetition of 'footprint on footprint' and in so doing creates the impression that the word has been physically cut in two by the line-break. At the same time he disaggregates one concept, the footprint, into two, foot and print. The line-break disrupts the syntax, but also destabilises meaning, drawing 'print' into association with 'word on word', suggesting the image of printed words. It also enacts a different temporality than that of the poem (and the walk) as a whole: the moment between one foot touching the ground and the next, the white space between one printed word and another, the distance between an action (the step) and its sign (the footprint).

Walking is contingent: direction, pace and length of stride can be altered between one step and another. Speech, too, is a series of contingencies, as Graham's poems make obvious through their syntax- and word-disrupting enjambments, portmanteaus and instances of arrestingly unusual metaphor. Furthermore, he claims that his creative process is similarly unpredictable, gaining impetus from a 'first intention' that is altered as it 'shatters itself and is replaced by the child of the new collision'.[24] The act of creating a poem, then, is less like a linear walk from A to B than like a meandering peregrination informed at every step by observations, obstacles and revelations. While he emphasises the unfolding and surprising stages of writing, Graham's poem also demands to be read step by step, line by line. The reader travels along the lines of 'Malcolm Mooney's Land', contemplating images as they would landmarks, coming to understand their provenance and possible meanings by reconstructing them in their mind. Towards the end of the poem, 'An old sulphur bear / Sawing his log of sleep' is one such stopping-place, where a rich imaginative and figurative world opens up as the senses and intellect are engaged: 'sawing his log' as a metaphor for snoring is so surprising that it requires the reader to pause and examine the logic of the association.[25]

For Rebecca Solnit, 'To write is to carve a new path through the terrain of the imagination, or to point out new features on a familiar route. To read is to travel through that terrain with the author as guide'.[26] Graham's construction of the route to follow through the poem leaves evident some of the decisions taken along the way. In 'Malcolm Mooney's Land' the account of an imagined walk provides a narrative structure along which the reader proceeds, but the poem also emphasises the semantic but non-narrative progression between each word and each poetic line, a movement of turning and returning which, as Ammons notes, finds its analogue in walking.

Lost in the forest: Susan Stewart

The walking pace of the poet, both literally and in the sense of the methodical foot-by-foot accumulation of sound and syntax, informs how the world is perceived and presented in the poem. The mimetic relationship between the rhythms of a poem and walking, the phenomenological experience of the walker in a landscape, and the attempt to interpret the signs perceived on a journey are all factors which are present in the 1995 collection *The Forest* by American poet Susan Stewart. Unsurprisingly, the most significant walks detailed in this collection involve treading and re-treading forest paths, both in the title poem and subsequently in 'Holswege'. The latter poem alludes to Martin Heidegger's collection of essays, *Holzwege*. A *Holzweg*, according to Heidegger, is one of many paths in a wood, is potentially a dead-end, and is best known to the foresters who work in this landscape.[27] The translators of a recent edition of *Holzwege* render the title as *Off the Beaten Track* in English, stating that the German idiom 'to be on a *Holzweg*' means 'to be on the wrong track' or 'off the beaten track'.[28] For Heidegger, poetry restores experience of the world through the revelation of the essential nature of things.[29] The image of the *Holzweg* can be interpreted as meaning that the thinker, and also the poet, should consider the world in the same way as they might follow paths through a forest – sometimes reaching dead ends and doubling back, sometimes following a path that seems to be familiar but is different from a previous route, and thus gaining overall knowledge of the forest by taking these paths rather than by taxonomising its trees. Stewart has discussed Heidegger's forest phenomenology in her critical work *Poetry and the Fate of the Senses*, stating that for Heidegger, 'the constant play among nearness, thingness, and farness is essential to our apprehension of our being in the world'.[30]

In Stewart's poem 'Holswege', the speaker walks through a chestnut wood, halting and turning, with 'the truth / of the light of day just above me'.[31] The poem is almost a sestina, made of six sestets that repeat end-words with some variations such as 'allée', 'alleluia' and 'allegory', followed by an envoi that recalls these line endings.[32] Throughout there are exceptions to the scheme, with lines ending on words that do not reappear, such as 'panicles' and 'follow'. These variations in the language mirror the feeling in the poem that meanings and perspectives are shifting and refracting in the wood – signs are inconsistent and barely perceptible. This is a poem about knowledge and the process of thought; the speaker is 'hoping that some feeble maxim was the truth', but two stanzas later concludes that:

It was no use, looking for closure
before the world was ready to yield it up. Better to follow the allée[33]

In the envoi, she is left rummaging for the key 'to the end of the terrible sentence, a turn, a light, a face, a truth'.[34] The poem ends with the act of finding out, although little has been found out other than the speaker's re-examinations of truth. The landscape is a process rather than a static image, and the poet finds a symbol of the mind in the physical environment.

Stewart's 'Holswege' is a useful way to approach the title poem of her collection, 'The Forest', which is also characterised by repetitions and the sensation of walking round in circles in a wooded landscape. The opening line, 'You should lie down now and remember the forest', recurs in the second stanza in parentheses, and 'remember' echoes through the following two stanzas.[35] The phrase 'No surface, skimming' occurs in the fourth and fifth stanzas, and several other phrases are repeated six lines after their first occurrence.[36] A tension is created between the order of this repetition and the lack of any clear meaning to it; in the fifth stanza the speaker admits that birds 'sing without a music where there cannot be an order'.[37] This forest is a place of contradiction and shifting meanings, and those contradictions are part of the meandering *Holzweg* experience of the poem, where even apparently simple statements might be paradoxes – for example, the first layer of the forest is described 'as it were firm, underfoot, for that place is a sea'.[38] This route through the forest hasn't led to a clearing – meanings are in flux and things are only half-seen or half-understood. Walking through it, like the repetitive and halting progress of the poem itself, isn't linear, in the sense of a logical, unidirectional trajectory.

Rather than recounting a real or imagined walk, Stewart's poem begins with the speaker telling a listener to 'lie down now' and in a meditative state to imagine the experience of walking in a forest. There is an almost liturgical sense of procession, resonant of medieval reading and meditative practices. In *The Craft of Thought*, historian Mary Carruthers shows that in the Christian monastic tradition, readers were instructed to approach scripture as they would a walk through a landscape, 'constantly in motion, all senses continually in play, slowing down and speeding up'.[39] Similarly, places were explored as a means of contemplation, whether landscapes, labyrinths or buildings.[40] But these places didn't have to physically exist. Like Stewart's forest, verbal or pictorial direction were sufficient to enable one to perform a 'mnemotechnical perambulation', a meditative walk in the imagination.[41] The medieval imagination, and its echo in 'The Forest', bring together physical and mental aspects of reading and walking, in a manner reminiscent of Ammons's conjunction of the poem and the walk.

The perambulation through the forest in Stewart's poem is sensually rich: the 'details you can bring back' are not merely visual, nor a rational quantification of the habitat, but include all the senses and impinge on the subconscious. The ground is 'black humus', stimulating smell and touch, as well as sight.[42] The image of the 'flecked birds' singing is both visual and aural. Similarly, 'the air has the texture of drying moss', on which there is 'a musk from the mushrooms and scalloped molds', an evocation of touch, smell and taste.[43] The poem evokes rich sensory images, but it also creates them. The lengths of the lines vary, but their complex syntax creates a rhythm redolent of slow physical progress through a forest, and this impression is furthered by frequent caesurae. The sounds of individual phrases also add to this effect: 'tangled with brambles', for example, creates a tangle on the tongue. Pauses slow lines down as if their movement has, like the walker in the forest, been caught on briars. In the line 'tangled with brambles, soft-starred and moving, ferns', the punctuation, metrical stresses and compressed syntax stall the reader's progress, terminating in the long pause of an enjambed stanza break.[44] To return to Ammons's comparison of poetry with walking, 'The Forest' is walk-like in its making 'use of the whole body': it has the 'rhythm, feeling, sound, and mind' of a particularly gnarly passage through dense trees.

Repetition slows movement through Stewart's forest. Words and phrases are dwelt upon, but their meanings remain elusive. The reader is led trance-like by the speaker, who invokes each sensory experience of the landscape: the poem's unfolding is out of the control of the person who is told to 'remember' the forest. Significantly, the poem takes place in the knowledge of the prior disappearance of the forest, presumably because of deforestation, and so the possibilities of interpretation and sensual experience are limited by time. The vision is framed by the opening lines: 'You should lie down now and remember the forest, / for it is disappearing –'.[45] This forest is briefly glimpsed although it's already destroyed.

In 'The Forest' it's not just the forest that is being lost, but also truth, expressed in a soon-to-be-forgotten narrative. The poem ends:

> Once we were lost in the forest, *so strangely alike and yet singular, too*, but the truth is, it is, lost to us now.[46]

The phrase 'the truth is', when reflexively considered by the next clause, 'it is', turns the idiom into a more profound statement about the loss of truth itself. Stewart suggests in this poem that if being lost in the forest – of following a *Holzweg* – no longer exists, then a form of thought itself no longer exists. All that is contingent on the speaker – the reader's navigation through the forest by a route that doubles back on itself, the existence of the forest itself – ends when the narrator falls silent. The vision concludes with the statement that the forest is lost. Although the attempt to close the distance between the world and the poem is suggested by the form of address in 'The Forest', Stewart ultimately pulls back from this possibility: the poem could be read an elegy for a Heideggerean pursuit of the essential nature of things.

'Wayfaring': Tim Ingold and Thomas A. Clark

In 'The Forest', meditation and memory are embedded in the phenomenological experience of walking among the trees, and *vice versa*. This connection of walking with thinking and knowing has been observed by many writers interested in walking. In *Wanderlust*, Rebecca Solnit argues that:

> Walking, ideally, is a state in which the mind, the body, and the world are aligned, as though they were characters finally in conversation together, three notes suddenly making a chord. Walking allows us to be in our bodies and in the world without being made busy by them [. . .]. Moving on foot seems to make it easier to move in time; the mind wanders from plans to recollections to observations.[47]

Solnit's point is partly about pace – walking is a slow means of travel in a busy, fast-paced world, and for that reason may open up different ways of perceiving the world, particularly because in the West a long walk is likely to be for leisure, rather than need. But she also perceives of the mind as aligned both with the body, and with the walker's environment. The mind, like the body, essays forth, wandering between observation and memory. Her emphasis on the embodied mind is shared by Frédéric Gros, who suggests that the regular rhythm of putting one foot on the other allows a person to come closer to a landscape than any other means of travel, and certainly closer than the stationary observer viewing scenes from a distance: 'The body becomes steeped in the earth it treads. And thus, gradually, it stops being in the landscape: it *becomes* the landscape.'[48]

One of the most ambitious theoreticians of the interconnections between the body, the mind and the walk is the anthropologist Tim Ingold, whose thinking about embodiment, movement and the senses attempts to elucidate the phenomenological experience of walking suggested by Solnit and Gros. Ingold differentiates two means of travel: transport and wayfaring. Transport is act of being carried across space, from one place to another. During transport, movement is simply a means of reaching a destination, and the journey should not alter the nature of the traveller or goods being transported.[49] In wayfaring, on the other hand, movement is more important than simply reaching successive destinations.[50] Unlike the passenger, who can rarely experience the environment other than visually, the wayfarer is sustained 'through an active engagement with the country that opens up along his path': movement and perception go hand in hand.[51] In contrast to functional transportation from A to B, wayfaring, like Ammons's 'useless', 'non-rational' poem, and indeed like the syntactic and semantic movement in Graham's and Stewart's work, is an ever-unfolding, unpredictable, contingent process. As a result, Ingold finds the dichotomy of abstract space and humanised place, introduced by thinkers such as Yi-Fu Tuan and Jeff Malpas, misleading: we don't live in a series of discrete places separated by nothingness, but rather along lines of movement 'through, around, to and from' countless places.[52] Each line is a way of understanding the world through lived experience, and place itself is an entwining of these lines, a knot of meaning.[53]

Many of Ingold's examples of wayfarers are semi-nomadic tribes, and walking is the primary means of wayfaring in his work. But the distinction between wayfaring and transport isn't simply about travel, it's about how people know the world in which they live. He states: 'I use the term *wayfaring* to describe the embodied experience of this perambulatory movement. It is as wayfarers, then, that human beings inhabit the earth.'[54] Inhabitation means 'moving *through* the world *along* paths of travel', and knowledge consists of the 'meshwork' of sensations, memories and encounters that happen on these paths.[55] Ingold is influenced by Carruthers's exposition of embodied medieval reading practices,[56] and his wayfaring represents the elision of physical and cultural aspects of embodied experience of the phenomenal world. Because of this, literal movement is an exemplar of how Ingold suggests organisms 'inhabit the earth', rather than a prerequisite. Although Ingold doesn't address a subject such as Gilbert's walk poem, his model of wayfaring, like the *Holzweg* experience of Stewart's 'The Forest', shows how the world may be understood via a mesh of phenomenological, cultural and ecological narratives rather than through a system of static units of meaning.

Walking through a landscape, for Ingold, means being involved in an 'all-enveloping experience of sound, light and feeling'; these forces, rather than anchoring us in a place, 'contrive to sweep us off our feet'.[57] This dynamic characterisation of landscape as a 'weather-world'[58] of movement, flows and atmospheric changes, rather than as a fixed entity to be comprehended by the gaze of a poet, chimes with contemporary ecopoetry's emphasis on the vitality, unpredictability and ambiguity of the natural world. Whilst Ingold's language here may hint at a sublime response to the non-human, he also acknowledges that landscape is cultural, 'taking on meanings and appearances in relation to people',[59] and points out that the suffix '-scape' contains connotations of 'shaping' – that is, physical engagement with the land by generations of people.[60] Paths are one such means of shaping the land, inscribing and ascribing it with lines of meaning.

Walking underlies much of the poetry of Thomas A. Clark, and the walks in his work involve what can be seen as both a meditative emptying of the self and an openness to the 'weather-world' and its non-human life. His *In Praise of Walking* is a sequence of detached sentences that blend aphorism, prose poetry and a lyric sensibility; it can be read as a manifesto for Clark's aesthetics of walking. It was originally published as part of the catalogue for *The Unpainted Landscape* (1987), a touring exhibition that featured the work of landscape artists, including Richard Long and Hamish Fulton, for whom walking is either an essential part of artistic practice (in the case of Long) or the artwork itself (for Fulton). In 2000 it was reissued as part of the collection *Distance and Proximity*. In it Clark writes that a walk is both movement and a process of deepening attentiveness: it is 'a mobile form of waiting', a closure of the distance between self and world through slow, patient progress on foot.[61] The gradual accretion of layers of meaning in *In Praise of Walking* may be a poetic equivalent of this process. For Clark, walking is not a form of transport from one destination to another, with places strung together like stepping stones across space. Rather, it is 'its own measure, complete at every point along the way'.[62]

Writing about the aphoristic 'Detached Sentences on Gardening' by Ian Hamilton Finlay, Clark comments that 'Finlay is here returning the sentence to its Pre-Socratic adventure, using it as a poetic probe rather than as a logical machine.'[63] Rather than a poem developing argument or self-expression through consecutive sentences, Finlay's 'Detached Sentences' remain intellectually open-ended, ambiguous, yet formally self-contained. Clark might have added that each is like a walk, in that it's a movement in thought that unfolds through changes of rhythm, as well as of sound and syntax. *In Praise of Walking* contains this sentiment in reverse: 'The line of a walk is articulate in itself.'[64] Clark's own short prose poems have the self-contained completeness typical of both a poem and a walk. Each poem might be understood as a discrete step, an isolated burst of intensity. Their accumulation doesn't form a single, logical prose argument, but is its own journey in image, idea and music. The unfolding of the sequence as a whole is like multiple iterations of the same walk, in which thought and sensation blend into each other. In Clark's later volumes of poetry, such as *Yellow & Blue* (2014), walking is less the explicit subject than the background to each poem: his short lyrics appear to record observations from a walk, or from multiple hypothetical walks, and taken together they are a sustained sequence which aligns mind, body and environment, what in Ingold's terminology could be seen as lines of movement which constitute knowledge of place.

In one section of *In Praise of Walking*, Clark writes: 'For the right understanding of a landscape, information must come to the intelligence from all the senses.'[65] This might be a riposte to the ideologically conservative tradition of landscape painting which emphasised a distancing, visual perspective, critiqued in studies such as W.J.T. Mitchell's *Landscape and Power* (2002). But seen through the lens of Ingold, Clark's statement can also be read as a vindication of the notion of wayfaring through a weather-world: movement facilitates participation in enveloping phenomena, in contrast with the insulation of transport. For Ingold, this participation is not necessarily predicated upon the five senses enjoyed by most able-bodied humans; rather, it is a model of experience that is broad enough to encompass the subjective worlds of individual people as well as different species; in Clark's poem 'all' is, arguably, equally open-ended.[66]

Graham's and Stewart's poems comprise imagined walks, and thus can't be said to be predicated on the embodied experience of the poet as speaker, which is one of the features of the walk poem identified by Gilbert. They nevertheless suggest similar openness to a weather-world, an imbrication of the mental, the cultural and the physical more subtle than Gilbert's Romantic implication that the walk poem is a way to close the distance between the poem and external nature. For all three poets, the duration, rhythm and incremental progress of going on a walk provide structure for poems in which lines of thought 'turn and return'. They support Ammons's notion that a poem is like a walk, but go beyond Ammons in their demonstration of how walking, thinking and the literary imagination are drawn together in the sensory and semantic aspects of their poems about travel on foot.

Notes

1 A.R. Ammons, 'A Poem Is a Walk', *Epoch* XVIII (1968): 116.
2 Ibid.
3 Ibid.
4 Ibid., 117.
5 Ibid., 119.
6 R. Gilbert, *Walks in the World: Representation and Experience in Modern American Poetry* (Princeton, NJ: Princeton University Press, 1991), 6.
7 Ibid., 22.
8 Ibid., 252.
9 Ibid.
10 T. Morton, *Ecology without Nature: Rethinking Environmental Aesthetics* (Cambridge, MA: Harvard University Press, 2007), 17, 205.
11 Gilbert, *Walks in the World*, 9.
12 W.S. Graham, *The Nightfisherman: Selected Letters of W.S. Graham*, ed. Michael and Margaret Snow (Manchester, UK: Carcanet, 1999), 192, 141.
13 T. Lopez, *The Poetry of W.S. Graham* (Edinburgh, UK: Edinburgh University Press, 1989), 86.
14 W.S. Graham, *New Collected Poems*, ed. Matthew Francis (London: Faber & Faber, 2005), 153.
15 Ibid., 154.
16 Ibid., 153.
17 Ibid.
18 Ibid., 153, 155.
19 Ibid., 155.
20 Ibid., 157.
21 R. Pite, 'Abstract, Real and Particular: Graham and Painting', in *W.S. Graham: Speaking Towards You*, ed. Ralph Pite and Hester Jones (Liverpool, UK: Liverpool University Press, 2004), 78.
22 Graham, *The Nightfisherman*, 379.
23 Ibid., 113, 341.
24 Ibid., 380.
25 Graham, *New Collected Poems*, 156.
26 R. Solnit, *Wanderlust: A History of Walking* (London: Granta, 2002), 72.
27 M. Heidegger, *Off the Beaten Track*, ed. and trans. Julian Young and Kenneth Haynes (Cambridge, UK: Cambridge University Press, 2002), v.
28 Ibid., ix.

29 M. Heidegger, *Poetry, Language, Thought*, trans. Albert Hofstadter (New York: Harper Perennial, 2001), 161–84, 209–27.
30 S. Stewart, *Poetry and the Fate of the Senses* (London: University of Chicago Press, 2003), 158.
31 S. Stewart, *The Forest* (Chicago, IL: University of Chicago Press, 1995), 39.
32 Ibid., 39.
33 Ibid., 39–40.
34 Ibid., 40.
35 Ibid., 5.
36 Ibid., 5–7.
37 Ibid., 6.
38 Ibid., 5.
39 M. Carruthers, *The Craft of Thought: Meditation, Rhetoric and the Making of Images, 400–1200* (Cambridge, UK: Cambridge University Press, 1998), 109–10.
40 Ibid., 254–61.
41 Ibid., 251, 354 fn. 77.
42 Stewart, *The Forest*, 5.
43 Ibid., 6–7.
44 Ibid., 6.
45 Ibid., 5.
46 Ibid., 7; Stewart's emphasis.
47 Solnit, *Wanderlust*, 5.
48 F. Gros, *A Philosophy of Walking* (London: Verso, 2015), 85; Gros's emphasis.
49 T. Ingold, *Lines* (Abingdon, UK: Routledge, 2016), 79.
50 Ibid., 78.
51 Ibid.
52 T. Ingold, *Being Alive: Essays on Movement, Knowledge and Description* (Abingdon, UK: Routledge, 2011), 148.
53 Ibid., 148–9.
54 Ibid., 148; Ingold's emphasis.
55 Ibid., 154; Ingold's emphasis.
56 Ibid., 198–9.
57 Ibid., 134.
58 Ibid., 135.
59 Ibid., 129.
60 Ibid., 126.
61 T.A. Clark, *Distance and Proximity* (Edinburgh, UK: Polygon, 2000), 16.
62 Ibid.
63 T.A. Clark, 'The Idiom of the Universe', in *Wood Notes Wild*, ed. Alec Finlay (Edinburgh, UK: Polygon, 1995), 136.
64 Clark, *Distance and Proximity*, 19.
65 Ibid., 21.
66 See Ingold, *Being Alive*, 76–88.

Works cited

Ammons, A.R. 'A Poem Is a Walk', *Epoch* XVIII (1968): 114–19.
Carruthers, M. *The Craft of Thought: Meditation, Rhetoric and the Making of Images, 400–1200*. Cambridge, UK: Cambridge University Press, 1998.
Clark, T.A. 'The Idiom of the Universe', in *Wood Notes Wild*, edited by Alec Finlay, 132–36. Edinburgh, UK: Polygon, 1995.
Clark, T.A. *Distance and Proximity*. Edinburgh, UK: Polygon, 2000.

Clark, T.A. *Yellow & Blue*. Manchester, UK: Carcanet, 2014.

Gilbert, Roger. *Walks in the World: Representation and Experience in Modern American Poetry*. Princeton, NJ: Princeton University Press, 1991.

Graham, W.S., *Malcolm Mooney's Land*. London: Faber & Faber, 1970.

Graham, W.S., *The Nightfisherman: Selected Letters of W.S. Graham*. Edited by Michael and Margaret Snow. Manchester, UK: Carcanet, 1999.

Graham, W.S. *New Collected Poems*. Edited by Matthew Francis. London: Faber & Faber, 2004.

Gros, F. *A Philosophy of Walking*. London: Verso, 2015.

Heidegger, M. *Poetry, Language, Thought*. Translated by Albert Hofstadter. New York: Harper Perennial, 2001.

Heidegger, M. *Off the Beaten Track*. Edited and translated by Julian Young and Kenneth Haynes. Cambridge, UK: Cambridge University Press, 2002.

Ingold, T. *Being Alive: Essays on Movement, Knowledge and Description*. Abingdon, UK: Routledge, 2011.

Ingold, T. *Lines*. Abingdon, UK: Routledge, 2016.

Lopez, T. *The Poetry of W.S. Graham*. Edinburgh, UK: Edinburgh University Press, 1989.

Morton, T. *Ecology without Nature: Rethinking Environmental Aesthetics*. Cambridge, MA: Harvard University Press, 2007.

Pite, R. 'Abstract, Real and Particular: Graham and Painting', in *W.S. Graham: Speaking towards You*, edited by Ralph Pite and Hester Jones, 65–84. Liverpool, UK: Liverpool University Press, 2004.

Solnit, R. *Wanderlust: A History of Walking*. London: Granta, 2002.

Stewart, S. *The Forest*. Chicago, IL: University of Chicago Press, 1995.

Stewart, S. *Poetry and the Fate of the Senses*. London: University of Chicago Press, 2003.

3   Photographic essay

Contouring alone and with a companion in the Dark Peak, Derbyshire between September 2014 and November 2017

Alison Lloyd

This photographic essay is an exploration of solitary walking, and convivial walking with companion Sara Wookey.[1] The photographs connect walking as an artistic process with an intuitive and personal exploration of 15 square kilometres of remote moorland in the Dark Peak.[2] Drawing on conceptual practices and a tacit response to place, I have constructed a series of intimate portraits. This area of the Dark Peak is an ideal place to stride out over heather, Derbyshire feather-moss and sphagnum mosses and practise using the map's contours to calculate distance and position in the landscape. This process has been called 'micro-navigation'. I appropriated the term 'contouring' to describe walking as an artistic practice. The contouring, when it is a solitary pursuit, is emphasized by the visible use of a cable release within the framing of the landscape. The essential tools of walking are often captured in the margins of the images. I 'mark time' through a close observation of my walking between setting up the camera on the flat stable surface of my rucksack, then walking across the rough terrain of moorland grasses and peat, to the final click of the shutter. When exploring walking with my companion, the convivial atmosphere of a late August day provided an opportunity to look closely at her engagement with the landscape through the camera's viewfinder.

Note

1 Sara Wookey's website is sarawookey.com
2 The Dark Peak is the name given to the Ordnance Survey map for the northern section of the Peak District National Park. The 15 square kilometres referred to here encompass Hope Forest Moor, Alport Moor, and Dale, an area west of Upper Derwent Valley, south of Bleaklow and north of the A57 or Snake Road.

Between Ramsley Reservoir and Big Moor, 30 August 2016

Big Moor, 30 August 2016

Birchin Hat, 7 October 2017

A short walk to High Neb, 1 March 2016

Grains in the Water, 24 July 2014

4 Walking and theatricality

An experiment in weathered thinking (*kairos*)

Carl Lavery

This chapter has two complementary sections, referred to in abstract terms as A and B, in the hope of evoking a journey through signs, the movement between two positions on a map, walking with the eyes, perhaps. The shorter opening section proposes a new ecological theory of walking constructed around a percolating constellation of concepts – *kairos*, intimacy, atmosphere, weather and theatricality.[1] The longer section practises that theory by giving an account of a piece of land art, *THEN/NOW*, located on the Forth & Clyde Canal in Glasgow. Here, walking becomes a textual experiment, a way of performing a peripatetic and durational mode of ecocriticism that seeks to expand how we engage with located or site-based art forms.

The overall aim of the chapter is to reconfigure our conceptual vocabulary so as to disturb the Kantian correlationism that still dominates the critical imagination. Instead, then, of equating '(human) thinking with (human) being', as correlationism tends to do, my approach is to develop a thinking in/of/from the outside,[2] one in which the generative materiality of the non-human takes its place in a relationship of 'cross-ontological fellowship'.[3]

A

The Greek word *kairos* is best grasped in English as a special form of time, in which the subject is confronted with a moment of utter importance, pure readiness, a kind of revelation or epiphany. A contemporary philosopher such as, say, Alain Badiou might see the *kairotic* as an event that 'advents', a catalyst for a process of becoming, a new kind of faithfulness.[4] For all its life-shattering potentiality, however, the evental qualities of *kairos* do not always manifest themselves in such dramatic ways. Not all of us are suited to playing the role of the hero, a (negative) possibility that inheres, interestingly, in the double etymology of *kairos*, a polysemous signifier that also translates as that most mundane of things: the weather. My own experiences of *kairos*, for instance, have tended to be subtle, minor flickerings of sense that have disclosed what I am content to risk calling a 'moment of originality'. In choosing that unfashionable and problematic word 'original',

I am referring to experiences that ask fundamental questions about what it means to live on the earth now, and which seem to come upon us as if from nowhere. These are questions that we stumble upon and irritate us, maybe even for a lifetime, without any type of agency or volition intervening on our part. Hence the paradox of the *kairotic* – to be original is always, in some senses, to be entirely unoriginal, for the stimulus to think is not necessarily something that concerns you or originates from your own cogito. Rather, originality – *kairos* – comes from the outside, an uninvited guest of sorts that falls upon you and discloses a gap in the very heart of things. Without you ever asking for it or knowing why, a barrier of sorts has been imposed between you and the world that seduces and fascinates your desire. To be original is to be dis-armed, in all the resonant senses of that word.

An example of my own disarmament through an encounter with *kairos* occurred on a path through the woods on the outskirts of Llanilar, a small village in mid-Wales where I lived for a time in the mid-2000s. On my daily walk with my dog Mali, a black cocker spaniel, I was suddenly struck by the following thoughts as I navigated a small bend below an old badger sett that banked the path. Why is it that walking, perhaps more than any other human activity, produces a sense of intimacy with a place or territory? And why is that intimacy so utterly impossible, refusing, as it does, ever to placate itself and exist as something finished and substantial? How strange that intimacy, the atmosphere that attaches subjectivity to the world by establishing a sense of familiarity, even homeliness, is always on the verge of taking off and dissolving into nothingness. Intimacy is processual and perennial, a practice without end. It takes you close only to disclose a primordial distance, a failure ever to possess or know the person, place or object that you have spent so long with.

Intimacy and walking share a common currency. For when we walk, we are not only establishing territory, we are also deterritorialised, our feet never quite meeting. While one foot strikes the earth, the other foot takes off into the air. To walk, then, is to exist in a nowhere, to know the world through an act of simultaneous arrival and departure, to be betwixt land and sky, to be always in movement, untimely. Although she is talking about a boat, the novelist Marguerite Duras gives as good an account of walking as any:

> On the planking, on the ship's bulwarks, on the sea, with the course of the sun through the sky and the ship, an unreadable and wrenching script takes shape, takes shape and destroys itself at the same slow pace – shadows, spines, shafts of broken light refocused in the angles, the triangles of a fleeting geometry that yields to the shadow of the ocean waves. And then, unceasingly, lives again.[5]

The walker shares the same fleeting, violent geometry as Duras's boat: someone whose movement through the air and across the land discloses the disruptive wave of intimacy. To walk, to be intimate, is to be open to the infinite, to affirm the double capture of a permanent becoming, to live in turbulence with things – their ecstasy, their *kairos*, their weather.

According to Gernot Böhme, the ecstasy of things produces atmospheres, a gaseous haze which alters the mood of walkers and envelops them in the pouring forth of a non-human world.[6] As the philosopher Michel Haar has it, in his brilliant analysis of Martin Heidegger's philosophy in *The Song of the Earth: Heidegger and the Grounds of the History of Being* (1993), this fundamental attunement to atmospheres, this *Stimmung*, effects a radical dispossession of the human. It does so, Haar continues, by disclosing the invisible enigma of the earth, its impossible presence, a materiality that touches us and engulfs us, but which moves away from us as it does so, never sitting still:

> *Stimmung* does not first provide access to a subjective interiority, nor to a self-enclosed bodily state. It is an attunement that we do not perceive first *in us*. Do we not say 'I am *in* such and such a mood', not 'such and such a mood is in *me*? More exactly it is *what* we occupy ourselves with, what we read or watch that interests us, stimulates us, bores us – in short that always *produces* these often changing dispositions [. . .]. *Stimmung*, the atmosphere, emanates from things themselves, and not from our subjectivity or from our bodiliness. In *Stimmung* the world presents itself as what touches us, concerns us, affects us [. . .]. [W]ithout the *Stimmung* that implicates us in the world there would be no knowledge, because there would be no desire to know. In order to want to know, it is necessary to have been affected, touched.[7]

Although walking, through its intimacy with the earth, is always a bodily encounter, there is nevertheless something else at work in it, too. As I have suggested, to walk is not only to occupy a place, to move through a territory, it is to absent oneself from oneself, to be open to the impress of things, the *Stimmung* that precedes knowing, refusing to be named as 'this' or 'that' emotion or state. When 'we' walk (and that 'we' is always individual and collective), we encounter an abyssal, silent force, a blind or stupid intimacy that accompanies us and which, I want to propose, is the fugitive source of all thinking and writing, the empty atmosphere in which our existence is wrapped. To walk, then, is to be everywhere and nowhere, to participate in a different kind of eternity: one in which the earth simultaneously pre-dates and succeeds us, a non-human temporality. The poet Lisa Robertson makes a similar point when, in an essay on reading and pilgrimage, she defines thinking as offering 'partial access [. . .] to an infinite and inconspicuous surface complexity which is not my own'.[8]

In this respect – and returning to Haar through a detour via Robertson – walking is not solely an art of enchantment,[9] and neither is it a purely phenomenological technique for flowing with the flesh of the world, being part of things, as so many theorists have proffered.[10] Rather, it is a non-human practice, something that undoes the (early) Heideggerian concern with the hand, the decidedly human organ that produces the world by metabolising nature for a technological purpose. In walking, by contrast, the foot is an organ that surpasses itself, always on the verge of taking off into an elsewhere, of becoming what Gilles Deleuze and Félix Guattari, after Antonin Artaud, term 'the body without organs'[11] – a decidedly apt phrase, I would propose, for the impress of that empty *Stimmung* or groundlessness which provokes original thoughts.[12] To walk, then, is not only to be ecologically attuned because one encounters 'nature' (whatever that signifier now means). More radically, it suggests, along with Deleuze and Guattari, that the earth is the non-human source of what we have for too long, and so disastrously, thought of as the exceptional domain of the human: art, culture, speech, consciousness and so on.

Such an ecological perspective throws new light on one of the key texts of 'walking theory' – Michel de Certeau's rich and complex essay 'Walking in the City', originally published in 1980. De Certeau's text is full of sophisticated propositions, analogies and metaphors that range from city planning to psychoanalysis to mythology, all things that I do not have space to do justice to here. Instead, for current purposes, I simply want to focus on – and problematise – the performative logic inherent in one of his central ideas: namely, the sense in which walking is famously compared to a pedestrian speech act:

> The act of walking is to the urban system what the speech act is to language or the statements uttered. At the most elementary level, it has a triple 'enunciative' function: it is a process of appropriation of the topographical system on the part of the pedestrian (just as the speaker appropriates and takes on the language); it is a spatial acting out of the place (just as the speech act is an acoustic acting-out of the language), and it implies differentiated positions, that is, among pragmatic 'contracts' in the form of movements (just as verbal enunciation is an 'allocution', 'posits another opposite' the speaker and puts contracts between interlocutors in action).[13]

Published in the aftermath of May 1968's supposed failure to change, radically, French society, de Certeau's thinking is an attempt to outwit the increasing disciplinarity and management of everyday life by an emergent neo-liberal ideology. As a way of achieving his goal, he posits walking as a speech act that replaces *langue* with *parole*, anonymity with individuality (style), prose with poetry. The overall objective is to contest what he calls the 'Concept city', a theory of urbanism which, like the view of New York from the old World Trade Center that opens de Certeau's essay, can be taken in with a single gaze and reduced to the panoptical scanning of masterful eye.[14]

While de Certeau is concerned, at all times, to draw attention to the groundlessness of the pedestrian speech act, the way in which, like gender, it must be practised again and again if is to have efficacy ('to walk is to lack a place. It is the indefinite process of being absent'), at no point in the essay does he ever discuss how the urban environment, in its material charge, might impact on or disturb the walker.[15] There are no smells, aches, noises or animals in his text; the focus remains resolutely anthropocentric. The point of Certeau's theory of performativity is to show how walking is like writing or speaking, disclosing alternative forms of grammar and syntax in the discourse of the city.

In order to add a sense of materiality to de Certeau's discursive theory of walking – and by extension to develop an ecology of walking that privileges the outside – I want to replace performativity with theatricality, a singular and singularising mode of disarmament that disturbs, in a more elemental and self-conscious manner, the ontological ground of being itself. Whereas performativity, as de Certeau suggests, always produces the city by 'manipulating spatial organisations'[16] so that the rules and codes constituting 'urban systematicity' are transgressed and re-appropriated by the walkers or *Wandersmänner* on the streets,[17] theatricality undoes the pedestrian subject. It does so by revealing, or better still, making a gap appear between the walker and the things they move through. As Samuel Weber explains, theatre has always been a suspect art because of how it challenges 'the self of self-presence and self-identity by reduplicating it in a seductive movement that never comes full circle'.[18]

In this exposure of non-identity, the walker, like the actor playing a role, is confronted with the presence of an earth that they are part of but unable ever to control or coincide with completely. Importantly – and this is very different from de Certeau – the strange, fugitive presence that theatricality discloses affects the subject, existing as the *Stimmung* that touches us with a non-human force and so establishes our impossible intimacy with the planet. To walk, then, is not only to lack a place in an urban system that is desperate to control and administer movement, it is to lack a proper sense of what the human is: to realise that one is always already non-human, an actor whose identity comes to them from the outside, from an attunement to a materiality that has neither origin nor end – a fact that perhaps explains why Antonin Artaud and Samuel Beckett were always so concerned to show the flesh and bones of the performer, to highlight their corporeal existence and mineral density.

In what follows in this essay, I seek to practise this theatricalised and materialised method of walking by providing a selective account of a year-long engagement with a piece of public art: Minty Donald, Nick Millar and Neil McGuire's THEN/NOW, situated on the Forth & Clyde Canal in the city of Glasgow. Playing on the double etymology of *kairos* ('opportune time' and 'weather)', I see my essay as an exercise in weathered thinking, a text whose logic is based on a methodology – an 'ecography' – that I advanced in a previous essay about walking the Paris Meridian in 2011.[19] Here, as then, I'm interested in experimenting with a mode of critical writing that would seek to map and express 'ecological experience'. Put simply, this is a type of sensate experience where a peripatetic body is folded into its environment and open to a series of incorporeal thoughts, feelings and becomings. This gives rise to a mode of criticism in which the art object is not approached as a discrete entity, something extracted from the material world in which it is located. On the contrary, the work is engaged in a series of material exchanges and entanglements. One should not be surprised to find that the writing ensuing from such a walking encounter is mobile, meandering and sometimes capricious. Like the site-based art object itself, the writing takes place in an expanded field; it is weathered, variable and heterogeneous.

In line with what I mentioned above, the essay is an example of theatricalised thought in motion and method. That is to say, it takes into account (a) a sense of temporality that one can never master, control or manage (theatre always repeats), (b) the presence of a body that moves in, across and through space and is affected and disarmed by that movement (the actor is always simultaneously here and elsewhere) and (c) a mode of relating that allows the outside to enter the inside, and vice versa (theatre always take place). Importantly, I do not see outside and inside in terms of a dialectic that can be resolved into a higher synthesis. On the contrary, inside and outside are in constant movement, never fixed and in perpetual oscillation. There is neither beginning nor end in this relationship – just an 'in-between' that never settles down, a kind of movement, something non-human.

B

January

THEN/NOW is in a tradition; it occupies a field – that of conceptual or post-minimal art that we associate with a number of land artists, such as Robert Smithson, Michael Heizer and Nancy Holt. But whereas much land art was concerned, like the eighteenth-century landscape gardener Capability Brown, with moving and disturbing the land for the sake of the perfect image, *THEN/NOW* is a slight work; its mode of operation on the canal is discreet – so discreet, in fact, that you can often miss it. In that respect, it is much closer to the work of contemporary eco- or public artists such as David Nash, Matt Baker and Jan Dibbets, each of whom moulds objects that can be moved, eroded and tampered with. This is work on a human scale that paradoxically and generatively points beyond the human to the earth systems that support it. Like a John Cage piece, *THEN/NOW* is decidedly non-heroic, a work that is desperate to get out of the way in order to let the world in, something that reverberates rather than absorbs. *THEN/NOW* is stubbornly anti-spectacle; it creates a kind of 'small displacement' when I am in the mood to receive it, or better still, when

Photographer: Brian Sweeney

everything I meet on my daily walk along the canal with my dog, Mali, attunes me to it. Much of this is accidental, *kairotic* – the sudden falling of snow, the play of light on the water, rain that makes me stop, dropping the dog lead. When I came across *THEN/NOW*, quite by chance, on a bright, frozen day in January 2016, I was disarmed by it.

March

THEN/NOW is made of two parts. A small engraving of the words 'THEN/ NOW' on the bank of the canal, and nine granite boulders on both sides of the bridge at Applecross Street. The surfaces of these 'erratics' have been sculpted to resemble, as in a scale model, the nine reservoirs that feed, or once fed, Glasgow. Depending on the weather, the hollows on the surface of the stones can either be filled with water, iced-up as solid blocks or, more rarely, left completely dry, containing, then, only cigarette papers and faint green rings, the traces of the rain that has accumulated in them over the winter. The stones have been weathered. After only four or five months on the canal, they already show the marks of time, atmospheric writing.

As I watched my fellow walkers on the canal engage with the works, I often witnessed a sense of perplexity and hilarity. It seemed to me

Photographer: Minty Donald

that they were seduced by the sculptures, trying to make sense of them, wondering about their status. I saw children, adults, and adolescents laughing, touching the stones, feeling the matter, being drawn in by their shape and form. They would also look at the flanks of the stone, and what they saw etched on the granite were the names of reservoirs: Lilly, Hillend, Johnstone, Woodend, etc. Crucially, though, there was nothing in the work to provide an obvious context for interpretation. There was a gap or interval between signifier and signified, and what filled this gap was nothing other than what Gaston Bachelard has termed in his great book on air and dreaming, 'the material imagination', an imagination that is affected, enchanted and produced by elemental matter.[20] If Bachelard is right in his psychoanalysis of the four elements (air, fire, water, earth), then there would appear to be some inextricable and ineradicable symbiosis between the earth and human creativity, something non-negotiable and atavistic, something that cannot be undone – earth as creative source, producing its own mythology, a poeticised materialism.

April

I was away from the canal for much of April, but what sticks in my mind is a clear blue day somewhere towards the middle of the month when I saw the stones become luminescent in the early Spring sunlight. They shone white like moonstones and seemed mysterious, alive, moving at a different pace from the rest of the percolating world. *THEN/NOW* is an open-air installation, a weather work, something that changes in time as it is buffeted, eroded and enfolded by the weather of Glasgow, by its geography of circumstance, by its 'aerography'. Even though it uses the dense elemental matter of stone and iron for its form of expression, *THEN/NOW* is not really a work about objects; rather, it seeks to gather the incorporeal stuff of the atmosphere around it, attuning us to the otherwise invisible play of pressure systems, temperatures, the always moving, transient passage of the sky.

May

The willow trees are opening. Sun, photosynthesis, leaves, green, a heron, swallows dancing through the gaps of the electricity pylons, and nine new cygnet swans taking to the water from their nest at Rockvilla – the new home of the National Theatre of Scotland. I focus on the word NOW that is written on the side of the canal nearest to the building, The Whisky Bond. It is reflecting its opposite – an upside down WON – on the calm, still surface of the water. I also know that there is an engraved THEN placed on the side of the canal where I am standing, under my feet, invisible to me. There is in this play of light and reflection, this temporal assemblage, something intriguing. The work makes me see that the present is never quite here, always on its way elsewhere, an impossible trace. The work's ability to put the 'present in crisis', to redistribute it, is what makes *THEN/NOW*

Photographer: Minty Donald

so ultimately 'theatrical'. For theatre is a medium that never stands still, a machine that places the performer in two incompatible spaces: the HERE of the body; the THERE of the character or persona. The present, of course, is caught in this fugitive space, lost in this shimmering movement, never quite here, never quite there. The ever-changing surface of the water makes it a perfect medium for *THEN/NOW*'s meditation on time, its theatricalised commitment to the present participle.

June

Much ecological thought today is seduced by what has been called neo-materialism, a type of materialism that stresses the living agency or vibrancy of matter. The logic at work in this attentiveness to the molecular and inorganic, to what is ordinarily left out of our discussions of the world, is to decentre the human, to show that it is just one actant in a network of energetic connections, feedback loops and flows. *THEN/NOW* is very much part of that debate. It draws our attention to the affective power of materials to create thought, to produce imaginings, maybe even existential territories. However, the work, whether consciously or not, does something else, too. In its invitation to think of the split between THEN/NOW, it cannot help but bring to mind a very different form of materialism, a kind of historical materialism that is sometimes forgotten by some proponents of new materialism.

For to walk on the canal, as I do every day, is to find oneself, necessarily, transported between past and future, between, that is, the two virtualities of ghost and phantom. The ghosts of infrastructure are everywhere: absent reservoirs, dammed up rivers, broken bodies, dead things, pollution, industrialism, slavery, the machine, the clock, alienation, work, schedules, disenchantment, insane metabolisms, Empire. And yet so too are the phantoms of the future: rising sea levels, ice melts, global warming, mass extinction events, acidification, vast people movements, water wars, the heat and horror of the Capitolocene. In *THEN/NOW*, the past and future are here, now, together in some blurred time ecology. In its mixity, the work supplies the very thing that new materialism overlooks: the preponderance of the human, and the return of history. In doing so, it discloses the paradox in new materialism: for if all matter is horizontally distributed and the human just an actant like any other, then how to account for the historical and barbaric role that capital plays in the production of the world? In an assemblage or non-linear history, not everything is equal.

June in Glasgow was hot. The water in the canal was strangely transparent, and dead fish – bream, carp, pike – floated to the surface, their bellies swollen and ready to pop. Green algae covered the canal. It stank. When they dug it out, it looked like solidified petroleum.

July

High summer but the rain and cloud have returned. Business as usual in Glasgow. As I walk through the low sky, dealing with its strange anonymity,

I think of the extraordinary images of the city captured by the photographer Raymond Depardon in the 1980s in a photo-shoot for the *Sunday Times*. Depardon's images were pulled from circulation because in their unsentimental realism; they conflicted with the glitzy image of the city promoted by the City Council as it was gearing up for the City of Culture extravaganza in 1990. A shame, because Depardon captures the light of Glasgow magnificently. He is so attuned to it; it is almost as if it blinded him, imprinting itself on his retina, a white eclipse.

Normally we do not see light. It is a medium that allows us to see other objects. To photograph the light as Depardon does, is precisely not to see it, but rather to allow oneself to be affected by it, to remain open to its impress. Thus Depardon is not so much capturing light as allowing himself to be captured by it, and then translating that capture into a series of 'mood-images'. Here the doubleness of language reinserts itself, for the word 'mood' relates to atmosphere, which, in scientific discourse, refers to the layer of air that surrounds the earth, and which is the medium in which weather takes place. To capture and be captured light, then, is to be attuned to something decidedly human – emotions, perceptions, feelings – and yet at the same time to be caught up in a series of impersonal, cosmic flows.

On the canal in July, everything is alive, too much, in excess, verdant. I wonder about what differentiates walking with a dog from walking with people. Of course, there are numerous stops to pick up shit, and to separate fighting dogs, but what stand out for me are the ways in which I am constantly moving between earth and sky, looking down, looking up, following Mali's movements in the undergrowth, and then watching her run towards the horizon. Might this movement, this inhabitation of the interstice, allow for a different thinking of time? Time here percolates and bubbles, it fizzes and schizzes; it does not flow in some arrow-like movement, the sequential, measured temporality of capitalist modernity.

August

A change in the light around mid-month – an exorbitant softness. The evenings shortening. Summer on its way out. Here in Glasgow, everything is pulling towards the West, towards the Atlantic, to the Americas, hurricanes, the Gulf Stream, great gyres in the Ocean. To love the weather is to give in to multiplicity, to realise that everywhere is always elsewhere, to give up on borders. As a meditation on time (*kairos*), THEN/NOW is also a mediation on space, a HERE/THERE. The same caesura, the forward slash, that diacritically and simultaneously connects and disconnects disparate, even opposed times and spaces. I am reminded of how, when we talk about theatre, we often describe the work as a 'piece' – an accurate word for an art form that can never be whole and that always changes its form in its necessary commitment to time. Paradoxically, given its usual location, theatre is the medium closest to weather, a vehicle that transports, an apparatus that is here and elsewhere, simultaneously and impossibly.

Photographer: Minty Donald

September

For the past two months, they have been a building a new cycle path by the Applecross Street Bridge. The work is almost finished now; all that is required is to lay some new turf around four of the *THEN/NOW* stones. The stones themselves look extraordinary as they sit in a field of brown mud. As in a Zen garden, they are objects that have retreated, mysteriously and massively, into their own immanence, and yet, at the same time, they radiate outwards and swirl vertiginously in the air, giving off a haze of atoms. Philosophers have long seen stones as inert matter, something to kick, maybe, or to carry like Sisyphus, but rock artists and geologists know better. For them, the lithic is a zone of seduction and attraction, a telluric reality that changes, erodes, and is marked by a million different temporalities, all of which form part of a non-linear history, vertiginous 'ancestralities' beyond human perception, even indeed life itself: 'I will call ancestral any reality anterior to the emergence of the human species – or even anterior to every recognised form of life on earth.'[21]

Every time I walk past them, the rocks change. They refuse to sit still. They erode and age.

In his 2004 book *Conversation Pieces: Community and Communication in Modern Art*, Grant Kester argues for a new methodology for understanding the objectives of certain kinds of community art that place the emphasis on process rather than product. This entails, Kester claims, a new focus on longitudinal enquiry, spending time with the work, seeing how it was made, and the changes it effects as it unfolds over time.[22]

A different but related argument for duration is made by the art critic T.J. Clark. In his 2006 text *The Sight of Death: An Experiment in Art Writing*, Clark explains how he arrived on a fellowship at the Getty Institute in Los Angeles not quite knowing what he would do. He soon found himself, however, magnetically attracted to two paintings by Poussin, *Landscape with a Man Killed by a Snake* and *Landscape with a Calm*, which he proceeded to visit on a daily basis for several months in the year 2000.[23]

While I would certainly not put myself in the same august company as Kester and Clark, my own peripatetic engagement with *THEN/NOW* is, perhaps, of a similar order. By walking past it every day for a year, I was interested in tracing the work's shifting shape, in tracking its transience and mapping the ways in which sculpture becomes theatrical, that is to say, temporal, always moving, committed to change. It quickly became apparent that the work was as much about the weather, the site and me as it was about itself. *THEN/NOW* was a medium, host and catalyst: it communicated information, allowed me to engage with the world, and produced a number of embodied but virtual thoughts. I have tried to give an account of the texture and motility of this thought through this writing, the way in which it could be as capricious and transient as the weather.

In doing so, I have tried to express what I call 'theatricalised knowledge' – knowledge that has neither origin nor end, is dependent on a material engagement with things, and troubles metaphysical notions of identity based on a close correlation or fit between human subject and non-human object. Fortuitously, the image that best renders this theatricalised engagement is of a pair of feet walking, one of which is stepping off the earth, the other alighting on it. In the gap between the feet – in the unrepresentable space caused by movement – the world enters the domain of thought. And it is in this impossible space, I want to wager, that a generative nexus emerges that brings together walking, theatricality and weather – all processes that are decidedly untimely and, for that very reason, the instigators of the *kairotic*, an intimacy that draws us close to things while simultaneously distancing us from them. Such an infinite and elusive play between proximity and distance, transience and duration, mind and matter is what I have sought to practise in my walks with, to and around *THEN/NOW*. Everything was a question of positions that moved.

Notes

1   Much has been written on the philosophy of walking, but no one has approached the 'ecosophy' of walking in the way I am proposing here. For more on philosophy and walking, see Frédéric Gros, *A Philosophy of Walking*, trans. J. Howe (London: Verso, 2015). For more on walking and ecology, see Jess Allen's work allinadayswalk.org.uk/about/about/ (accessed 5 January 2018).

2   Quentin Meillassoux, *After Finitude: An Essay on the Necessity of Contingency*, trans. Ray Brassier (London: Bloomsbury, 2008), 10.

3 Jeffrey Jerome Cohen, *Stone: An Ecology of the Inhuman* (Minneapolis, MN: University of Minnesota Press, 2015), 8.
4 Alain Badiou, *Being and Event*, trans. O. Feltham (London: Continuum, 2007).
5 Marguerite Duras, *The North China Lover*, trans. L. Hafrey (New York: New Press, 1994), 25.
6 Gernot Böhme, 'Atmosphere as the Fundamental Concept of a New Aesthetics', *Thesis Eleven* 36 (1993): 121.
7 Michel Haar, *The Song of the Earth: Heidegger and the Grounds of the History of Being*, trans. R. Lilly (Bloomington, IN: Indiana University Press, 1993), 37
8 Lisa Robertson, *Nilling* (Toronto, Canada: Book Thug, 2012), 13.
9 This is opposed to my previous argument for walking and enchantment in my essay 'Mourning Walk and Pedestrian Performance: History, Aesthetics, Ethics', in *Walking, Writing and Performance: Autobiographical Texts by Deirdre Heddon, Carl Lavery and Phil Smith*, ed. Roberta Mock (Bristol, UK: Intellect, 2009), 49–51.
10 See many of the essays in Tim Ingold and Jo Lee Vergunst, eds, *Ways of Walking: Ethnography and the Practice on Foot* (Aldershot, UK: Ashgate, 2008).
11 Gilles Deleuze and Félix Guattari, 'November 29, 1947: How to Make Yourself a Body without Organs', in *A Thousand Plateaus: Capitalism and Schizophrenia*, trans. B. Massumi (Minneapolis, MN: University of Minnesota Press, 1987), 149–66.
12 A good way to think of the body without organs is to consider it as an excessive, vibratory body, a body that has gone beyond the limits of the skin
13 Michel de Certeau, *The Practice of Everyday*, trans. S. Rendell (Berkeley, CA: University of California Press, 1984), 98.
14 De Certeau, *The Practice of Everyday Life*, 91–100.
15 Ibid., 103
16 Ibid., 101.
17 Ibid., 105.
18 Samuel Weber, *Theatricality as Medium* (New York: Fordham University Press, 2004), 8.
19 Carl Lavery, 'Performing Paris: An Ecography of Meridians and Atmospheres', in *Performing Cities*, ed. Nicolas Whybrow (Basingstoke, UK: Palgrave Macmillan, 2014).
20 Gaston Bachelard, *Air and Dreams: An Essay on the Imagination of Movement*, trans. E. Farrell and C. Farrell (Dallas, TX: Dallas Institute of Humanities and Culture, 2011), 7.
21 Meillassoux, *After Finitude*, 10.
22 Grant Kester, *Conversation Pieces: Community and Communication in Modern Art* (Berkeley, CA: University of California Press, 2004), 67.
23 T.J. Clark, *The Sight of Death: An Experiment in Art Writing* (New Haven, CT: Yale University Press, 2006), 1–15.

Works cited

Allen, Jess. allinadayswalk.org.uk/about/about/ (accessed 5 January 2018).
Bachelard, Gaston. *Air and Dreams: An Essay on the Imagination of Movement.* Translated by E. Farrell and C. Farrell. Dallas, TX: Dallas Institute of Humanities and Culture, 2011.
Badiou, Alain. *Being and Event.* Translated by Oliver Feltham. London: Continuum, 2007.
Böhme, Gernot. 'Atmosphere as the Fundamental Concept of a New Aesthetics'. *Thesis Eleven* 36 (1993): 113–126.

Clark, T.J. *The Sight of Death: An Experiment in Art Writing*. New Haven, CT: Yale University Press, 2006.

De Certeau, Michel. *The Practice of Everyday*. Translated by Stephen Rendell. Berkeley, CA: University of California Press, 1984.

Deleuze, Gilles and Félix Guattari. 'November 29, 1947: How to Make Yourself a Body without Organs', in *A Thousand Plateaus: Capitalism and Schizophrenia*, trans. B. Massumi, 149–66. Minneapolis, MN: University of Minnesota Press, 1987.

Duras, Marguerite. *The North China Lover*. Translated by L. Hafrey. New York: New Press, 1994.

Gros, Frédéric. *A Philosophy of Walking*. Translated by John Howe. London: Verso, 2015.

Haar, Michel. *The Song of the Earth: Heidegger and the Grounds of the History of Being*. Translated by R. Lilly. Bloomington, IN: Indiana University Press, 1993.

Ingold, Tim and Jo Lee Vergunst, eds. *Ways of Walking: Ethnography and the Practice on Foot*. Aldershot, UK: Ashgate, 2008.

Kester, Grant. *Conversation Pieces: Community and Communication in Modern Art*. Berkeley, CA: University of California Press, 2004.

Lavery, Carl. 'Mourning Walk and Pedestrian Performance: History, Aesthetics, Ethics'. In *Walking, Writing and Performance: Autobiographical Texts by Deirdre Heddon, Carl Lavery and Phil Smith*, edited by Roberta Mock, 25–56. Bristol, UK: Intellect, 2009.

Lavery, Carl. 'Performing Paris: An Ecography of Meridians and Atmospheres'. In *Performing Cities*, edited by Nicolas Whybrow, 56–78. Basingstoke, UK: Palgrave Macmillan, 2014.

Meillassoux, Quentin. *After Finitude: An Essay on the Necessity of Contingency*. Translated by Ray Brassier. London: Bloomsbury, 2008.

Robertson, Lisa. *Nilling*. Toronto, Canada: Book Thug, 2012.

Weber, Samuel. *Theatricality as Medium*. New York: Fordham University Press, 2004.

5 *Ghosts of the Restless Shore*
A personal pilgrimage

Mike Collier

Introduction

In this chapter, I examine elements of my practice that might be described as pilgrimages, explored through my role as Principle Investigator of WALK.[1] I introduce an artistic intervention that I call *conversive pilgrimage* and show how the idea of pilgrimage is closely linked to the activity of walking, suggesting that 'the volume and depth and intensity of the world is something that only those on foot will ever experience'.[2] Following an introduction about the idea and experience of pilgrimage, the main part of my essay presents a series of linked (one might say rhizomatic) notes and recollections of one particular project, *Ghosts of the Restless Shore*, presented as memories that collapse traditional ideas and experiences of time. Here, I focus on a four-day phenomenological walk in 2015 along the Sefton Coast were I was born and raised. The structure of this section is based on an eighteenth-century essay tradition in which friends set out on a walking tour and discuss a range of subject matter from natural history to philosophy and culture. Central to this part of the essay are four text-based works listing everything seen and heard on the walk. Here, the lists presented can be seen as 'memorials': these very specific 'lists' of flora and fauna celebrate local ecologies and can be seen as 'pilgrimage shrines'. Finally, I summarise my reasons for adopting *conversive pilgrimage* and walking as a creative and research methodology, suggesting that the lists of flora and fauna created and shared on these secular pilgrimages embody the appreciation or understanding of 'things in their singularity'[3] – a way to bridge the dualism between culture and nature, allowing us to engage with ethical issues that confront us in the Anthropocene.

Names which scintillate in the mind and engage our feelings[4]

When I use the words 'landscape'/'soundscape' or 'nature' in this essay, I refer to both the rural and urban ideas of landscape. My walks and pilgrimages deliberately take place in both the city and the countryside. They seek to redress the Cartesian bifurcation of culture and nature, Nature, in this inclusive sense, is inherently creative and fluid. The poet Kay Syrad explains that culture is a veil through which we describe nature:

> The edge is the division
> What is known is always from the past
> Through knowledge, the new is a reworking of the old
> The sum total of knowledge is culture
> Culture is the veil through which we describe nature
> The process of nature continues despite our analysis
> Our analysis is part of the process of nature
> The process of nature must include the actions of man
> Whether or not they are destructive
> Man's description of nature as something separate – out of town – where
>   the edge is the division between 'nature' and 'culture', is an illusion.
> 'Nature' and 'Culture' are the same thing.
> There is no division.[5]

My use of the list (a central feature of this chapter) as a form of art can be seen both as a meditative monument to a particular place and as an embodiment of 'things in their *singularity*'. I like the possibility that this word 'singularity' also references *sing*ing with respect to the spoken or sung word. These lists of mine should be read/sung out aloud, each word 'rooted in the felt experience induced by specific sounds and sound-shapes as they echo and contrast with one another [. . .], a particular way of "singing the world"'.[6] These names of flora and fauna can draw us 'into a world where art meets science, often producing names which scintillate in the mind and engage our feelings'.[7] Furthermore, these individual words, spoken together, map a very specific landscape. They allow us the intellectual and emotional space to fill in the gaps between the words – to imagine what this land-scape/soundscape might be like; and so we can become participants in the imagined world summoned up. These place-specific lists are indicative of a very particular habitat – 'lists that anyone with a little knowledge of plant-life and ecological habitats might identify with the Sefton Coast'.[8] Robert Macfarlane explains that:

> we once had a wonderfully rich and expressive range of words for our local landscapes [. . .] [but that] [a]s more people are brought up to live in towns and cities, the land beyond the city fringe has increasingly become understood as consisting of large, generic, units ('field', 'hill', 'valley', 'wood'). It has become a *blandscape* [. . .]. As we further deplete our ability to name, describe and figure particular aspects of our landscape, our competence for understanding and imagining possible relationships with non-human nature is corres-pondingly depleted.[9]

Conversive pilgrimage

The words 'pilgrim' and 'pilgrimage' are derived from the Latin *peregrinus* (from *per*, 'through', and *ager*, 'field' or 'land', so 'pilgrimage' literally means 'through the land'). Pilgrimage might therefore imply 'a physical journey, as well as state of inner reflection'.[10] Although the journey can take many forms, in general walking is central to the act of pilgrimage. As Rebecca Solnit writes:

> While walking, the body and mind can work together, so that think-ing becomes almost a physical, rhythmic act; [. . .] past and present are brought together when you walk, as the ancients did or relive some event in history or your own life by retracing its route.[11]

People go on pilgrimages for almost as many reasons as there are pilgrims. A pilgrimage can be undertaken individually – perhaps as a journey of self-discovery – or it can be a sociable activity, allowing us to enjoy the company of others we meet on our journey. Many cultures have pilgrimages that involve eye-wateringly large numbers of pilgrims, for example the Kumbh Mela Hindu pilgrimage is one of the largest gatherings of people in the world. At any given place, the Kumbh Mela is held once in twelve years; an estimated 120 million people visited Maha Kumbh Mela in 2013 in Allahabad over a two-month period, including over 30 million on a single day, on 10 February 2013 (the day of Mauni Amavasaya).[12]

As an artist, my work draws on my 'practice' of *conversive pilgrimage* walking, or more properly, meandering; the research for my studio-based collaborative artwork is 'conducted' through such secular 'pilgrimages' – walks or meanders which are inclusive, involving artists, natural and social historians, poets, sound artists as well as students and the public. I often find that the shared experiences gained when walking with others generate new knowledge about flora and fauna encountered and noted during the walk, along with diverse individual perceptions and social observations that inevi-tably emerge as the conversations between walkers/pilgrims develop and the walk unfolds in its place-specific way.[13]

These walks encourage participants to experience the world with their heart and through all their senses. Participants gather and share the knowledge that comes directly from experience (from the wildness of the world) – a process called *biognosis*, meaning 'knowledge from life' – research and knowledge which I hope encourage people to care more about their environment and therefore to effect positive change. All of this experience serves as material for thought, layered intuitively into the fabric of the work I construct back in the studio.[14] Making such work is a different, but parallel and equally embodied, conversive experience, and I invariably work collaboratively with the poets, sound artists, glass artists, photographers, natural historians and composers who have walked with me when making new, place-based work.

In *Walking* (1851), Thoreau defines 'the art of Walking' as 'a genius [. . .] for *sauntering*', describing the etymology of *saunter* as derived from '*à la Sainte Terre*', that is, 'going to the Holy Land'.[15] The walk, then, becomes a sort of pilgrimage, a kind of religious or quasi-religious ritual. Although not religious myself, I respect, and am interested in, non-institutional religious thought and philosophy. My own experience, shared with many fellow walkers, is that pilgrimage is not about affirmation – that is, confirming long-held imaginings about a place, space or faith. It is about discovery . . . what Tim Ingold describes as knowledge 'grown along the way'.[16] It provides us with an opportunity to step out of the non-stop clutter of our everyday lives, to seek a time of embodied reflection. I also share a view with many artists and writers/poets that our creative life is a journey of exploration and discovery – a pilgrimage of embodied, physical and creative reflection underlining that we are part of a more-than-human, creative world.

Ghosts of the Restless Shore

> The Sefton coast is a haunted place, where the past can suddenly reappear, bursting into the present, the way a gust of wind in a ghost story flings open a loose window and rushes into the room. Concealment and revelation are its talents. It knows how to throw a covering of sand over a wrecked ship, to suck it down into its underground chambers and keep it there.[17]

I want to now focus in detail on one key, personal pilgrimage – a walk along the Sefton Coast from Waterloo to Southport with my brother Tim (a wildlife photographer), sound artist Dr Robert Strachan, poet Jake Campbell and natural historian John Dempsey of the Sefton Coastal Landscape Partnership. Following this walk, we created a multi-media exhibition of visual and sound art presented at the Atkinson Gallery in Southport and published a book about the project with essays written by each of the artists.[18] For this section, I have edited elements of the catalogue texts and presented them as an invented narrative. In doing so, I am mindful of the Japanese Haiku master Matsuo Bashō's travel narrative *A Narrow Road to the Deep North*, in which:

> he often changed the chronological order of his journey to enhance the artistic effects of his poems. His meandering handwritings on the manuscripts, occasionally patched up with revised sheets, suggest not only his rambling journey, but also reconstructed the process of recollection and self-examination as a poet [. . .] inspired by the vicissitudes of nature and by living in the flow of time and life.[19]

The lists of flora and fauna that punctuate this narrative honour everything seen and heard on each of the four days of the pilgrimage and have been edited from a larger piece which included the derivation of local place names and mythological information about the natural history encountered. They are a memorial to the ecology of this very specific, liminal landscape/soundscape.

I was born in Sefton – a suburban conurbation and industrial landscape between the plains of Lancashire and the sea – and I lived there for eighteen years. It is the place that shaped many of my ideas about how we experience and perceive the world. For some years, Tim and I had talked about walking the Sefton Coastal Path together, enriching and deepening our knowledge of this seminal place in our lives. It was to be a kind of pilgrimage. As well as walking with Robert, Jake and John, we were joined by over thirty members of the public at different points along our journey, an experience which became communal and collaborative as we meandered and shared experiences of this special place.

Walk one: 12 July 2014: Waterloo Station to Hightown Station – 4.4 miles

Tim: 'This coast is a place that holds many memories and has shaped who I am. With family ties close to the coast in Crosby I've continued a distant yet powerful relationship with the twenty or so miles that take you from Gormley's *Another Place* at Seaforth to the wild open reaches of the salt marshes of Southport. Each time I visit family I find myself drawn to the coast, always preferring winter when the vast horizons seem endless and you can spend all day without coming across a soul.'

John: 'As a small boy looking out on the grey vastness of Liverpool Bay, I'd struggle over autumn dunes, settle down to be buffeted in a north westerly, then scour the waves for shearwaters, petrels and skuas through binoculars that first saw action on the racecourses and dog tracks of southern Ireland, before the passing of my Uncle Jim meant they came to me [. . .]. The romance of a bundle of feathers winging off to the southern Atlantic to wander deserted oceans while we batten down the hatches for a northern winter grabbed my attention at eight years of age, as surely as the thought of the trade routes and the potential of "destination anywhere" did when I learnt more about the incredible maritime history of Liverpool Bay.

I've always been a sucker for an horizon, or to be more accurate, what lies beyond it.'

Robert: 'I have been drawn to this coast by the richness of the area's natural and social history to be found in the most minute detail as well as its imposing seascape and landscape. The dunes, meadows and woods are alive with an incredible richness of flora and fauna and the focus of the eye and ear upon its intricacies bring this diversity to life. The environment itself affords different levels of engagement; different modes of exploring the world around us. The suspension of everyday modes of time and attention leads us to look closely, to be engulfed in a constant sonic environment that suspends linearity or to exercise selective attention in the way we listen to the environment.'

12 JULY. STARTED 10.00 AM AT WATERLOO STATION AND FINISHED 4.00 PM AT HIGHTOWN STATION. WEATHER WARM (20 DEGREES), LITTLE WIND, SUNSHINE AND BRIGHT. SEA BUCKTHORN; COMMON CENTAURY; EVENING PRIMROSE; CLUSTERED DOCK; SPEAR-LEAVED ORACHE; SEA BEET; SEA SANDWORT; KNOTTED PEARLWORT; BLADDER CAMPION; MEADOW RUE; SEA RADISH; SEA ROCKET; SEA KALE; BITING STONECROP; MEADOW SWEET; SALAD BURNETT; TUFTED VETCH; TARE; EVERLASTING PEA; HARE'S FOOT CLOVER; MEADOW VETCHLING; RIBBED MELILOT; WHITE MELILOT; REST HARROW; BIRD'S-FOOT-TREFOIL; HOP TREFOIL; RED CLOVER; WHITE CLOVER; MEADOW CRANESBILL; DOVE'S FOOT CRANE'S BILL; CUT-LEAVED CRANE'S BILL; SEA SPURGE; COMMON MALLOW; ROSEBAY WILLOWHERB; SEA HOLLY; WILD CARROT; ANGELICA; HEMLOCK WATER DROPWORT; WILD PARSNIP; ALEXANDERS; FENNNEL; SEASIDE CENTAURY; HEDGE BINDWEED; COMFREY; HOUND'S TONGUE; VIPER'S BUGLOSS; COMMON STORK'S-BILL; HEDGE WOUNDWORT; SELF HEAL; BETONY; POLYPODY FERN; COMMON CORDGRASS; MULLIEN; COMMON TOADFLAX; EYEBRIGHT; SEA PLANTAIN; HAREBELL; ISLE OF MAN CABBAGE; GOLDEN ROD; SCENTLESS MAYWEED; SEA ASTER; YARROW; COLTSFOOT; MUGWORT; RAGWORT; CREEPING THISTLE; SPEAR THISTLE; HAWKWEED; COMMON SPOTTED ORCHID; NORTHERN MARSH ORCHID; PYRAMIDAL ORCHID; BEE ORCHID; YELLOW RATTLE; ROUND-LEAVED WINTERGREEN; HOUSE SPARROW; COMMON TERN; BLACK-HEADED GULL; LESSER BLACK-BACKED GULL; HERRING GULL; LINNET; GOLDFINCH; LITTLE OWL; WHITETHROAT; WILLOW WARBLER; SEDGE WARBLER; PIED WAGTAIL; STARLING; REDSHANK; CURLEW; OYSTERCATCHER; HERON; SHELDUCK; KESTREL; CARRION CROW; MAGPIE; MEADOW PIPIT; SWIFT; HEDGE SPARROW; BUTTERFLIES AND MOTHS SEEN INCLUDE: COMMON BLUE; SMALL HEATH; SIX SPOT BURNETT; GATEKEEPER; RED ADMIRAL; SMALL TORTOISESHELL; SMALL SKIPPER; SMALL HEATH; MEADOW BROWN; SMALL WHITE; GREEN VEINED WHITE; NATTERJACK TOAD.

Walk two: 13 July 2014: Hightown Station to Freshfield Station – 4.7 miles

Tim: 'Do you remember the many afternoons spent walking along Fisherman's Path, following the pinewoods through Massam's Slack and onto the shore between Freshfield and Ainsdale? Mum would have her *Illustrations of The*

British Flora by W.H. Fitch and W.G. Smith in tandem with the *Handbook of The British Flora* by George Bentham and Sir J.D. Hooker (she would hand colour the illustrations and date them in the book), and Dad his 35mm Ilford Sportsman camera. We would have open spaces and places to explore as well as things to collect.

Memories are created out of such experiences and shaped by time. They are reinforced, embellished, never quite forgotten and always building, one upon another; layers of memories.

When I was about ten, I was adventurous, a little headstrong and far too sure of myself. More dangerously, I was old enough to believe I could explore, yet be safe. In this dune system, paths are everywhere and to a raw ten-year-old the landscape was huge and identical whichever way you looked; and at ten who wants a path anyway? Even today finding a spot you earmarked for re-visiting at a later date is unusually difficult. So I got lost, really lost, hopelessly lost, lost for a full day – and at ten that's an eternity.'

John: 'The literary giant Nathaniel Hawthorne strode these same dunes during his time as American consul in Liverpool, and maybe steered Herman Melville through pipe smoke and advice to the shores of genius that lie in *Moby Dick*, who knows?

Some experts suggest Hawthorne hated his time here.

If true, that's something I could never let pass [. . .] how can the dunes and sands not grab you? How can you not be impressed by the scale of the place, the isolation that seems to actively resist permanent structures?

The remains of a few shipwrecks, like the skeletons of beached dinosaurs, are all that seem to last for any length of time on the sands.'

13 JULY. STARTED 10.30 AM AT HIGHTOWN STATION PASSING ROUND FORMBY POINT AND FINISHED 4.00 PM AT FRESHFIELD STATION. WEATHER WARM AGAIN (22 DEGREES), CLOUDLESS SKY, NO WIND, BRIGHT SUNSHINE. SOAPWORT; BUTTERCUP; MEADOW RUE; MARE'S TAIL; ISLE OF MAN CABBAGE; HEDGE MUSTARD; SEA RADISH; SEA ROCKET; HAIRY BITTER CRESS; SEA-KALE; WILD MIGNONETTE; WELD; HIMALAYAN BALSAM; YELLOW-WORT; MUGWORT; RED CAMPION; SEA CAMPION; BLADDER CAMPION; SEA SANDWORT; SPEAR-LEAVED ORACHE; SEA BEET; SEA PURSLANE; DOVE'S-FOOT CRANE'S BILL; RESTHARROW; RED CLOVER; HOP TREFOIL; HARE'S-FOOT CLOVER; TUFTED VETCH; SMOOTH TARE; MEADOW VETCHLING; SEA PEA; RIBBED MELILOT; BIRD'S-FOOT TREFOIL; KIDNEY VETCH; FIELD ROSE; DEWBERRY;

(continued)

(continued)

SILVERWEED; MEADOW SWEET; BROAD-LEAVED WILLOWHERB; ROSEBAY WILLOWHERB; PURPLE LOOSESTRIFE; SEA SPURGE; SWEET CICELY; ANGELICA; FENNEL; SEA HOLLY; WILD CARROT; BROAD-LEAVED DOCK; SORREL; YELLOW LOOSESTRIFE; COMMON CENTAURY; SEASIDE CENTAURY; HEDGE BINDWEED; EYEBRIGHT; YELLOW BARTSIA; RED BARTSIA; SELFHEAL; GREEN ALKANET; VIPER'S BUGLOSS; HOUND'S TONGUE; COMFREY; LADY'S BEDSTRAW; TEASEL; RAGWORT; GOLDEN ROD; FLEABANE; BLUE FLEABANE; SCENTLESS MAYWEED; SPEAR THISTLE; CREEPING THISTLE; KNAPWEED; BURDOCK; GOATSBEARD; CAT'S-EAR HAWKWEED; HAREBELL; YELLOW RATTLE; DUNE HELLEBORINE; MARSH HELLEBORINE; PYRAMIDAL ORCHID; BEE ORCHID; EARLY MARSH ORCHID; GRASS-OF-PARNASSUS; SOUTHERN MARSH ORCHID; COASTAL HEDGE BINDWEED; BROOKWEED; POPPY; EVENING PRIMROSE; PRICKLY SALTWORT; CARLINE THISTLE; MONTBRETIA; CLEAVERS; BURNET ROSE; WOOD SAGE; WILD STRAWBERRY; WILD THYME; EARLY FORGET-ME-NOT; WILD PARSNIP. BUTTERLIES SEEN: SMALL WHITE; GREEN VEINED WHITE; GATEKEEPER; COMMA; DARK GREEN FRITILLARY; GRAYLING; RED ADMIRAL; SMALL TORTOISESHELL; SIX SPOT BURNETT; SPECKLED WOOD; LARGE HEATH; SMALL SKIPPER; MEADOW BROWN. ALSO SEEN: EMPEROR DRAGONFLY AND COMMON GREEN GRASSHOPPER. BIRDS SEEN OR HEARD INCLUDE: MISTLE THRUSH; SHELLDUCK; OYSTERCATCHER; BLACK-HEADED GULL; HERRING GULL; LESSER BLACK-BACKED GULL; LINNET; GOLDFINCH; BLACKCAP; WILLOW WARBLER; STOCK DOVE; JAY; MAGPIE; ROOK; CARRION CROW; SKYLARK; MEADOW PIPIT; WHITETHROAT; KESTREL; RAVEN; SPARROWHAWK; PIED WAGTAIL; CHIFFCHAFF; TREE CREEPER; COAL TIT; COMMON TERN; REED BUNTING; SWIFT; HOUSE MARTIN; STARLING.

Walk three: 19 July 2014: Freshfield Station to Ainsdale Station – 4.4 miles

Tim: 'Layered memories of the Sefton Coast have built up from each of my visits over the period of my life, lately separated by prolonged periods of real time, yet stacked up together to produce a seamless continuity of imagined time.

Taking home an oiled Guillemot from the Alt Estuary, attempting to clean it up with soft detergent and feeding it fish of various types; stroking a windblown and exhausted Little Stint by the boat yard at Hightown; telephoning that sage of birding in the North West, Eric Hardy, on coming across a Black Tern and Spoonbill, then seeing them reported in his column in the *Liverpool Daily Post*; being shat upon by over 5,000 Pink-footed Geese whilst on my bike birdwatching around the Flea Moss lanes; more recently seeing my first Great-white Egret coming into roost at the marina in Southport along with over forty Little Egrets on a cold February evening. These are more than memories and, like being lost in the dunes, they are perceptible in who I am today.'

John: 'Pink-footed Geese darken October skies in staggering numbers – their calls are ingrained in the subconscious of anyone who has lived here for any length of time.

They spend their days commuting from the safety of roosting sites out on the Alt and Ribble estuaries, where no fox can catch them unawares on the open sand and mud, to the rich peaty fields of the Lancashire mosslands that surround the dune system.

But they'll still go back to Iceland to breed, leaving a vacuum in grey skies that is filled each spring with Swallows and Swifts, albeit in numbers that diminish each year.'

Mike: 'I remember when I was a kid, I used to spend many days searching the dunes for Natterjack Toads. Smaller than the common toad, what it lacks in size, it more than makes up for with a loud rasping croak that echoes around the dunes on spring nights, as the males go in search of a mate. It is the nosiest amphibian in Europe and its ratcheting call has brought it two local nicknames: the Birkdale Nightingale and the Bootle Organ. I remember these sounds very clearly. The Natterjack's voice is a more-than-human sound that is "of the earth", but that reaches to the stars.'

John: 'A chorus of Natterjacks – "Birkdale Nightingales" or "Bootle Organs", depending on your neighbourhood loyalties – is almost primeval on a mild and cloudy spring night.

It is certainly eerie.

The sound is as inseparable from this coast as the Marram Grass that binds the dunes, or the skittering trails left behind by startled Sand Lizards on hot May mornings.

To lose the chorus would be unthinkable.'

As we walked, Jake would be making notes. Each evening, he would begin writing poems which he would then read to us the next day as we meandered through the dunes.

Jake: 'The Natterjack Toads or Bootle Organs that I describe in this poem are as much a part of the story of this coast as wartime Operation Starfish (the lighting of dummy fires north of Liverpool to divert German bombs away from the important docks and factories on the Mersey) was.'

Bootle Organ

> Let the sun stub out the day,
> darkness grab us in its vice.
>
> Put a spark to the pyre, lads;
> the dance of flame on creosote.
>
> Cut the cable to the city, lads;
> wear the night like a cloak.
>
> Make yourself a Natterjack, lads;
> belly to the dunes.
>
> Luftwaffe tear through paper dusk;
> embers glow in eyes of toads.
>
> Let this replica city rush
> and rise to meet them, lads.
>
> The lick of bindweed burning;
> the city's pulse in your throat.
>
> Stay low, lads, stay starfished;
> stay silent and wait.
>
> They'll be gone as the Bootle Organs
> go up like sirens.

John: 'I find that the wild flowers draw you in as the days lengthen – dune slacks full to bursting with a dizzying array of species, some extremely rare, yet flourishing in this incredible eco-system.

Trying to put a name to them all is overwhelming – their life stories luring you off again into other spheres.

But seeing them in flower afresh each year is like meeting up with old friends.

Evening Primrose trumpets yellow everywhere in the dunes from midsummer into late autumn, yet its origins are in the New World – seeds came over in ballast on ships from North America.

American GIs arriving in the North West in WW2. Evening Primrose. The same.'

19 JULY. STARTED 10.30 AM AT FRESHFIELD STATION AND FINISHED 4.00 PM AT AINSDALE STATION. WEATHER WARM AGAIN (22 DEGREES), BUT DARK, GREY, THREATENING SKIES ALONG THE COAST; NO WIND, HEAVY ATMOSPHERE – THE PROMISE OF RAIN. SEA BUCKTHORN; EVENING PRIMROSE; COMMON CENTAURY; SEASIDE CENTAURY; KNOTTED PEARLWORT; EARLY MARSH ORCHID; LESSER CELANDINE; PYRAMIDAL ORCHID; BEE ORCHIDS; MARSH HELLEBORINE; DUNE HELLEBORINE; LESSER SPEARWORT; WATERCRESS; WELD; GRASS-OF-PARNASSUS; BITING STONECROP; TORMENTIL; EVERLASTING PEA; REST HARROW; BIRD'S-FOOT TREFOIL; RED CLOVER; ROUGH CLOVER; SEA STORKSBILL; SEA SPURGE; HIMALAYAN BALSAM; DUNE PANSY; ROSEBAY WILLOWHERB; GREAT WILLOWHERB; BROAD-LEAVED WILLOWHERB; PURPLE LOOSESTRIFE; MARSH PENNYWORT; SEA HOLLY; ROUND-LEAVED WINTERGREEN; DEW BERRY; HOUND'S TONGUE; SELF HEAL; WATERMINT; COMMON TOADFLAX; RIBWORT PLANTAIN; YARROW; RAGWORT; BLUE FEABANE; SPEAR THISTLE; CREEPING THISTLE; YELLOW RATTLE; KIDNEY VETCH; JAPANESE ROSE; WOODY NIGHTSHADE; CREEPING WILLOW; MARRAM GRASS; RED FESCUE; SAND SEDGE. ALSO SEEN: SEA POTATO; SAND MASON; COMMON CRAB; SHORE CRAB; RAZOR SHELLS. ALSO SEEN: COMMON DARTER; COMMON BLUE; GRAYLING; GATEKEEPER; MEADOW BROWN; GREEN-VEINED WHITE; CINNABAR MOTH CATERPILLAR; DARK GREEN FRITILLARY. ALSO SEEN: NATTERJACK TOAD; RED SQUIRREL; BAR-TAILED GODWIT; COMMON TERN; SANDWICH TERN; SWIFT; SWALLOW; LINNET; OYSTERCATCHER; CORMORANT; BLACK-HEADED GULL; HOUSE SPARROW; GREAT BLACK-BACKED GULL; LESSER BLACK-BACKED GULL; WHITETHROAT; CARRION CROW.

Walk four: 20 July 2014: Ainsdale Station to the RSPB Centre at Marshside, Southport

Robert: 'The landscape invites us to look down, at, or into the minutiae of detail in plant life, as well as immersing ourselves in the open sky and engulfing seascape. We train our ears on the difference in soundscape of birds and insects, masking the low frequency sound-bed of the waves and wind.'

John: 'I crawl around on my hands and knees, dampness and cold ebbing into my joints, in search of Petalwort on cold winter days, just as collectors driven by a fascination for mosses did in Victorian times.

The search for this tiny lower plant is all engrossing, a planet shrunk to a few millimetres of dune earth, a world in miniature, yet you can feel the hunt still developing into a towering obsession.'

Robert: 'I find that scale is incredibly important to the way in which we experience this landscape. The seascape offers visual and aural perspectives which are vast and uninterrupted in comparison to constant variations in sound and vision of the urban milieu to which it is so close. And this is clearly part of our attraction to it. The seasonal flocking of humans to the shoreline since the advent of tourism has been essentially sensory in nature.'

Tim: 'Memories: when I'm not here, in my mind, I can still taste the salt in the sea air of the Sefton Coast; pick up the aroma of the sweetness of the pinewoods and feel the change underfoot as I move across the bomb rubble (tipped to act as erosion protection), onto firmer sand and then sinking mud and out towards the incoming tide at Burbo Bank; hear the "wink wink" of individual Pink-feet on a still, frozen early morning and the undercurrent of low drumming conversation as they amass in the feeding fields behind the sand banks that provide a safe haven for their nightly roosts; the lower pitched "knut" of tightly packed feeding Knots which flock together with Black and Bar-tailed Godwits, Dunlin, Sanderling, Grey and Ringed Plover and the odd migratory surprise; wind-rush through marram; gun fire from the firing range at Great Altcar; the baleful "clink clink" of the folded mainsail against the mast supports of the boats anchored in the Alt.'

Robert: 'We visit the coast to inhale the air, to smell the salt, to experience light in a manner that is extraordinary and takes us out of our everyday existence. We visit to listen to the rolling of the waves on the shoreline, to feel the wind in our hair. Each of these responses to the sensory affects of the environment has become part of the socially constructed set of signifiers relating to how we interact with our surroundings. Through our interaction with the shoreline we deliberately place ourselves in an altered perspective with the world, into a different sense of scale, based in a different light, immersed in a different sound world. In doing so we also move into a different sense of time, we tap into the rhythms of the rolling waves, we let the sounds of nature slow us in a physical and mental entrainment.'

Tim: 'Memories: altered perspectives; storms, fog, wind, rain, baking hot uncomfortable days, days when even the sea at Southport froze; spring and neap tides, birds photographed or just seen, lists made, sunrises, sunsets, night forays, subtle shifts of light over short stretches of time and profound changes of the shape of the restless shore over longer periods of time.'

WALKING THROUGH THE SANDS OF TIME: 20 JULY. STARTED 10.00 AM AT AINSDALE STATION AND FINISHED 4.00 PM AT WELD ROAD CAR PARK WHERE A MINIBUS COLLECTED THE WALKERS AND TOOK THEM TO THE RSPB RESERVE AT MARSHSIDE, SOUTHPORT. WEATHER WARM (23 DEGREES), LITTLE WIND AGAIN, BRIGHT AND SUNNY. CLUB RUSH; SEA MAYWEED; SEA BEET; COMMON SPIKE-RUSH; SLENDER SPIKE-RUSH; FLAT SEDGE; BLUNT FLOWERED-RUSH; SPEAR-LEAVED ORACHE; SEA PLANTAIN; SEA ASTER; THRIFT; MARSH SAMPHIRE; HARE'S-FOOT CLOVER; SEA-BLITE; SEA BUCKTHORN; MEADOW CRANESBILL; RESTHARROW; WILD RADISH; SANICLE; SEA HOLLY; BEE ORCHID; COMMON TWAYBLADE; DUNE HELLEBORINE; MARSH HELLEBORINE; COMMON SPOTTED ORCHID; PYRAMIDAL ORCHID; EARLY MARSH ORCHID; ROUND-LEAVED WINTERGREEN; GRASS OF PARNASSUS; YELLOW-WORT; FLEABANE; YELLOW RATTLE; COMMON CENTAURY; SEASIDE CENTAURY; EYEBRIGHT; RED BARTSIA; RAGWORT; GOLDEN ROD; SPEAR THISTLE; KNAPWEED; HAREBELL; EVENING PRIMROSE; RIBBED MELILOT; BIRD'S-FOOT TREFOIL; KIDNEY VETCH; JAPANESE ROSE; DEWBERRY; ROSEBAY WILLOWHERB; SEA SPURGE; ANGELICA; FENNEL; ASPARAGUS; COMMON STORK'S-BILL; KNOTTED PEARLWORT; MARSH PENNYWORT; YARROW; WATERMINT. ALSO SEEN: SEA POTATO; DOG WHELK; MERMAID'S PURSE; RAZOR SHELL; GOOSE BARNACLES; SMOOTH NEWT; ASPARAGUS BEETLE; NORTHERN DUNE TIGER BEETLE; SIX SPOT BURNETT MOTH: GRAYLING; GATEKEEPER; DARK GREEN FRITILLARY; GREEN-VEINED WHITE; LARGE WHITE; SMALL SKIPPER; SMALL HEATH; MEADOW BROWN; EMPEROR DRAGONFLY; COMMON DARTER; BLUE-TAILED DAMSELFLY. BIRDS SEEN OR HEARD INCLUDE: BLACK-TAILED GODWIT; DUNLIN; RINGED PLOVER; KESTREL; WHITETHROAT; REED BUNTING; LINNET; SNIPE; AVOCET; BUZZARD; KINGFISHER; RUFF; COMMON SANDPIPER; LITTLE EGRET; HERON; SWIFT; SWALLOW; HERRING GULL; BLACK-HEADED GULL; GREAT BLACK-BACKED GULL; MAGPIE; HOUSE SPARROW; CARRION CROW; CANADA GOOSE; COOT; MOORHEN.

Concluding reflections

For me, pilgrimage is about embarking on a journey of discovery that takes me out of myself; it is not an inward looking process. I often walk in the footsteps of others, and usually with natural historians, sound artists, photographers and local people, because they have different things to tell me about the landscape we meander through. And 'meander' is the correct term to use for this slow walking. I allow plenty of time to stop, talk, listen, backtrack, share memories and slow down.

Most of my walks or pilgrimages are relatively local and have some sort of personal significance. This may have something to do with the knowledge that it is becoming increasingly impossible to disconnect the idea of pilgrimage from modern-day capitalism – the shrine of money and commerce. Pilgrimage 'package holidays' are now offered to a variety of destinations, for example, a ten-night walk along the Camino de Santiago or 'Way of St James' – a collection of pilgrimage routes from all over Europe to the Cathedral of Santiago de Compostela in north-western Spain where the remains of the saint are thought to be buried (offered by Pura Aventura).[20]

I suggest that *meandering* and *field-work* undertaken on local and personal pilgrimages can create a space to consider living in and experiencing the world we are accustomed to differently, developing within each of us a sense of embodied identity. I have organised a number of 'local' 'pilgrimage walks' (each one accompanied by up to thirty people) – pilgrimages that were inherently sociable, their meandering format inviting conversation and the sharing of knowledge even (or perhaps especially) among strangers. 'It is only after walking in a landscape that I can learn to see, and to sense, that landscape through my body, for the act of walking is sensing that landscape at a human pace'[21]; and we must first learn to trust in our senses (in my experience, most natural historians with good field craft do exactly this); but we should also recognize that our 'sense' of the world is enriched by the discovery and accumulation of scientific knowledge and personal narratives; and that our participation *within* the landscape/soundscape can be honed and deepened by these discoveries[22] . . . and discovery, I argue, is key to the idea and experience of pilgrimage.

These pilgrimages are 'phenomenological and involve the 'gathering of synaesthetic, material and social sensory experiences as they unfold [. . .] in the duration of the walk'[23]. After each walk, I share the lists of flora and fauna encountered with my fellow walkers – meditative 'shrines' to the specificity of place and the 'sensuous singularity of things'. As a human being with a sense of ethical responsibility, I hope that my work might 'offer a linguistic mode that holds [. . .] potential for tuning us to environmental ethics in the Anthropocene'.[24] We need to begin to see and experience flora and fauna not as an unlimited and infinite human resource, but as entities in their own right, entities which sense, react, grow, care, share a 'sense' of community and feel pain. We need to release ourselves 'from the dichotomy of regarding nature either as a combination of *processes* or *things*; we need to recognize that nature is a communion of subjective, collaborative beings that organize and experience their own lives'.[25] I would suggest that the idea and experience of embodied and *conversive pilgrimage* can enhance and expand the ecological imaginary in such a way that we might be open to considering non-human agency and subjectivity. Perhaps this is an impossible task, but that, to me, is what pilgrimage is about: about challenge of one kind or another; and like all good pilgrimages, the 'goal' may be unobtainable – it is what we learn and share on the journey that matters. Pilgrimages are 'not to be taken lightly' . . . they can open us up to 'new possibilities as well as effect an emotional and spiritual purification'.[26] A pilgrimage can collapse time and space, develop creative non-hierarchical rhizomatic networks of shared thinking and ideas. It can make us feel more alive, more a part of the world in every sense and not separate from it. It can be a celebration of the joy of being . . . and being alive on the earth.

Notes

1 WALK (Walking, Art, Landskip and Knowledge) is a research centre at the University of Sunderland exploring the way we creatively experience the world as we walk through it.
2 Robert Macfarlane, 'Rites of Way: Behind the Pilgrimage Revival', *The Guardian*, 15 June 2012. Available at: www.theguardian.com/books/2012/jun/15/rites-of-way-pilgrimage-walks. Accessed 16 August 2019.
3 Jane Bennett, *The Enchantment of Modern Life: Attachments, Crossings and Ethics* (Princeton, NJ: Princeton University Press, 2001), 157.
4 Peter Marren, *Rainbow Dust* (London: Square Peg, 2015), 130.
5 Kay Syrad, *Chris Drury, Silent Spaces* (London: Thames & Hudson, 1998), 6.
6 David Abram, *The Spell of the Sensuous* (New York: Pantheon Books, 1995), 76.
7 Marren, *Rainbow Dust*, 130.
8 Mike Collier, 'Picturing Language Back into the Land', in Mike Collier (Ed.), *Ghosts of the Restless Shore* (Sunderland and Sefton, UK: Arts Editions North and Sefton Council, 2015), 90
9 Robert Macfarlane, 'A Counter Desecration Phrasebook', in Di Robson and Gareth Evans (Eds), *Towards Re-enchantment* (London: Art Events, 2010), 115.
10 James Harpur, *The Pilgrim Journey: A History of Pilgrimage in the Western World* (Oxford, UK: Lion Books, 2016), 6.
11 Rebecca Solnit, *Wanderlust: A History of Walking* (London: Verso, 2011), 5.
12 *Wikipedia*, 'Kumbh Mela'. Available at: https://en.wikipedia.org/wiki/Kumbh_Mela, 2018. Accessed 6 May 2018.
13 Carol McKay, 'Walking Otherwise: One Foot after Another'. Paper presented to the *Association for Art History Conference*, Milton Keynes, 29–31 March 2012.
14 Ibid.
15 Henry David Thoreau, *Walking* (Thomaston, ME: Tilbury House Publishers, 2017), 1.
16 Macfarlane, 'Rites of Way: Behind the Pilgrimage Revival'.
17 Jean Sprackland, 'Introduction', in Mike Collier (Ed.), *Ghosts of the Restless Shore* (Sunderland and Sefton, UK: Arts Editions North and Sefton Council, 2015), 5.
18 Mike Collier (Ed.), *Ghosts of the Restless Shore* (Sunderland and Sefton, UK: Arts Editions North and Sefton Council, 2015), 30–107.
19 Kaz Oishi, 'Two Recollective Journeys to the North: Bashō and Wordsworth', in Mike Collier (Ed.), *Wordsworth and Bashō: Walking Poets* (Sunderland and Grasmere, UK: Arts Editions North and the Wordsworth Trust, 2014), 51.
20 Pura Adventura, 'Camino de Santiago: The Way, Our Way'. Available at: www.pura-aventura.com/spain/camino-de-santiago. Accessed 6 May 2018.

21 Christopher Tilley, 'Walking the Past in the Present', in A. Árnason, N. Ellison, J. Vergunst and A. Whitehouse (Eds), *Landscapes Beyond Land* (Oxford, UK: Berghahn Books, 2012), 29.
22 David Abram, *Becoming Animal* (New York: Pantheon Books, 2010), 307.
23 Tilley, 'Walking the Past in the Present', 29.
24 Alan Macpherson, 'Sensuous Singularity: Hamish Fulton's Cairngorm Walk-texts', *Critical Survey*, 29(1), 2017: 12.
25 Matthew Hall, *Plants as Persons: A Philosophical Botany* (Albany, NY: State University of New York Press, 2011), 169.
26 Harpur, *The Pilgrim Journey*, 7.

Part II

Walking with

People, places, politics

6 "This world that walks"

Cultural destruction, cultural renewal, and social justice on the trails of North American Indigenous removal

Amy Hamilton

In 2015, Diné youth organized a series of walks to commemorate the 150-year anniversary of the removal trail their ancestors endured and to protest fracking and other environmental hazards on their traditional homelands.[1] Called *Nihígaal bee Iiná*, "Our Journey for Existence," the walks extended across the Navajo Nation to each of the Diné's four sacred mountains, demonstrating how walking can articulate an ethics of social justice.[2] Laura Red Elk (Diné), one of the organizers of *Nihígaal bee Iiná* explained, "We are journeying back to our original selves including our responsibility . . . to protect the land and take care of it . . . . [W]e are returning to our original leadership by letting the mountains determine how we walk on the land."[3] Red Elk and her fellow walkers join a long tradition of American protest marches, from the 1963 March on Washington for Jobs and Freedom led by Martin Luther King, Jr. to the 2017 Women's March. Protest marches have played a central role in Indigenous social and environmental justice movements, such as the Trail of Broken Treaties (1972), the recent Water Walks performed by the Anishinaabe, the Blackfeet, and various bands of the Sioux, the Oceti Sakowin's (Great Sioux Nation) 2,000-mile relay to Washington, DC (2016), and the Native Nations Rise march (2017) to protest the encroachment of oil infrastructure on tribal lands.

Like the Trail of Broken Treaties, which addressed contemporary issues of sovereignty alongside removal histories, *Nihígaal bee Iiná* linked current threats to tribal sovereignty and environmental health to a long history of colonization, a history that includes the forcible removal of Indigenous peoples from their traditional homelands and that continues today through what Rob Nixon calls "stationary displacement," the loss of land to pollution and environmental hazards even as it is still inhabited.[4] In commemorating the Diné removal trail, referred to as the Navajo Long Walk, the organizers celebrated the resilience of their ancestors by reclaiming the act of walking. *Nihígaal bee Iiná* walkers remapped vital connections between people and land by moving in a ceremonial pattern between the sacred mountains.

In reenacting a nineteenth-century removal in a contemporary context, *Nihígaal bee Iiná* points both forward to the impact of current social and environmental threats, and backward through Indigenous histories of dislocation and trauma, embodying tropes found in Indigenous texts that reveal the entanglement of walking and justice. The removal trails worn into the US land by the footsteps of thousands of Indigenous peoples bear witness to the devastation of hundreds of communities by the land-greedy US government. Yet the removal trails do not signify the end of Indigenous cultures. Indigenous authors demonstrate how the removal trail walkers and their descendants not only recount pain and trauma, but also reclaim walking as a site for cultural renewal and continuance. Acoma poet Simon Ortiz has described the need to make the events of colonialism "significant and realized in the people's own terms" as "bring[ing] about meaning and meaningfulness."[5] In stories of Indigenous removal, walking serves the contradictory role of both shattering communities and providing a path back to self-determination and cultural coherence.[6] In addition to memorializing what was lost, the trails also testify to the incredible resilience of the walkers.

Walking and removal trails

Throughout the nineteenth century, removal trails crisscrossed the land that is now the United States. The most well-known is the Trail of Tears, more accurately Trails of Tears.[7] Regulated by the provisions of 1830 Indian Removal Act,[8] thousands of Indigenous people were forced to walk the land between the American Southeast and "Indian Territory" (today's Oklahoma). Members of at least thirty tribes were removed from their homelands in the East, including the Cherokee, Muscogee, Chahta, Chicaza, and Seminole people. Paula Mitchell Marks estimates that the US forced more than 100,000 eastern Indigenous people from their traditional homelands in the first half of the nineteenth century.[9] Along the grueling, several-months-long journey to Indian Territory, thousands of walkers perished.[10]

As the US extended its reach westward, the policies of the Indian Removal Act were felt thousands of miles from the land it was originally enacted to claim. Thirty years after the act was signed, the US army's "scorched earth" campaign destroyed food stores and planting grounds around *Dinétah*, the Navajo homeland, which compelled thousands of Diné to surrender at Fort Defiance. On March 4, 1864 the first of between 8,000 and 11,000 Diné began the nearly three-month Long Walk from their homeland in the four corners region to a small reservation at Fort Sumner in eastern New Mexico.[11] Four years later, and in response to deplorable conditions in Fort Sumner and the petitions of Diné leaders, a new treaty was drafted and the dislocated Diné returned to a small reservation within *Dinétah*. By that time, nearly a third of the Diné who walked to Fort Sumner had died as a result of murder by US army troops, illness, depression, severe weather, and starvation.[12]

Prior to the removal era, Indigenous peoples enjoyed mobility over large tracts of land. Far from inhabiting a static world, they shifted in response to circumstances such as environmental conditions, seasonal changes, and confrontations and confederations among groups.[13] Gerald Vizenor (Anishinaabe) suggests that the ability to move is intimately connected to self-determination and cultural autonomy. "Native sovereignty," he states, "is the right of motion."[14] In an attempt to control both actual movement and the *meaning* of movement, Euroamericans forced Indigenous nations along brutal removal trails to then restrict their movement on reservations and further impede sovereignty. Yet Indigenous understandings of movement remained embedded in Indigenous worldviews, stories, and ceremonies, even in the face of forced movement. Vizenor links mobility to the very source of Native cultures, suggesting that movement within stories and across land is inseparable from individual and tribal identity: "Natives have been on the move since the creation of motion in stories; motion is the originary."[15] Or, as Reid Gómez (Diné) puts it, "There is no finished story because like the people, [story] too is always in motion."[16] Vizenor and Gómez trace the strands of story, movement, and identity to a common origin, demonstrating how worldview is intimately bound to land and the potential for change.

The importance of walking in many Indigenous American cultures complicates the experience and narration of walking on removal trails. In family stories and contemporary literatures, movement along removal trails is variously understood as the source of intense suffering *and* a practice of reintegration and survival. Walking is experienced as physical pain and emotional devastation, and yet it is also paired with ceremonial movement and traditional story cycles. The apparently simple act of human walking is layered with multiple meanings and messages in and through these stories.

Demonstrating the interconnections of movement, family, memory and survival, Diné poet Luci Tapahonso connects to her ancestors through the memory of the Navajo Long Walk. Her poem "In 1864" combines a nested perspective and first-person narration to create a sense of immediacy for an event that occurred more than one hundred years before the poem was written. The speaker tells her daughter stories as they drive along part of the Long Walk route. She moves from her own perspective to her aunt's, and finally to that of her great-grandmother, who walked the trail. The speaker tells us, "My aunt always started the story saying, 'You are here / because of what happened to your great-grandmother long ago,'"[17] before shifting to the voice of her great-grandmother. This nesting of voices across generations connects the Long Walk to the present. When the great-grandmother remembers, "All of us walked, some carried babies. Little children and the elderly / stayed in the middle of the group. We walked steadily each day, / stopping only when the soldiers wanted to eat or rest,"[18] the use of first-person plural collapses time and generations so that the atrocities of the walk exist within the memory of individuals living now.

Tapahonso ends her poem with an emphasis on survival and possibility, repeating her aunt's conviction: "'This is why we are here,' she would say to us. 'Because our grandparents prayed and grieved for us.'"[19] She follows this statement with what the people gained from their imprisonment at Fort Sumner:

> it was at Bosque Redondo that the people learned to use flour and now
> fry bread is considered to be the 'traditional' Navajo bread.
> It was there that we acquired a deep appreciation for strong coffee.
> The women began to make long, tiered calico skirts
> and fine velvet shirts for the men.[20]

The speaker comforts her daughter by focusing on the fortitude of a people who were able to find ways to withstand catastrophic loss and to maintain and even strengthen their community. The Long Walk must be remembered because of the great pain the Diné experienced as well as for way the walkers and their descendants integrated the experience into the long history of the Diné and their movement over land.

While Tapahonso's poem is rooted in Diné history and cosmology, the legacies of removal trails have been explored by poets and writers from many Indigenous communities. The most widely known removal story, the Trail of Tears, is the context for Chicaza poet Linda Hogan's poem "Tear." In this piece, Hogan explores the complicated legacies of the Trail of Tears through the "tear dresses" made along the walk. Not trusted with "scissors or knives,"[21] the speaker tells us, the women tore the cotton in straight lines along the grain of the fabric. The name of the dresses has a triple meaning, pointing to the literal tears of the fabric, the ways the tears mimic "the straight lines / like the roads we had to follow / to Oklahoma,"[22] and the homograph of "tears / it was impossible to hold back, / and so they were called / by this other name, / for our weeping."[23] "Tear," then, links the Chicaza to the land, to their history, to their walking, and to one another across time. As a place of rupture, the "tear" marks the experience of loss and mourning expressed in "tears." As an action in dress-making, the "tear" is part of reorientation and re-creation.

Hogan, like Tapahonso, shares her people's removal story through a complex use of perspective. The poem begins with the speaker telling us that the events of the poem occur in "the time before / I was born."[24] Yet in the second stanza, the speaker shifts to telling the story of the trail in the first person. She emphasizes her placement alongside the travelers: "Above us, lightning split open the sky. / Below us, wagon wheels cut land in two. / Around us were the soldiers."[25] This placement insists on the coherence of the people and their integration with the land. The poem strongly asserts that the Trail was not traveled in vain and that the people were stronger than the destructive forces allied against them. The speaker's memory of the Trail of Tears is populated by ancestors who "walk inside me. This blood /

is a map of the road between us. / I am why they survived . . . I am the tear between them / and both sides live."[26]

The violence of the removal trails leaves a trace in human and land of the material and psychic impact of forced walking, demonstrating how human bodies are intimately and inextricably entangled with the substance of the world. This entanglement, what Stacy Alaimo calls "trans-corporeality," suggests that "the body is never static because its interactions with other [human and more-than-human] bodies always alter it."[27] In the stories of Indigenous removal trails, trauma and loss exist alongside and within the living reality of the descendants of those who were forced away from land and home. The feet of the walkers march through the poems, reminding readers of the emotional, cultural, and material impact of removal, demanding justice.

Pushing the Bear along the Trail of Tears

Cherokee writer Diane Glancy's *Pushing the Bear: A Novel of the Trail of Tears* (1996) elaborates the themes in Tapahonso and Hogan's poems, illustrating the intimate melding of body, land, and story. In the novel, the experience of walking the Trail weaves from despair to determination, from prostration to protest. Glancy's novel follows the path of the third detachment of Cherokee along the approximately 900-mile northern route to Indian Territory. The novel transforms the violence and fragmentation of forced movement into a source of renewal, identity, and power. Here, walkers survive through their ability to remember and embody their physical and spiritual connection to the land and therefore their communal sense of identity.

The novel is organized spatially, following the path the characters walk. Each section begins with the date the Cherokee enter a new state, the name of the state, and a map representing a segment of the Trail of Tears.[28] Each geographically designated section is divided into brief accounts from several of the trail walkers, their stories overlapping. Whereas Tapahonso and Hogan use first-person narration to place removal trails within living memory, Glancy employs multiple voices to indicate the novel's connection to Indigenous storytelling traditions and to offer an alternate understanding of the meaning of the Trail of Tears in Cherokee history. The more than forty narrators of *Pushing the Bear* suggest multiple ways of experiencing and surviving removal. Some of the voices are historical figures, others are fictional characters representing the real people who walked the Trail, and still others are communal voices, such as "Voices as They Walked," "Voices in the Dark," and even "The Soldiers." Together, these voices tell the story of a community of walkers, not a single character.

As the voices chronicle their experience on the Trail, they constantly return to descriptions of their painful walking bodies. Unable to articulate their pain in simple descriptive language, the voices in *Pushing the Bear* turn to the physical agent or cause of their pain, walking, to describe and therefore limit and control suffering.[29] Walking as the cause of pain is also a site to contain pain. The most frequent narrator, a Cherokee woman named Maritole, describes her experience of the Trail in this way: "Nothing but our feet walking west. The wagons slipping, people crying, soldiers hitting horses, some of them screeching under the whip."[30] The first sentence incorporates the description of violence and fear that follows, restricting the walkers' experience to only "feet walking" and thereby providing a site for expressing the pain and fear that are too vast and incomprehensible to articulate.

Faced with the irrationality of the Trail, the walkers struggle to understand their experience, but walking resists easy explanations. Knobowtee and other voices satirize rosy interpretations of the Trail offered by leaders to encourage the people forward:

> "You sound like Chief Ross," Knobowtee said. "You know how he goes on"
>
> . . .
>
> "Let's not be discouraged," Quaty said under her breath.
> Now Knobowtee had others talking like him.
>
> "'*We must forgive each other, O-ga-na-ya. That's what we learn on the trail. Anger is our enemy.*'" Who was Knobowtee mocking now in his North Carolina dialect?
> Someone made a choking sound.
> "We become human beings through our trials"
> "We learn how to feel the soldiers' bayonets," Anna Sco-co-tah said.
> "We learn how to walk and walk," Mrs. Young Turkey said.
> . . .
> "We learn to walk," My mother sat beside Aneh, my sister.
> "Yep," Knobowtee answered. "Walk."[31]

The characters bitterly mock the advice of Cherokee leaders and missionaries invoking Christian platitudes, revealing such coping methods to be simplistic and misleading. Questioning his brother O-ga-na-ya's adoption of these interpretive methods, Knobowtee undercuts inadequate attempts to encourage the walkers and thereby reduce the significance of the Trail into a single interpretation. It is impossible to contain the Trail in trite phrases such as "we become human beings through our trials" or "anger is our enemy." In place of such hollow and deceptive bromides, the only idea large enough to contain the horrors and complexities of the Trail is "we learn to walk." The phrase recalibrates the walkers' relationship to movement and its meaning. "We learn to walk" explodes the attempt to interpret the Trail by offering an image that is deceptively simple but able to invoke the physical, personal, cultural, and psychic movement of the people.

In resisting simple interpretations, the walkers begin to insist on their right to define the significance of the Trail. Walking provides an opening for resistance, a way of creating a different trail even as the walkers follow the path delineated by the US army. "Walk steadily," Maritole's father advises her, "and maybe you can forget you walk."[32] Later, Maritole hears her ancestors urging her to keep going: "They said to keep walking. [They] told me the road would come to an end and I would see a new land."[33] Maritole's father and ancestors hint at another option, the prospect that Maritole can *choose* how to walk. After Maritole hears her ancestors' voices, she relates: "When I got up the following morning, I tied a rope around the waist of my skirt and trousers to keep them up. I marched on holding my father's hand or Luthy's hand."[34] By tying up her pants and aligning herself with her family, Maritole takes control of walking the Trail. Another of her fellow walkers, Terrapin Head, makes a similar decision: "[M]y legs pump as if my heart was in them. My feet slip in the snow. My hands pump. My head slarps. Har. I am Big-heart-walking-all-over."[35] Terrapin Head gives himself a new name rejecting captivity in favor of agency, "walking-all-over." Further, like Maritole holding her family members' hands and walking as a unit, Terrapin Head envisions the parts of his body uniting in the rhythm of footsteps. The walkers shift the meaning of walking; rather than walking in pain and delirium, they choose to walk in strength and community.

Reimagining walking as a potential site for strengthening communal identity allows the walkers to draw connections between the power of walking and the power of story, both of which are bound to the land. As she walks, Luthy perceives the connections among language, land, and walking. She muses, "*I am part of the earth as I walk. I am the harvested crops . . .. It doesn't matter if I walk or cause the walking.*"[36] Unlike the trite interpretations the walkers mock, Luthy's vision establishes a complex understanding of walking, agency, and trans-corporeality. Language and story enter a nuanced relationship with land and bodies. By connecting land and language with the moving bodies of the Trail walkers, Luthy places the specific experiences of the walkers within a larger framework that "*travels through time.*" This connection, Luthy silently reasons, "*[is] in the corn. It's in the boys. All the same. It doesn't matter.*"[37] Luthy's comment "*It doesn't matter*" is not a statement of despair and defeat; rather, it is a realization that her personal experience is reflected and reinforced by a larger communal experience. Her family's life is part of the community and the land. Anna Sco-so-tah articulates this connection by referring to the Cherokee as the earth itself: "We were the land. The red clay people with mouths that would talk."[38] Maritole also understands this connection when she notices a leaf rustling in the wind: "It was telling the story of our march. I would have the tongue of a leaf. I would tell our story."[39] Language opens a space for Luthy, Anna, and Maritole to voice their experience on the Trail and their physical enmeshment with the land.

As they engage language to combat disconnection and dislocation, Maritole and the other walkers trace the contours of traditional stories on the Trail. One of the most prominent of these is the Cherokee story of Selu, the woman who brought them corn. In the story, Selu sacrifices herself for her sons and directs them to:

> clear a large piece of ground in front of the house and drag my body seven times around the circle. Then drag me seven times over the ground inside the circle, and stay up all night and in the morning you will have plenty of corn.[40]

The boys follow her instructions, and where her blood falls, corn grows.[41]

The walkers understand Selu's blood as a parallel to the blood they leave in their tracks and as a reminder that through her blood Selu's trans-corporeality is made manifest as she is integrated into the earth. The story of Selu draws together the Cherokees' ideas about the land and communal strength by reminding the walkers of their long experience with and connection to the land. Maritole's father tells his fellow walkers, "We can feel the corn move our bodies. We can get up. We can go on."[42] Knobowtee looks at the line of people walking behind him and imagines them as "kernels on a corn cob,"[43] an image similar to Maritole's vision of the walkers "crowded together row after row like corn in a field."[44] The story of Selu combats the fracturing effect of the Trail by insisting on the continued connections between the walkers and between the walkers and the land.[45] Another Trail walker, Alotohee, explains that story, "brings the land inside, too. . . . [The walkers] carry the cornfields with [us]."[46] Selu's gift of story and corn represents a longstanding promise between people and land, and illustrates that the Cherokee have survived and will continue to survive through reliance on these relationships.

As the narrative voices find significance and empowerment in stories such as Selu's gift of corn, they draw connections between their physical movement over the land and the narrative movement of story and language. According to Knobowtee, "The stories fueled my walk. Yes."[47] They learn, as the spirit of Maritole's mother suggests, *"Riding on your voices you can walk."*[48] Storytelling yields a space for articulating and interpreting walking, and also facilitates and mirrors that walking. As the walkers cross into Indian Territory, Knobowtee notes, "We'd make a way into it with our words."[49] Storytelling has vitality beyond the figurative or metaphoric; language *acts*. The fluidity of language and story makes survival possible, a dynamic action that the narrative voices connect to the complex movement of walking itself. Language makes a way into the new land, it creates a path, it provides fuel and energy, and it acts as a foundation for walking. Whereas the pain and fear of walking once actively destroyed language, through storytelling, language can also reimagine walking and create a path to the new land.

Out of the vitality of language, the walkers begin to understand the strength in redefining the Trail and claiming the ability to walk. Addressing "the people who seemed to be giving up," Knobowtee says, "We walk together and we're strong . . .. We walk all day. At night our feet still walk. . . . Say to one another, we move like wind in the cornstalks. Something happens when we walk."[50] Even in the midst of pain, something vital is reformed through the fluidity of movement. The walkers find strength and the possibility of renewal in learning to walk correctly. Knobowtee explains, "I could almost believe we were walking a holy walk. As a unit. A people. One kernel following another. Our voices united. If we could be one in our walking, we would make it to the new territory."[51] "Right walking" is connected here to "right speaking." N. Scott Momaday (Kiowa) suggests, "in a profound sense our language determines us; it shapes our most fundamental selves; it establishes our identity and confirms our existence, our human being."[52] Knobowtee takes this equation further by claiming that the generative act of speaking extends to movement. Survival is dependent on the way embodied experience is imagined and narrated. When Maritole asserts that she "*want*[s] to walk,"[53] she recognizes that walking can be a space for recovering communal identity from being rendered an object of history. Through the communal act of remembering and retelling stories, Maritole and her fellow walkers discover the powerful effects of claiming walking as a site of cultural expression and reconstitution.

Walking and social justice

Indigenous memories and stories of removal trails resonate in unexpected ways with contemporary social protest marches. It might be tempting to understand these histories as solely tragic examples of colonialism and Indigenous genocide. Indeed, the violent and devastating treatment Indigenous nations continue to experience at the hands of settler-colonists and the US government cannot be minimized. Yet stories of the removal trails also teach us about the incredible strength and determination of Indigenous peoples in the face of threatened cultural annihilation.

In the years before her death in early 2019, Anishinaabe elder Josephine Mandamin, the Water Walker, led a yearly peregrination around the Great Lakes and other major waterways, "to raise awareness that our clean and clear water is being polluted . . .. Water is precious and sacred."[54] Importantly, the walks, which have continued after Mandamin's passing, "are conducted through Anishinaabe (First Nations, Native American) ceremonial protocols and ways of understanding the natural world."[55] The water walkers demonstrate the interconnectedness between protecting the water and protecting the people. In other words, social justice is inseparable from environmental justice, and walking is an embodiment of that enmeshment. Mandamin and her fellow walkers understand the intimate links between human and more-than-human bodies. Like Maritole, they see the land as inseparable from themselves. Maritole explains: "In the mountains (East). In the new territory (West). There would be . . . a remnant. The land was their power. They were of the earth.

The turtle island. They were the . . . everlasting people."[56] Through walking, Maritole and the Cherokee and Mandamin and the water walkers reclaim and renew this deep relationship. As Michael Davis suggests, "For the walker, movement is not ancillary to knowing . . .. Rather, moving *is* knowing."[57]

In the context of settler-colonialism, tracing the paths of Indigenous social and environmental justice to the removal trails reveals walking's place in a long history of resistance and "survivance."[58] Ecocritic Joni Adamson argues that we need "'constellations of practice' to help us see deep time, scale and intricately entangled relationships between human and nonhumans that may be relatively invisible to most humans."[59] Walking, with its deep-rooted and profound ties to social justice, offers us a site for such a practice. Indigenous land knowledge emerges through long experience and story, exemplified by material walking bodies. How human bodies move through space both determines and is determined by a complex nexus of cultural systems and stories and the material reality of both bodies and land. When forced plodding becomes intentional striding, walkers reassert their subjectivity and insist upon a complex vision of land, migration, and colonialism in which walking opens space for social justice.

Notes

1 "Nihígaal Béé Íina: Our Journey for Existence," www.indiegogo.com/projects/nihigaal-bee-iina-our-journey-for-existence.
2 Broadly speaking, social justice refers to the equitable distribution of rights and resources. Within an Indigenous context, social justice takes on the additional meaning of identifying and reclaiming the lands and lifeways that settler-colonialism stole and/or disrupts.
3 Lyla Johnston, "Young Navajos Stage 200 Mile Journey for Existence," www.idlenomore.ca/young_navajos_stage_200_mile_journey_for_existence.
4 Rob Nixon, *Slow Violence and the Environmentalism of the Poor* (Cambridge, MA: Harvard University Press, 2011), 19.
5 Simon Ortiz, "Towards a National Indian Literature: Cultural Authenticity in Nationalism," *Multi-Ethnic Literature of the U.S.* 8(2) (1981): 9.
6 A more complete analysis of the relationships among walking, land, and story is developed in my book, Amy T. Hamilton, *Peregrinations: Walking in American Literature* (Reno, NV: University of Nevada Press, 2018).
7 Daniel F. Littlefield Jr. and James W. Parins, eds., *Encyclopedia of American Indian Removal* (Westport, CT: Greenwood Press, 2011), xv. Littlefield and Parins write that the term "Trail of Tears" "was fashioned and emerged as a metaphor for the removal experience" during the second decade of the twentieth century. "Made popular primarily by Cherokee women college students in the 1910s and 1920s, the term found its place in serious history by the 1930s."
8 *Indian Removal Act of 1830*, www.calhum.org/files/uploads/program_related/TD-Indian-Removal-Act-1830.pdf. Congress passed the Indian Removal Act in May of 1830, allowing the US president to extinguish Indigenous claims to lands east of the Mississippi in exchange for public domain lands in the West. While specifically targeting eastern lands, because it encoded removal and relocation in federal law the Act paved the way for similar violent patterns elsewhere as Euroamerican settler-colonists continued to push their way into the contested landscape of the West.

9 Paula Mitchell Marks, *In a Barren Land: American Indian Dispossession and Survival* (New York: William Morrow, 1998), 90.

10 William L. Anderson, *Cherokee Removal: Before and After* (Athens, GA: University of Georgia Press, 1991), 83, 93; Littlefield and Parins, *Encyclopedia of American Indian Removal*, 45; "Trails to the Past," www.rootsweb.ancestry. com/. Anderson writes: "no detailed information is available as to exactly how many Cherokee died during the ordeal; only speculations exist." He goes on to state that "the figure of 4,000 deaths has generally been accepted by more recent scholars" (*Cherokee Removal*, 84), though he suggests that this number is simply an estimate handed down from one scholar to another. Anderson then examines known population numbers and proposes a new number based on his own projections (which appear to be solid). He ultimately argues, "[a] total mortality figure of 8,000 for the Trail of Tears period, twice the supposed 4,000, may not be at all unreasonable." Littlefield and Parins contend that the Chicaza experienced relatively low mortality rates on the Trail, particularly because they avoided "epidemic diseases such as cholera that attacked other tribes and were vaccinated either on the trail or upon their arrival against smallpox." However, a website maintained by the Chickasaw Nation contends, "more than 500 Chickasaw died of dysentery and smallpox" on the Trail.

11 Lawrence Cheek, *The Navajo Long Walk* (Tucson, AZ: Rio Nuevo, 2004), 41.

12 Luci Tapahonso, *Sáanii Dahataał: Poems and Stories* (Tucson, AZ: University of Arizona Press, 1993), 7.

13 Marks, *In a Barren Land*, xviii.

14 Gerald Vizenor, *Fugitive Poses: Native American Indian Scenes of Absence and Presence* (Lincoln, NB: University of Nebraska Press, 1998), 182.

15 Ibid., 55.

16 Reid Gómez, "The Storyteller's Escape: Sovereignty and Worldview," in *Reading Native American Women: Critical/Creative Representations*, ed. Inés Hernández-Avila (Lanham, MD: AltaMira, 2005), 159.

17 Tapahonso, *Sáanii Dahataał*, 33–34.

18 Ibid., 51–53.

19 Ibid., 79–80.

20 Ibid., 83–87.

21 Linda Hogan, "Tear," in *Book of Medicines* (Minneapolis, MN: Minneapolis Coffee House, 1993), 11.

22 Ibid., 15–17.

23 Ibid., 19–23.

24 Ibid., 1–2.

25 Ibid., 6–8.

26 Ibid., 30–32, 37–38.

27 Stacy Alaimo, *Bodily Natures: Science, Environment, and the Material Self* (Bloomington, IN: Indiana University Press, 2010), 13.

28 Amy J. Elias, "Fragments that Rune up the Shores: Pushing the Bear, Coyote Aesthetics, and Recovered History," *Modern Fiction Studies* 45(1) (1999): 199. It is important to note that the novel's structure highlights Euroamerican conceptions of land and space that are in conflict with Indigenous cosmologies. By prefacing each section of the novel with Euroamerican epistemologies, Glancy calls attention to the place of the Trail of Tears within the official American histories of westward progress and the myth of the noble savage who obligingly vanishes as Euroamericans settle the land. Elias argues that the structure of the novel "point[s] to how time and space are newly joined in an unnatural reversal of traditional Native American land/time values. What would be a natural link between time (as myth) and space (as landscape) for the Cherokees had become a surreal, nightmarish terrain, unnaturally segmented by surveyor's lines and cut off from their mythic history."

29 Elaine Scarry, *The Body in Pain: The Making and Unmaking of the World* (Oxford: Oxford University Press, 1987), 13. Scarry contends, "Though there is ordinarily no language for pain, under the pressure of the desire to eliminate pain, an at least fragmentary means of verbalization is available . . .. These verbal strategies revolve around . . . the language of 'agency.'"

30 Diane Glancy, *Pushing the Bear: A Novel of the Trail of Tears* (New York: Harcourt, 1996), 73.

31 Ibid., 98–99.

32 Ibid., 103.

33 Ibid., 210.

34 Ibid.

35 Ibid., 79.

36 Ibid., 214.

37 Ibid.

38 Ibid., 179.

39 Ibid., 172–73.

40 James Mooney, *James Mooney's History, Myths, and Sacred Formulas of the Cherokees* (Fairview, NC: Bright Mountain Books, 1992), 244.

41 Ibid., 242–45.

42 Glancy, *Pushing the Bear*, 83.

43 Ibid., 62.

44 Ibid., 31.

45 Joni Adamson, "Seeking the Corn Mother: Transnational Indigenous Organizing and Food Sovereignty in Native North American Literature," in *Indigenous Rights in the Age of the U.N. Declaration*, ed. Elvira Pulitano (Cambridge, UK: Cambridge University Press, 2012), 28. Joni Adamson argues that through the frequent references to Selu and corn, the novel illuminates the close connection between humans and land: "The earth regenerates the human body when people eat corn and, when they die, humans return to the earth and the cycle continues."

46 Glancy, *Pushing the Bear*, 98.

47 Ibid., 144.

48 Ibid., 72.

49 Ibid., 227.

50 Ibid., 219.

51 Ibid., 62.

52 N. Scott Momaday, *The Man Made of Words* (New York: St. Martin's Griffin, 1998), 103.

53 Glancy, *Pushing the Bear*, 228.

54 "About Us," www.motherearthwaterwalk.com/.

55 "For the Earth and Water Walk 2017," www.motherearthwaterwalk.com/?p=2873.

56 Glancy, *Pushing the Bear*, 151.

57 Michael Davis, "Walking Together into Knowledge: Aboriginal/European Collaborative Environmental Encounters in Australia's North-East, 1847–1850," in *Humanities for the Environment: Integrating Knowledge, Forging New Constellations of Place*, ed. Joni Adamson and Michael Davis (London: Routledge, 2017), 189.

58 Gerald Vizenor, *Manifest Manners: Narratives on Postindian Survivance* (Lincoln, NB: University of Nebraska Press, 1999), vii. Vizenor defines survivance as "an active sense of presence, the continuance of native stories, not a mere reaction, or a survivable name. Native survivance stories are renunciations of dominance, tragedy, and victimry. Survivance means the right of succession or reversion of an estate, and in that sense, the estate of native survivancy."

59 Joni Adamson, "Gathering the Desert in an Urban Lab: Designing the Citizen Humanities," in *Humanities for the Environment: Integrating Knowledge,*

Forging New Constellations of Place, ed. Joni Adamson and Michael Davis (London: Routledge, 2017), 114.

Works cited

"About Us". www.motherearthwaterwalk.com/.

Adamson, Joni. "Gathering the Desert in an Urban Lab: Designing the Citizen Humanities." In *Humanities for the Environment: Integrating Knowledge, Forging New Constellations of Place*, edited by Joni Adamson and Michael Davis, 106–19. London: Routledge, 2017.

Adamson, Joni. "Seeking the Corn Mother: Transnational Indigenous Organizing and Food Sovereignty in Native North American Literature." In *Indigenous Rights in the Age of the U.N. Declaration*, edited by Elvira Pulitano, 228–49. Cambridge, UK: Cambridge University Press, 2012.

Alaimo, Stacy *Bodily Natures: Science, Environment, and the Material Self*. Bloomington, IN: Indiana University Press, 2010.

Anderson, William L. *Cherokee Removal: Before and After*. Athens, GA: University of Georgia Press, 1991.

Cheek, Lawrence. *The Navajo Long Walk*. Tucson, AZ: Rio Nuevo, 2004.

Davis, Michael. "Walking Together into Knowledge: Aboriginal/European Collaborative Environmental Encounters in Australia's North-East, 1847–1850." In *Humanities for the Environment: Integrating Knowledge, Forging New Constellations of Place*, edited by Joni Adamson and Michael Davis, 181–94. London: Routledge, 2017.

Elias, Amy J. "Fragments the Rune up the Shores: Pushing the Bear, Coyote Aesthetics, and Recovered History." *Modern Fiction Studies* 45(1) (1999): 185–211.

"For the Earth and Water Walk 2017." www.motherearthwaterwalk.com/?p=2873.

Glancy, Diane. *Pushing the Bear: A Novel of the Trail of Tears*. New York: Harcourt, 1996.

Gómez, Reid. "The Storyteller's Escape: Sovereignty and Worldview." In *Reading Native American Women: Critical/Creative Representations*, edited by Inés Hernández-Avila, 145–69. Lanham, MD: AltaMira, 2005.

Hamilton, Amy T. *Peregrinations: Walking in American Literature*. Reno, NV: University of Nevada Press, 2018.

Hogan, Linda. "Tear." In *Book of Medicines*, 59–60. Minneapolis, MN: Minneapolis Coffee House, 1993.

Indian Removal Act of 1830. www.calhum.org/files/uploads/program_related/TD-Indian-Removal-Act-1830.pdf.

Johnston, Lyla. "Young Navajos Stage 200 Mile Journey for Existence." www.idlenomore.ca/young_navajos_stage_200_mile_journey_for_existence.

Littlefield, Daniel F. Jr., and James W. Parins, eds., *Encyclopedia of American Indian Removal*. Westport, CT: Greenwood, 2011.

Marks, Paula Mitchell. *In a Barren Land: American Indian Dispossession and Survival*. New York: William Morrow, 1998.

Momaday, N. Scott. *The Man Made of Words*. New York: St. Martin's Griffin, 1998.

Mooney, James. *James Mooney's History, Myths, and Sacred Formulas of the Cherokees*. Fairview, NC: Bright Mountain Books, 1992.

"Nihígaal Béé Íina: Our Journey for Existence." www.indiegogo.com/projects/nihigaal-bee-iina-our-journey-for-existence.

Nixon, Rob *Slow Violence and the Environmentalism of the Poor*. Cambridge, MA: Harvard University Press, 2011.

Ortiz, Simon. "Towards a National Indian Literature: Cultural Authenticity in Nationalism." *Multi-ethnic Literature of the U.S.* 8(2) (1981): 7–12.

Scarry, Elaine. *The Body in Pain: The Making and Unmaking of the World.* Oxford, UK: Oxford University Press, 1987.

Tapahonso, Luci. *Sáanii Dahataał: Poems and Stories.* Tucson, AZ: University of Arizona Press, 1993.

"Trails to the Past." www.rootsweb.ancestry.com/.

Vizenor, Gerald. *Fugitive Poses: Native American Indian Scenes of Absence and Presence.* Lincoln, NB: University of Nebraska Press, 1998.

Vizenor, Gerald. *Manifest Manners: Narratives on Postindian Survivance.* Lincoln, NB: University of Nebraska Press, 1999.

7 The trouble with Munro bagging

Summiting as erasure in the Highlands of Scotland

Christos Galanis

Introduction

Walking is political. Tracing where, why, and how we walk reveals contestations of territory, power, positionality, and memory that are negotiated on an ongoing basis – both within and between communities. To walk is not only to create and inscribe; it is also to erase and obscure.

My ethnographic research on hillwalking in the Scottish Highlands, and specifically on Munro bagging, studied the ways in which these walking practices and their representations draw strongly upon the objectification of mountains, positioning them as passive, interchangeable summit-objects to be classified and collected. Further, Munro bagging arguably perpetuates erasing and obscuring the modes of relation, memories, and ontologies of pre-modern (mainly Gaelic-speaking) inhabitants of these still-contested upland landscapes. Drawing upon interviews I conducted with Munro baggers in Scotland, this chapter further makes visible how, far from being a neutral, apolitical leisure activity, hillwalking in the Highlands and its representations may be understood to be (often unwittingly) reproducing human exceptionalisms and Anglo-Modern supremacisms. As a consequence, the full richness and complexity of pre-modern relations between human and mountain have largely been obscured – and at times systematically repressed – in favor of imperialist Victorian myths of wilderness, discovery, and conquest. In turn, this narrow and prescriptive regime of conquering or collecting Highland summits perpetuates a poverty of the imagination and eclipses alternative walking practices that might allow for more reciprocal and mutually nourishing qualities of relationship to be explored and modeled.

Further, while I have engaged with the most relevant Anglo scholarship on these issues to date, I have also referenced Gaelic-language sources, both academic and folkloric, in order to bring other voices and tongues into the conversation. In this chapter, I hope not only to offer a critique of Munro bagging that is arguably long overdue, but also to shed light on pre-modern folkloric walking practices in the Highlands that too often go unremembered and unrepresented. However, while this subject and these histories stir up much passion in myself and others, my intention is not to shame or blame individuals. While conducting my field-work, several of my Munro bagging informants became good friends over time, and overall the groups and individuals I spent time with treated me with kindness, expressing much interest and support for this line of research. Underlying so many of these connections and conversations was most of all a mutually recognized love of mountains. The differences and disagreements lie mainly in how that love is practiced and represented.

Finally, in resonance with the ontological turn in related discourses, I suggest that the pre-modern, formerly dominant Gaelic culture of the Highlands – even though it had long before been converted to Christianity – still retained echoes of animistic relationships with mountains, relating to them as persons or spirits imbued with agency and the capacity for communication and reciprocity. From within the growing body of 'new animist' literatures, Graham Harvey argues that "places are not only environments and ecologies but persons, individuals, agents, active and relational beings, participants in the wider ecology of life".[1]

Unlike modern materialist ontologies, animist positionings of personhood, or aliveness, are not based on rigid ontological taxonomies. Rather, they are more often situated on a case-by-case basis through relationship, consent, and mutuality. For example, Alfred Irving Hallowell's study of the Ojibwa First Nations culture in Canada describes how some stones are perceived as alive, while others not.[2] The relative difference lies in which stones, if any, 'turn' towards you and engage with you – and you to them. The fundamental paradigm is relationship and mutuality, not class and division. As Harvey suggests:

> The ethical implication of animist worldviews is that no "environment" is given to us, or to any other persons, and that whatever we need we must seek in the give and take of relationships and actions and in honest engagement with a diverse community of similarly needy and desiring persons.[3]

By obscuring pre-modern Gaelic inhabitants and practices, cultures of summiting and their representations can often serve to further erase and disrupt pre-modern animist ontologies that have been part of these landscapes for millennia. In what follows, I trace how Munro bagging can be situated within a larger historical project of systematically disciplining and eradicating pre-modern animistic folk walking traditions in Scotland. That larger project has arguably been underway since at least the early 1500s. Over the course of the 16th century, spiritually inflected folk walking traditions took a decisive turn as the Reformation banned the practice of pilgrimage altogether. Many of the pilgrimage sites could be traced to sacred wells, springs, mountains, stones, or sites of healing. For some time, popular resistance to the ban was attempted, but in turn the clergy and state pushed back even harder. For example, in 1571 all pilgrims trying to make their way to a sacred shrine near Peebles had their path blocked by ministers and magistrates.[4] Yet contestations of folk walking traditions continued. During May Day celebrations in Aberdeen, officials tried their best to police the crowds, but the worshippers managed to escape across a river. There, they "danced to music and visited an ancient well with allegedly restorative waters, leaving ribbons, pins or lace as a thanksgiving".[5] By the end of the century, the absolute repression of any and all spiritual folk practices was introduced, and in 1602 attendance of church "was made mandatory according to an Act of Parliament and there were fines for not attending".[6] The celebrating of all festivals and holy days other than Sunday church services was banned as well – including Christmas. And yet still into the 1600s communities resisted the prohibitions that sought to keep them from walking to the sacred sites that their ancestors had visited for perhaps thousands of years before them:

> When holy days could not be celebrated during the week, people chose to absent themselves from Sabbath sermons to celebrate in the countryside instead. The [church] would also have been alarmed that pilgrimages to wells were still taking place . . . in areas such as Moray in 1611.[7]

As a consequence, over the last few centuries one would have been hard pressed to find any pilgrims making their way across these upland landscapes. When Alastair McIntosh recently made a pilgrimage across his home island of Lewis and Harris in the Outer Hebrides, he felt it wiser to introduce himself as a poacher, lest he encounter ridicule or resistance.[8] If you go out into the countryside on any given day in Scotland today, what you will most likely encounter are hillwalkers – hikers whose primary goal is to summit prominent peaks in the landscape. If go into many areas of the Highlands and Islands specifically, what you're likely to encounter are a subset of hillwalkers who are called Munro baggers. Representing what is likely the most popular of all outdoor leisure activities in the Highlands, the singular goal of Munro bagging is to summit all 282 mountains over 3,000ft. Reflecting its cultural pedigree, 'bagging' as a term is derived from hunting, signifying a successful kill and the subsequent hauling of a trophy, or carcass, in a bag. Bagging has also been used as a euphemism for the sexual conquest of a woman. These details may begin to paint a picture of the development of summiting culture that increasingly encroached into the Highland mountains during the 18th and 19th centuries, finding its apogee at the height of Victorian British expansionism in the period preceding World War I.

Victorian headwaters

A brief biography of Sir Hugh Munro himself – the man who first published the table of mountains that would later become the 'Munros' – is as good a context as any for tracing the colonial Victorian headwaters of Munro bagging as a practice. Born in London in 1856 and educated at Cambridge, he was the 4th Baronet of Lindertis, an estate in Angus, Scotland to which Munro would return throughout his life. His great-grandfather, Sir Thomas Munro, was made 1st Baronet of Lindertis for his service as an officer in support of crown and corporate interests through the East India Company, going on to serve as governor of Madras in occupied India. Hugh Munro himself served with the cavalry corps in colonial South Africa during the Basuto War of 1880–81, assisting in putting down indigenous resistance to colonial British rule.[9] Well-travelled from a young age, his biographers often remark on his love of collecting and taking possession of intriguing finds from across the British colonies, including fossils, butterflies, African ritual objects, animal trophies, and a monkey. A young Munro was also said to have collected a 'black boy' from South Africa and brought him home with him as a playmate.[10] By the 1890s, Munro had become a founding member and eventual president of the Scottish Mountaineering Club, publishing an article in 1891 in the club's journal in which he presented his now famous list of mountains. Munro never did get to complete his list. With two mountains to go at the outbreak of World War I, he was too old to enlist, yet volunteered with the Red Cross to aid Allied soldiers. He subsequently died in 1919 in the post-war influenza epidemic. The practices of administering the vast British Empire and those charged with its expansion and sustainment are mirrored in the sorts of leisure practices that developed and were made popular during Munro's lifetime. Whether trainspotting, birding, big-game hunting, egg-collecting, or mountaineering, these distinctly middle- and upper-class Victorian practices raised the tasks of ordering and collecting to the level of highest nationalistic virtue.

Being the first to summit prominent peaks became a national obsession in England. The country's zeal for first climbs surpassed all other European countries and was instrumentalized through a kind of 'mountain modernism' by Anglo-British-led expeditions from the Alps to the Himalayas. Peter Hansen has extensively traced the ways in which the summiting of previously untouched peaks in foreign territories was used by Anglo-Britain to inscribe and normalize the supremacy of both modernity and the 'Anglo-Saxon race' above the supposedly more primitive and less evolved indigenous inhabitants down below.[11] By daring to set their boots upon summits that had previously been respected by indigenous locals as the exclusive, untouchable abodes of powerful mountain spirits, Anglo-British mountaineers would represent their successful return from conquering the highest peaks in Switzerland, India, or Kenya as proof that the local animistic indigenous cultures and their now obsolete Gods and primitive spiritual practices were never anything more than child-like fears and superstitions. While popularly represented still to this day as a universalized and 'natural' human proclivity for adventure and exploration, Victorian mountaineering culture and its fixation on summiting provided a topographic teleology for Anglo-modern supremacism that was in turn used to affirm and justify the necessity of

Anglo-British projects of occupation, re-education, and 'improvement'. By the mid- to late 19th century, summiting culture progressively penetrated into the Scottish Highlands as well, projecting myths of exploration and discovery onto mountain landscapes that had until very recently been inhabited for millennia. My research is the first to connect these histories of imperial Anglo-British mountaineering with the Highlands of Scotland and the practice of Munro bagging itself, foregrounding the ways in which Anglo-British summiting culture has been instrumentalized not only in the contestation of territories, but also of ontologies.

My desire for doing so is not to conjure villains, but to bring critical attention to the ways in which Munro bagging can obfuscate pre-modern Gaelic history and culture and perpetuate the objectification of mountains as passive objects to be collected and possessed. I have also striven to strike a balance between representing the pre-modern Gaelic communities of the Highlands fairly, without romanticizing them as innocent, passive victims of lowland Anglo oppression. The histories of inter-ethnic and intra-ethnic strife in Scotland are complex and well beyond the grasp of any single text. While far too many people have been displaced from the Highlands who would not have chosen to leave their beloved mountains and glens, many others in turn were enthusiastic for the opportunity to sail to newly conquered lands and seek fortune, power, and territory. Such gains almost always came at the expense of those indigenous communities who were already there before. These complex histories of both internal and external colonization, with Highlanders simultaneously embodying both positions, make the Highland mountain landscape a densely tangled site of myth and memory. In resonance with Lucy Taylor's study of the nationalist Welsh colony of Y Wladfa in Patagonia, my approach is aligned with a growing body of literature that seeks to trouble and complexify the tendency to position imperial Britain as a singular and coherent monolithic entity.[12]

Quantified mountains and the inscribing of wilderness

The ways in which Munro baggers have practiced and documented the sport since its inception through to the present has often been hyper-quantitative and technical. As a typical example pulled from the archives of the Scottish Mountaineering Club, an anonymous completist documents his time walking in the mountains as follows:

Bristol, 7 June 1989

I took 152 separate expeditions (1.83 Munros per expedition)

I walked 2,692km (1,672 miles)

I climbed 171,380m (562,000ft or 106½ miles)

My actual walking time was about 958 hours

69% were not occupied by other walkers

78% gave me a view from the top. (Another future target might be to get a view from the other 22%!)[13]

The most exclusive of the many hundreds of Munro bagging clubs across Britain is the Munro Society Club (MSC). Its membership is open only to those who have completed their Munros, conferring a sense of authority upon its members. Reflecting this sense of authority is a program for quantifying Munros devised by the MSC called the Mountain Quality Indicators of Environment and Experience (MQI).[14] It is a quasi-scientific surveying method for assessing mountains, where members rate mountains in several categories with numerical values ranging from 1 to 4, seeking to quantify, classify, and compare Munro mountains. The contents meanwhile reveal a fascinating window into the moral and aesthetic values of the club members themselves. For example, the sight of livestock, marked trails, wind farms, tree felling, charity walks, tourists, or signage of any kind are consistently referenced as degrading the experience. Any sort of 'un-natural' sounds are likewise cause for low marks, including the sound of distant airplanes or helicopters, barking dogs, conversation, and in one instance, even the sound of distant bagpipes. One reviewer downgraded the mountain for having strong mobile phone reception, while at the same time revealing that they chose to climb that particular mountain on that day because their employer needed them to be on call. While it may be tempting to dismiss such projects as nothing more than the digressions of a few eccentrics with too much time on their hands, it should be noted that the MSC and related mountaineering and Highland tourism organizations represent some of the most powerful and best-organized groups in terms of influencing Scottish land use and conservation policies.

But perhaps most compelling of all in the MQI surveys is the tendency to only assign the highest score (4 out of 4) when there are no signs whatsoever of previous human presence in the landscape. While ancient sheep folds or cairns are generally tolerated more than structures built in the last hundred years, even older ruins bring the score down to at least a three, if not lower:

Category:	Notes:	Score from 1-4:
Human Influence pre 1900	No real evidence of past human influence. Route taken was remarkably free of old fencing, walls, buildings.	**4**
Human Influence post 1900	Radio mast on hill across River Dee and wooden electric pylons at Linn of Quoich, but these were soon left behind. Extensive, but good quality & well maintained, estate roads network up Glen Quoich. Trail markers and sensor across track early in walk. What appeared to be a relatively new, but high standard, path up An Diollaid. Native tree planting on hillside up west side of Glen Quoich. Some old tree stumps seen early on the walk.	**3**

Figure 7.1 Example of scoring Ben Avon

Source: Mountain Reports. "Mountain Quality Indicators." www.tmsmountainreports.net/index.php?mqi.

Category:	Notes:	Score from 1-4:
Human Influence pre 1900	No evidence of historical human influence on hillside	4
Human Influence post 1900	Tarmac road in Glen Etive. Telegraph poles. Fences around house at Coileitir. Restored house. Bridge over R. Etive (MOD). Wooden bridge over Alit nam Meirceach. Walkers paths throughout entire route. Summit cairn. Heavy erosion on Allt Mheuran path. No noise pollution. No litter.	2

Figure 7.2 Example of scoring Glas Bheinn Mhor

Source: Mountain Reports. "Mountain Quality Indicators." www.tmsmountainreports.net/index.php?mqi.

William Cronon has argued that the very concept of wilderness itself – of virgin landscape untouched and uncorrupted by human influence – is an obsessively managed geographic myth, a symptom of modern existential alienation that reflects a deep psycho-spiritual need for an idealized topology that preserves a timeless, Edenic purity, unblemished by the complexities of history and consequence:

> Wilderness represents a flight from history . . . a place outside of time . . . it is the place of youth and childhood, into which men escape by abandoning their pasts and entering a world of freedom where the constraints of civilization fade into memory . . . wilderness offers us the illusion that we can escape the cares and troubles of the world in which our past has ensnared us.[15]

Post-colonial analyses of European colonization have soundly refuted the legal and moral grounds of *terra nullius* – the doctrine that, to this day, has been used to justify the legal seizure of foreign territories that were perceived as uninhabited or uncultivated. Similar arguments were invoked to justify the evacuation and privatization of the Highlands, while the displacement and migration (both willing and unwilling) of countless Gaelic-speaking communities means that today, less than 2% of Scotland's population are fluent in Gaelic.[16]

An emptied place is not the same as an empty place

In my time with baggers, many related how even running into other baggers could potentially ruin an otherwise enjoyable day out in the mountains. This was consistent with how Munro baggers typically view themselves as possessing a higher capacity than mere 'tourists' for accessing the wildness they perceive to be afforded by the Highlands. This dividing line between Munro bagging and tourists – most often negotiated through a cultivated aesthetic sense of 'taste' – reflects a deeply ingrained relationship between summiting an 'empty' landscape and a claim of proprietorship that is fairly consistent throughout Munro bagging culture.

Here is an exchange with several members of an Edinburgh-based hill-walking club during a weekend club meet near Invergarry where I asked them to explain why it was so displeasing to encounter others on the hills:[17]

Me:	I'm curious, what is it . . . what's the enjoyment for example in not seeing other people?
Harriet:	'Cause it's more landscape to myself! [group laughter] It's all mine!
Ben:	You don't want someone behind you the whole day having a conversation, 'cause you might as well be at home . . . or in your office . . . you want peace and quiet.
Mike:	I'd still rather be the only group . . . even if you were up there as a group.
Eva:	Even if you're with a group, you're with people who you know, and they're people that you want to be with – what you don't want is people that you don't want to be with [laughter] – you go, "The hell with you!"
Mike:	I guess it comes down to a sense of accomplishment – like you feel like you've accomplished something when you get to the summit. If you get to the summit, and there's another two hundred people and a café and a train, it kinda detracts from the whole: "I've achieved something by getting to the top of this particular little bit of the world."
Me:	But why . . . I'm really curious? Because you're climbing, you're doing this physical thing that you enjoy, but then how does the presence of people, or trains, or cafés degrade the experience?
Ben:	Because it makes it spoiled.
Mike:	It makes it un-special.
Gretchen:	It makes it a tourist attraction.
Jeremy:	It takes away the sense of isolation . . . a wilderness . . . if there's loads and loads of other people, you're never gonna feel very isolated.
Eva:	You get to see a place that many people don't get to see, and you've had to make an effort to be there, so you don't really wanna be met by loads of other people who also go there too . . . It's like a competition.
Ben:	If you've spent four hours walking somewhere to get there, and a train pulls up and six hundred people get out . . .
Mike:	You'll think, "Why did I bother walking up that if these people just got the train?" And we don't kid ourselves that we're the only people that have ever been up there – you shouldn't think that – but there is a certain sense of . . . exclusivity about it. I mean, there are fewer people that have been to all the peaks of Scotland than have been to all the peaks of the Lake District, or whatever else.

My informants consistently reported strong pleasure in this sense of isolation and emptiness they could only acquire higher up the mountains, far away from the visual and auditory presence of other humans. Several told me that looking down from peaks were the only times in their life that they "truly felt alive". Although they clearly didn't believe themselves to be the first ones to step foot on these peaks, it's also clear that they were identifying with a peripatetic imaginary of exploration and discovery; an imaginary whose conjuring threatens to be dispelled by the presence of other humans, both past and present. Gavin Carver describes how in the world of "exploration and discovery, the mapping, [and] measuring . . . of a thing is a significant performance of ownership and an extension of the imperial hand into a remote, impenetrable frontier land".[18] I came to find that Munro bagging often lends itself to a problematic sense of proprietorship.

Further, it normalizes an imagined supremacism of Munro bagging over other methods of relating to mountains both in the present and the past. My informants described how the pleasure they derived from summiting was not only from the sheer exertion and aliveness they felt; a significant aspect of their enjoyment came from how they positioned themselves in comparison and competition with those who didn't summit. By summiting, they perceived themselves as both physically and socially 'above' non-baggers who didn't expend the time and energy to rise to the top, or else 'cheated' by using mechanical transport.

Munro bagging often traffics within a hierarchy where the higher you walk, and the more mountains you conquer, the greater your status. Walking as an act of acquiring territory and status is not only a competition with tourists, but between baggers as well. Some of my informants described how they employed the number of mountains bagged as a metric for measuring social status and determining who they would or would not walk with:

Ben: You think of where you fit into the scale in the sport . . . and, so you only want to associate with people in your class or above it, and you don't want where you are to be devalued by people much lower down, 'cause you like to feel you're doing something special. It might be a bit of that.

Me: Is there a sense of hierarchy?

Ben: Yes yes . . . that's what I mean . . . I think everyone has a sense of where they'd like to think they are . . . a status guide.

Mike: You feel you belong to a more elite club if you've made it to the top of a specific thing.

I've come to find that Munro bagging is more than just the innocuous form of sport and nature appreciation that it is commonly represented as. My concern is that the continued normalizing of conquering and collecting mountains risks perpetuating human exceptionalism by seeing mountains as inert objects or playgrounds. In Scotland, it contributes to the perception of the Highlands as an empty wilderness, an aesthetic resource or 'eco-service' to be managed primarily for the gaze of tourists and elites. However, an *emptied* place is not the same as an *empty* place. The following section further traces how the expansion of imperial territory, the erasure of colonized cultures, and the construction of the idealized mountain summiting body are often cited and iterated through summiting practices.

The summiting body of imperialism

The Victorian era saw the rise of an ethic of character-building meant to turn out morally upright British citizens whose virile bodies stood in for the idealized body of the empire itself. Summiting was believed to produce an ideal rugged manliness that contrasted with the 'effeminate French' across the Channel while also building a national Anglo-Saxon ethic better suited to imperial projects abroad:

> [the English] focused their energies on the completion of first ascents. [They] attributed the dominance of Alpine climbing to the English-British national character. [English mountaineers] "afford a very striking example of the pre-eminence of our own countrymen over all others in matters requiring determination, intrepidity, and skill" *Fraser's Magazine* reflected on "how thoroughly English all this is, and how indicative of that rambling, scrambling, exercise-loving disposition" of the English. "If there is talk of an unknown land into which no Englishman has penetrated", *The Times* observed, "he must be the first to visit the place."[19]

Hansen further describes how:

> Mountain climbing helped to legitimize exploration and the broader imperial expansion by transforming imperialism from an abstraction into something tangible and readily accessible to ambitious professional men ... adventure stories became "the energizing myth of imperialism", inspiring Englishmen "to go out into the world and explore, conquer, and rule".[20]

While mountaineering was popular in many European countries at the time, it was Anglo-Britain which pursued it most fiercely, culminating in the eventual summiting of Mt. Everest in 1953. The British mountaineering body was positioned as the paragon of masculinity, with high-altitude landscapes territorialized as being the sole domain of men. They largely remain so in Munro bagging culture, where men by and large outnumber women in hillwalking groups. However, the gendering of mountains as masculine social spaces is relative and culturally specific. For example, even though it was the British who introduced mountaineering culture to Japan in the late 19th century, it is increasingly middle-aged women who 'collect' prominent summits there, in an amalgam of Victorian mountaineering and ancient Buddhist and Shinto pilgrimage traditions.[21]

Mountaineering culture was also a vector for the production of dualistic racialized identities within Scotland itself, positioning the Anglo-Saxon (Lowlander) as superior to the Gael (Highlander). For example, the anatomist Robert Knox called for the "quiet and gradual extinction of the Celtic race", a race that should be "forced from the soil" and have their lands sold "to Saxon men".[22] Though Scottish himself, Knox identified himself as a 'Saxon', railing against the Gaelic Highlander as an impediment to Saxon progress and drawing up comparisons between white US Americans and African American slaves: "To me the Caledonian Celt of Scotland appears a race as distinct from the Lowland Saxon of the same country, as any two races can possibly be . . . as negro from American."[23]

Knox's further description of the Highland character could be interpreted as the debased foil to the ideal Saxon specimen the British mountaineer was perceived to embody:

> idleness, indolence . . . the most dreadful of all human conditions. See [the Gael] cling to the banks of rivers, fearing to plunge into the forest; without self-reliance; without self-confidence . . . a hatred for order and patient industry; no accumulative habits; restless, treacherous, uncertain.[24]

Knox provides here a window into the racist ideology that contributed to the formation of the imperialistic Lowland 'Saxon' subject and his supposed superiority. Where the Gael is idle, the Saxon is ambitious. Where the Highlander is frightened and cautious in wilderness, the Lowlander is fearless and intrepid. Where the Celts are impatient and incapable of order and detail, the Anglo-British are measured and deliberate. For Knox and those of this mindset, the capacity for accumulating, listing, and categorizing the objects of the natural world was a sign of greater evolutionary development and racial superiority. Functioning as an initiation into imperialism that traffics in self-mastery and self-improvement, the mapping, conquering, and collecting of summits was both an ideological *and* physical training exercise for implementing superiority over not only nature, but of other 'races' with whom imperial Britain was vying for power and territory at the time.

The commissioner of the Sutherland Estate, James Loch (1780–1855) advocated for a state-administered program of colonization in the Highlands, similarly arguing that the Gaelic race and its inferior temperament presented an obstacle to the march of civilization and the improvement of society. Loch set out a vision for the colonization, displacement, and re-education of Gaelic Highlanders, where eventually "the children of those removed from the hills will lose all recollection of the habits and customs of their fathers".[25] Loch's vision has largely come true. The mountains are now largely silent and still, save for the footsteps of 'day trippers' slogging their way up a summit or two. What I hope to make legible with such historical perspectives is a framework for understanding the manner in which popular walking practices are not born and developed in a vacuum. Rather, they are thoroughly drinking from the complex currents of their formative days. Below, I describe how these insufficiently troubled waters continue to flow through contemporary Anglo-British media and literature.

Echoes from the mountains

During the course of the popular 2017 documentary film *Mountain*, and similarly across much Anglo-mountain literature, we are often presented with the narrative that up until 300 years ago, 'we' didn't dare venture into the mountains. In this telling, it was only once early Anglo-British explorers of the 18th century 'discovered' Alpine landscapes and steeled their nerves in order to penetrate these lonely high places that "slowly the blank spaces on the maps were filled in".[26] But as we've seen above, these weren't blank spaces. They were often spaces *inscribed* with emptiness after the fact.

What is actually being described is not the filling in of blank space, but the making legible of foreign territories that imperial Britain was making incursions into. And rather than encountering virgin wilderness, local resistance to being 'discovered' was often fierce, as native populations well understood what would soon be trailing along behind the slow, measured footsteps of surveyors and mapmakers. Take, for instance, Ireland *circa* 1603–1609, where the life of Anglo-Irish mapmaker Richard Bartlett came to a gruesome end: "When he came to Tyrconnell the inhabitants took off his head, because they would not have their country discovered."[27] By situating 'us', the viewers, within a normative positionality of Anglo-British imperialism, the imperial gazing subject is in turn positioned as a synecdoche for universal human progress and evolution itself.

However, my own experiences of meeting and interviewing Gaelic-speaking elders in the Highlands themselves, or in turning to Gaelic-sourced scholarship, were to position mountains and the Highlands within a vastly different history. Rather than vacant theaters waiting for the cast from the south to arrive and animate them, in the pre-modern Gaelic culture of the Highlands, "high places were commonly used as assembly sites for many ceremonies of importance, whether the occasion was legal, restive, religious or social".[28] Far from shunning or fearing mountains, what's revealed is a deep and ancient relationship between Highland Gaelic culture and the high places by which they were nourished in body and spirit for thousands of years. Multiple sources suggest how large communal fires on prominent peaks would provide the ceremonial setting for various Gaelic festivals that marked the agrarian calendar. The earliest ever written account of such a celebration is from the life of St. Patrick himself, when in 433 CE he lit a massive bonfire during Beltane on top of the Hill of Slane, ritually inaugurating the Christian conversion of Celtic Ireland by usurping the competing Beltane fire that had been lit by the indigenous Druidic priests.[29]

Further, Neolithic burial monuments on prominent peaks from over 6,000 years ago are among the very oldest archeological evidence in the Highlands. On the summit of Tinto Hill, at an altitude of 2,336ft lay the ruins of a substantial Bronze Age cairn measuring 20ft high by 140ft in diameter. The cairn and burial mound on the summit of Cairnpapple Hill at 1,024ft was used and re-used as a major ritual site for over 4,000 years.[30] Such overwhelming evidence makes clear that Anglo-British imperial histories of wilderness and virginal mountain summits do not correspond with reality; they only correspond with an imperial geographic imaginary.

Finally, my research also uncovered accounts of largely forgotten folkloric Gaelic walking practices that provide an alternate history to the myths of exploration and discovery, where the summiting of mountains appears to have been long practiced as an outpouring of grief for the loss of loved ones. In several Gaelic songs of lament, references are made to the protagonist "ascending and descending the peaks" in what seems to be a widely understood ritualized peripatetic mourning practice.[31] As well, a Gaelic poem going back at least to the 8th century tells us that high places were traditional places of ritual mourning, describing "men, women, and children / beating their hands without cease / in lament on the hills".[32] Another lament, likely from the 1500s, has as its chorus: "I climb the pinnacle of the crags / I descend the pinnacle of the crags / Very sad am I".[33] Such glimpses into the pre-modern Gaelic Highlands suggest that mountains were in fact deeply woven into the fabric of life, and that their summits were sites of both memorial and celebration for possibly thousands of years.

Conclusion

My troubling here of Munro bagging culture seeks to provoke better questions around how those of us who love walking in high-altitude landscapes and care deeply for mountains might relate with them in a more ethical, mutually nourishing manner: as persons and companions, rather than as objects to be collected, or resources from which eco-system services are extracted. By further integrating new animisms into discourses and praxes of conservation and mountain ecologies, might it be possible to compost the well-defended borders that modern culture has erected between objects and persons? Might we instead foreground a radically intersubjective – or even *intra*-subjective – ethics? One grounded in care, dialogue, hospitality, protocol, ceremony, and mutuality between human and mountain, all negotiating difference in an emergent world of more or less social (and also anti-social) persons with no 'objects' or 'environments' in sight? What might come to be once we allow ourselves to imagine that mountains might indeed *need* something from us, such as our respect, our care, our rituals of gratitude, or the unique creative expressions of beauty that humans are capable of? How might dance, music, film, poetry, visual art, or even research and writing serve to care for and nourish mountains?

Walking practices are indeed political. The practices we normalize and the ones we erase have consequences for not just human life, but other-than-human life as well. One bagger I interviewed who had just completed all his Munros confessed to me that it was a relief to complete the list, largely because it meant he was now finally free to visit mountains that weren't on the list, or to return and linger for a longer time on the ones he felt most drawn to when he was racing to tick them off. This suggests to me that what for some may be a useful and enjoyable structure for spending time outdoors can become for others an internalized disciplining of imagination that eclipses all other qualities of relationship outside of completing a task.

A Canadian friend of Scottish descent once told me a story about 19th-century Highland immigrants in the Canadian prairies and how they were heartbroken from missing their mountains, having now found themselves surrounded in every direction by endless flat grasslands. One way they coped was to write songs for fiddle that acted as gifts for their mountains back home. The tunes completed, they would transcribe them and send the sheet music by post to friends or relatives back home in Scotland. The fiddlers back home would learn these tunes and then hike up into the mountains and perform them as lamentations, so that the mountains might know through a beautiful bespoke song from far away that they were loved and missed. We are well to be reminded that there are many ways, and many reasons, to walk a mountain.

Acknowledgments

Blessings and gratitude to Dr. Michael Newton for your mentorship, for your passion and love of Gaelic language and culture, and for sharing these with me through your scholarship and our conversations: "*Cuiridh mi clach air a' chairn* / I shall add a stone to your Cairn".

Much love and respect to Dr. Kirsten Pai Buick and Dr. Ray Hernández-Durán for your respective love and guidance over all these years, for your fierce commitment to nurturing and modeling critical scholarship, and for first teaching me to see landscapes as knowledge, power, and memory.

Notes

1 Harvey, Graham. *Animism: Respecting the Living World*. London: Hurst & Co., 2005, 109.
2 Hallowell, A. Irving. *Ojibwa Ontology, Behavior, and World View*. New York: Columbia University Press, 1960.
3 Graham Harvey, "Animals, Animists, and Academics," *Zygon* 41(1) (March 1, 2006): 12.
4 Maureen M. Meikle, *The Scottish People 1490–1625*. Morrisville, NC: Lulu. com, 2015.

5 Ibid., 293
6 Ibid., 291
7 Ibid., 294
8 McIntosh, Alastair. *Poacher's Pilgrimage: An Island Journey*. Edinburgh, UK: Birlinn, 2016.
9 The Munro Society. "Biography of Sir Hugh Munro – 1856–1919," 2017.
10 Dempster, Andrew. *The Munro Phenomenon*. Edinburgh, UK: Mainstream Publishing, 1995.
11 Hansen, Peter H. "Modern Mountains: The Performative Consciousness of Modernity in Britain, 1870–1940." In Martin Daunton and Bernhard Rieger, eds., *Meanings of Modernity: Britain from the Late-Victorian Era to World War II*. Oxford: Berg, 2001, 185–202.
12 Taylor, Lucy. "Global Perspectives on Welsh Patagonia: The Complexities of Being Both Colonizer and Colonized." *Journal of Global History* 13(3) (November 2018): 446–68.
13 Lund, Katrin. "Making Mountains, Producing Narratives, or: 'One Day Some Poor Sod Will Write Their Ph.D. on This,'" *Anthropology Matters* 8(2) (2006): 1–12.
14 Mountain Reports. "Mountain Quality Indicators." www.tmsmountainreports. net/index.php?mqi.
15 Cronon, William. "The Trouble with Wilderness: Or, Getting Back to the Wrong Nature." *Environmental History* 1(1) (January 1, 1996): 16.
16 "Scotland's Census 2011." www.scotlandscensus.gov.uk/.
17 Field-work was undertaken for doctoral study at the University of Edinburgh in compliance with research ethics approval. Names have been replaced and aliases used throughout.
18 Carver, Gavin. "Between Nothing and Everything: The Summit of Mount Everest." *Performance Research* 18(3) (2013): 16.
19 Hansen, Peter H. "Albert Smith, the Alpine Club, and the Invention of Mountaineering in Mid-Victorian Britain." *Journal of British Studies* 34(3) (1995): 314.
20 Ibid., 322
21 Nakata, Michihiko, and Janet D Momsen. "Gender and Tourism: Gender, Age and Mountain Tourism in Japan." *Malaysian Journal of Society and Space* 6(2) (2010): 63–71.
22 Robert Knox (1850), quoted in Mackinnon, Iain. "Colonialism and the Highland Clearances." *Northern Scotland* 8(1) (2017): 35.
23 Ibid.
24 Ibid.
25 James Loch, quoted in ibid., 37
26 Peedom, Jennifer. *Mountain*. Documentary film, 2017.
27 Russell, Charles W. *Calendar of the State Papers, Relating to Ireland, of the Reign of James I. 0: 1611–1614*, Vol. 4. London: Longmans, Green, Reader, & Dyer, 1877, 280.
28 Newton, Michael. "The Sense of Place in the Gaelic Tradition as Localised in Strath." *John Muir Trust Journal & News* (1998).
29 Dumville, David. *Saint Patrick, A.D.493–1993*. Woodbridge, UK: Boydell Press, 1993.
30 Wrightham, Mark, and Nick Kempe, eds. *Hostile Habitats – Scotland's Mountain Environment: A Hillwalkers' Guide to Wildlife and the Landscape*, first edition. Edinburgh, UK: Scottish Mountaineering Trust, 2006.
31 Newton, Michael. "Notes on the Symbolism of Mountains in Scottish Gaelic Tradition." *John Muir Trust Journal & News* (July 1996).
32 Ibid.
33 Ibid.

Works cited

Carver, Gavin. "Between Nothing and Everything: The Summit of Mount Everest." *Performance Research* 18(3) (2013): 15–18.

Cronon, William. "The Trouble with Wilderness: Or, Getting Back to the Wrong Nature." *Environmental History* 1(1) (January 1, 1996): 7–28.

Dempster, Andrew. *The Munro Phenomenon*. Edinburgh, UK: Mainstream Publishing, 1995.

Dumville, David. *Saint Patrick, A.D.493–1993*. Woodbridge, UK: Boydell Press, 1993.

Hallowell, A. Irving. *Ojibwa Ontology, Behavior, and World View*. New York: Columbia University Press, 1960.

Hansen, Peter H. "Albert Smith, the Alpine Club, and the Invention of Mountaineering in Mid-Victorian Britain." *Journal of British Studies* 34(3) (1995): 300–324.

Hansen, Peter H. "Modern Mountains: The Performative Consciousness of Modernity in Britain, 1870–1940." In Martin Daunton and Bernhard Rieger, eds., *Meanings of Modernity: Britain from the Late-Victorian Era to World War II*. Oxford: Berg, 2001, 185–202.

Harvey, Graham. "Animals, Animists, and Academics." *Zygon* 41(1) (March 1, 2006): 9–20.

Harvey, Graham. *Animism: Respecting the Living World*. London: Hurst & Co., 2005.

Lund, Katrin. "Making Mountains, Producing Narratives, or: 'One Day Some Poor Sod Will Write Their Ph.D. on This.'" *Anthropology Matters* 8(2) (2006): 1–12. https://anthropologymatters.com/index.php/anth_matters/article/view/69/134.

Mackinnon, Iain. "Colonialism and the Highland Clearances." *Northern Scotland* 8(1) (2017): 22–48.

McIntosh, Alastair. *Poacher's Pilgrimage: An Island Journey*. Edinburgh, UK: Birlinn, 2016.

Meikle, Maureen M. *The Scottish People 1490–1625*. Morrisville, NC: Lulu.com, 2015.

Mountain Reports. "Mountain Quality Indicators." www.tmsmountainreports.net/index.php?mqi.

Muhr, Kay. "Bealtaine in Irish and Scottish Place-names." *Journal of Scottish Name Studies* 10 (2016): 38.

Nakata, Michihiko, and Janet D. Momsen. "Gender and Tourism: Gender, Age and Mountain Tourism in Japan." *Malaysian Journal of Society and Space* 6(2) (2010): 63–71.

Newton, Michael. "Notes on the Symbolism of Mountains in Scottish Gaelic Tradition." *John Muir Trust Journal & News* (July 1996). www.academia.edu/11710823/Notes_on_the_Symbolism_of_Mountains_in_Scottish_Gaelic_Tradition.

Newton, Michael. "The Sense of Place in the Gaelic Tradition as Localised in Strath." *John Muir Trust Journal & News* (1998). www.academia.edu/11710683/The_Sense_of_Place_in_the_Gaelic_Tradition_as_localised_in_Strath.

Peedom, Jennifer. *Mountain*. Documentary film, 2017.

Russell, Charles W. *Calendar of the State Papers, Relating to Ireland, of the Reign of James I. 0: 1611–1614*, Vol. 4. London: Longmans, Green, Reader, & Dyer, 1877.

"Scotland's Census 2011." www.scotlandscensus.gov.uk/.

Taylor, Lucy. "Global Perspectives on Welsh Patagonia: The Complexities of Being Both Colonizer and Colonized." *Journal of Global History* 13(3) (November 2018): 446–68.

The Munro Society. "Biography of Sir Hugh Munro – 1856–1919," 2017. www.themunrosociety.com/biography-of-hugh-munro.

Wrightham, Mark, and Nick Kempe, eds. *Hostile Habitats – Scotland's Mountain Environment: A Hillwalkers' Guide to Wildlife and the Landscape*, first edition. Edinburgh, UK: Scottish Mountaineering Trust, 2006.

8   *Black Men Walking*

An interview with Dawn Walton and Testament

Pippa Marland and Anna Stenning

Introduction

Black Men Walking, written by Testament (a.k.a. Andy Brooks) and directed by Dawn Walton, toured theatres to huge acclaim in 2018, selling out 71 of 84 shows around the UK, and reaching an audience of nearly 10,000 people. The play was produced by Walton's company Eclipse, 'the foremost Black-led national production company in the UK', and was the first national touring production to be born from Revolution Mix, Walton's initiative to bring 500 years of hidden Black British history to theatre, film and radio. The play is inspired by the Sheffield Black Men's Walking Group, and is set in the Peak District of Northern England. It focuses on three men, all of whom are experiencing some kind of crisis in their lives, and a young woman the men encounter as they walk through increasingly rough weather in the Peaks. This chapter presents the edited transcript of a face-to-face interview with Dawn Walton and the written replies to an email interview with Testament. The questions were co-devised by the editors of this collection, and concern the evolution of Eclipse, Revolution Mix, and *Black Men Walking*, the challenges of staging a play about walking, the significance of walking itself, hidden Black histories, race and racism in the British countryside, gender and generational perspectives and the play's reception in the UK.

Interview with Dawn Walton, in conversation with Pippa Marland, 19 December 2018, Eclipse, The Workstation, Sheffield

Could you say a little about Eclipse and Revolution Mix, and how the ideas for *Black Men Walking* came into being?[1]

DW: I started Eclipse eight years ago in Sheffield, and in 2014 I launched a movement called Revolution Mix, my ambition to deliver the largest amount of new Black British work. We make work in theatre, film and radio, with a group of writers we've been committed to over a number of years, developing a body of work with a jumping-off point for 500-plus years of Black British history – the real hidden, some may say erased, histories of Britain. So we've been working with these writers and with various ideas, and the pieces we've created either use the hidden history at the front, as a story in itself, or use it as the backdrop to another story.

Most of my ideas come from frustration. I'm a bit frustrated at the notion that the Black population in Britain just arrived here a mere 70 years ago on the *Windrush* – it's a bit of a lie, really, and a very convenient one, I think, in terms of pecking orders, opportunities, and all those things. Eclipse is about equality – and inequality – and in order to understand those things you have to look at the history, see where they come from, and understand the roots of them before you can make them right again. That's all the hard politics of it, if you like. But on the basic level, we care about telling great stories, and when I launched Revolution Mix nobody was telling those stories. There's actually been several movements since, for example David Olusoga's *Black and British: A Forgotten History* for BBC2, and we now seem to be in the middle of a very vibrant movement to rediscover all those histories, so that's exciting.

When we were researching *Black Men Walking*, it was clear that there was a lot of Black history in Yorkshire – like nowhere else, really – Black Roman emperors, the Bangle Lady found just over there in York. Here in Sheffield we have Samuel Morgan, the Black actor who was based here in the 1860s and 70s and died here. We were quite fascinated with that history. A lot of the Revolution Mix pieces relate to the modern era – our most recent production, *The Princess and the Hustler*, is set in 1963, around the Bristol bus boycott, and there are other ones set in the 1970s, all around a specific time – but I wanted something that moved us away from the idea that Black history was in one place, at one particular moment in time, something that was much more epic, that took in a span of history, and there was a great opportunity to do that in Yorkshire, with all those stories.[2]

The second thing was, we have an audience development group process, which is about creating ambassadors everywhere we go, and we employ those ambassadors to advocate for Eclipse. They make sure that the people who would normally be the last to know about a show are the first. Amongst our ambassadors were members of Sheffield's Black Men's Walking Group. They invited me to come for a walk with them, and in the course of that walk the idea grew to create *Black Men Walking*. I wanted to work with a Yorkshire-based writer, so I invited Testament along, and we walked the land with these walkers. There was a particular moment I recall when we were on a Roman road, and I was panting and puffing up this slightly steeper bit, and I was looking at my feet, as you do sometimes when you're walking and you're a little bit out of breath. And I can remember someone was talking, so that I could make it – so I didn't have to do the talking (they're very generous, this group) – and I said to him, 'What is this road, it's really straight?' and he said, 'Oh, it's the Roman road,' and there was a moment of remembering Septimius Severus [the first Black Roman Emperor, who led a campaign in northern Britain in 208 CE] and looking at my own feet and seeing Septimius Severus's sandals, as I imagined them, next to my feet – and at that moment I looked around at Testament, and we were there, really. We knew that there was something we could make to do with that walk and those men in that proximity. So we then sat in a room and threw paper at each other until *Black Men Walking* formed itself over about 18 months.

What were the challenges of setting a play about movement and walking in nature in the static and enclosed space of a stage? What opportunities did the focus on walking provide?

DW: Well, it's one of my favourite bits of it, actually. For the last 20 years I've worked with a movement director, on and off, called Steve Medlin, and I knew I was going to work with Steve on this. Steve is a physical theatre artist, amongst other things – a mime artist, some would say, Lecoq-trained – and I knew, as we were developing this piece, that I wanted the characters to do the real walk in almost real time, so that's what we did. We held a series of workshops that were not just about developing the text, but were about developing the movement. There was a physical language to be found. But because they have to be able to talk and walk at the same time, we needed a technique, needed to create something that looked really realistic, but didn't use all their energy. We also wanted to show them meeting certain obstacles on the walk, and again they would use very basic, very simple physical theatre techniques to create the illusion of a stile, gates and so on. All those mechanisms just became part of the language of the piece. We simplified some of this in order to tell the story, so as not to take away from the fact that there was actually a drama going on, but the drama was also in the walking.

The set was also extremely effective. How did you go about designing that?

DW: The design in itself is really interesting. I kept saying, 'I want something that's epic, it's got to be epic,' even though the set wasn't a massive physical piece. And so, in Simon Kelly's beautiful design, there was this kind of earth strata at the back, which symbolises a connection with the land – and with that land over time – and greenery and millstones [remnants of 19th-century corn milling in the area]. There was also a gradient in the walk – an uphill and downhill bit and two layers. But the one incongruous thing was, because I wanted it to feel like these histories just came through time and landed, we used the device of a mirror, so that when you lit it differently, you could suddenly see through it, and you could see that the history characters in the play came out from this mirror, almost like a Tardis. Also, when you light it in certain ways, the audience can see themselves in it, and indeed each other – you can see other members of the audience, so there's that sense that 'we're all in this' as opposed to it being just something you come to as a voyeur. That was the thinking.

One of the things that I thought was really, really important in this body of work that we're making was not just to make work in which the subject was new and challenging, but which was formally challenging – to break down the barriers of traditional theatre, in a sense. It doesn't just have to be in big ways, but in small ways too, so presenting a piece of work where there are three *older* Black men on stage – I have never, ever seen that. And they *walk* – again, I've never seen that.

There's a slightly comic element in the play around the North/South divide, a feeling of, 'We're tough Northerners.' There's also a strong sense of the importance of being in rural places. Can you say a bit about those elements of the work?

DW: I'm not sure it's something I really set out to explore, specifically, but Andy [Testament] and I, we're not originally from the North – we've both adopted the North, so we're conscious of those differences. But what was interesting was the response to the play: people from walking groups contacted us from all over the country, and there were people who talked about walking in the North, but there were equal numbers of people talking of walking down South, Black walking groups that were forming as a result of it – which was really wonderful – or that existed that people didn't know about. There's a women's walking group that walks through the back of Croydon and out into Surrey that I knew nothing about.

Particularly if you're Black, I would say – I'll talk about it from a purely Black perspective – I think what's really important about that rural setting is the safety of it: it's a safe space, there's no interruptions from other forces, other than Nature itself. So what was really striking about those men, walking with them, was the sort of love in them, really. They loved each other, and supported each other, and it was a place where they could release the valves of being Black and British: the micro-aggressions, tensions, things you experience that are covert, but you feel them. And you'll bat them away, whatever; they're not awful, violent things, but they're micro things that you're very conscious of – the unconscious biases that you experience, the double look that you get. The guys talk about these things in the play . . ..

Yes, that comes across very clearly. You also show how those tensions are there even in rural areas, when the characters meet other people. I'm thinking of the scene where the men see the policeman and then talk about the exchange afterwards:

RICHARD: I'm sure he approached us to genuinely warn us about the
             weather and the roads and so on.
MATTHEW: Yes.

Beat.

THOMAS: Still you think, don't you?

**And later there's the discussion between Ayeesha and Matthew, where she
asks him what he's doing in the countryside. It's overtly comic, but clearly
has serious undertones:**

AYEESHA: Um . . . Black people really live in the cities, innit though?
             Countryside's not for us. I don't get it . . .
MATTHEW: It's a safe space you see?
AYEESHA: Safe space! I wouldn't like to go into a pub round here.
MATTHEW: Oh, I think you'll find it's not like that anymore. Not round
             here anyway. We're just black men . . . Walking in the
             countryside –
AYEESHA: Walk into one of those pubs and you'd be black men
             running.

**There's also a character in *White Open Spaces* who describes the country-
side as a 'violent, nasty place'[3] Is there a tension between the idea of the
countryside as a 'safe space' and one that harbours its own forms of danger?**

DW: The original podcasts were responding to Trevor Phillips' description a
decade previously of the 'passive apartheid' of the countryside, and we were
comparing that moment when he said it and this moment ten years later,
asking whether there was any difference.[4] So we retold the three original
pieces and commissioned three new pieces, and the question was, which
ones were then, and which were now? I don't know of anyone who can
really answer that question, which tells you quite a lot. I think if you are
Black in the countryside, you have a different kind of visibility, and when the
characters in *Black Men Walking* talk about going into a pub, that's real –
that is an experience that's not just me, but many of us have had: people
looking at you like you shouldn't be there.

   When we were making the trailer, actually, the actors were going out for
a walk with the walking group, and the walking group took off at quite a
pace that day. I was talking to camera people and I sent the actors on to go
and catch up with the group, so I was trailing behind with my assistants and
this guy stopped me, and said, 'Are you looking for that group that went
past here five minutes ago?' and I said, 'Oh yeah, I am – I take it they were
Black?' 'Yeah, yeah, yeah – they went that way.' So he immediately identified me as part of this group, and then he said, 'Why are you walking out
here – are you, like, a church group or something?' And he was American,

which was really funny, because *he* was on a trip, *he* was, if you like, the interloper at that moment, but *we* were, in his mind, the interlopers. He couldn't make it work in his head that Black people go out for walks – *it's an extraordinary thing – in the countryside!*

So we're aware of this sense, this expectation, that you don't have Black people in the countryside – this is basically what he was saying – and we deal with it all the time. There are certain areas you can walk into and you can see the negativity straight away, and the countryside is one of those places. My company Eclipse has always been really clear that this idea that there are spaces where Black people can't be, or aren't welcome – or don't exist – nine times out of ten, it's just not true. There's always somebody there; if you haven't met them, it doesn't mean they don't exist.

Could you say a little more about the centrality and importance of walking itself for the walking group and for the characters in the play?

DW: Well, they walk for health – physical health, mental health, all those things come with walking, and I think if you experience micro-trauma, or any of those issues constantly, and you're managing that, then a good walk can be restorative. It was also important in the play in terms of reclaiming a whole history, which is a big thing – it was a way of walking it into the room, walking it into a space. It is a really physical act that people seem to appreciate. In telling that story, there's something about the energy of it, the length of it – it's about travelling as much everything else, but it's you, your body that's doing the travelling, taking that epic journey through time.

Despite the title of the play, one of the four central protagonists is a woman – a young rapper called Ayeesha. Could you say a little about the role of this character?

DW: There is an inter-generational conversation that happens within the Black community that hasn't really been put on the stage before. I don't think that the experiences of my parents' generation, my generation or the generation that's coming after me are different; the problems and the challenges and the barriers to the Black community across all three generations remain, but they take slightly different forms, and the way to handle them has shifted. Class comes into this as well. The three men would describe themselves as, and are, middle-class – by their own definition and by societal definitions. So it was not only interesting to put a younger character in there, but a younger working-class character, going, 'What are you all talking about, going walking in the country? Why the hell do you do this?' It made them think about what they were doing as well, because they're a little bit, you know, 'We walk, we're the guys, we do this thing, we're extraordinary because . . .'. And to get someone to actually come in and make them re-think it a little bit was great.

And for it to be a young woman . . .

DW: For it to be a young woman was awesome, because the men's instinct was, 'We're going to protect you, we're going to save you,' and of course this isn't necessarily the case; they need her as much as she needs them, and that's the message. There's something loving in Andy's writing – he looks for the love, and he looks for the humour as well . . . his humour is about wanting to share love, if you like. I think that's inherent in his personality, and it comes through his writing as well. So there's something really wonderful, to bring this woman who has a specific skill, who is a very specific challenge to that male, older-generational thinking – she just wipes it away. Also, you don't often see class played out within the Black communities. It's one of my obsessions. You'll see class played out between a Black community, who are working-class, and a white middle class, but you don't see it explored within the Black community itself.

Black Men Walking **is ultimately a refreshingly joyful and optimistic play. Do you think this is one of the reasons behind its success?**

DW: I think that really is Andy. I mean, I don't necessarily share the 'everything should finish well' point of view, but he's an optimist and he wants people to feel good at the end of it, when they come out of a space, and I think that's just who he is. So my job at that point is to respect that. I mean, there's another version, isn't there? There's another version that doesn't end so well, actually, and that might have been equally as successful as a story. But he just wants people to feel good, and I think it's about opening people up; they feel good, but they're also receiving something that they would never have thought of.

Did *Black Men Walking* **fulfil the objectives of your Revolution Mix, 'to place Black narrative at the heart of British theatre'?**

DW: Yes, and very, very deliberately. If you think about this walking group, in which people are still stared at as if it's something unusual, and the Black British stories that people just don't know about – those two really work well together, they complement each other perfectly; so, hidden histories, people reclaiming the land. There's a line in the play where the characters say they walk the land to claim the land, and that's what those real walkers talk about: 'It is our space as well – we are Yorkshire dwellers.' Most of the men that go on that walk once a month from Sheffield are born and bred in Sheffield; they're Yorkshiremen, so it is their land – more so than mine, as a Londoner – and they walk it to claim it. Also, if you think culturally and historically, we're very connected to the land; my parents grew up in the countryside on their island, and people that come from African heritage, their families lived in rural settings. This is nothing unusual, so it's strange when people find the idea of Black people walking the land weird. There's no part of our culture that isn't close to the land.

How was the play received, and what kinds of audiences did you attract?

DW: We know that Eclipse is very good at is bringing in new audiences. I think there's this sort of expectation, because we're a Black theatre company, that all of our audience would be Black. Well, why would it be? Most theatres don't have Black audiences, so why would we bring in this mass of an entirely Black audience? The inference in that is that Black work is only for Black audiences. That is a ludicrous idea. But what we've known, anecdotally, for years is that our work appeals to, as I describe them, 'the *so-called* "Hard to Reach"' . . . if you reach out, you'll find them, and we're very good at that. And at the other end, we score really highly on what's known as 'experience seekers', people who go to the theatre very regularly, but actually don't necessarily want to see another Shakespeare, probably don't want to do panto. They want to see something that's new, that they wouldn't have seen anywhere else; they're looking for a new experience, something that makes them think a bit differently about the world. We appeal to both sets of those audiences.

For the *Black Men Walking* tour, we had an independent consultant pool all the data from the box offices of the tour venues and then analyse it. They delivered a 24-page report to us, and we then sent the report to an independent artist and asked her to illustrate that data, so what we have is a really beautiful document which I call 'The "R" Word'.[5] It basically analyses and illustrates the data in a really beautiful and accessible way. The report showed that 21.4 per cent of our audience self-identified as BAME against a UK average for theatre tours of 4 per cent. Actually, the best example of it was the opening night at the Arnolfini in Bristol, which was quite incredible. We have a great audience development officer down there, who basically used to be one of our audience members, but we've employed her now. We have those relationships all over the country. So two months before the show, she would have had an event and invited interested parties, and those audiences booked. What was interesting to me was, when I went to see it, there was a lot of Black audience members at the front, and they were very excited and really celebratory, stamping feet and getting really excited about the show. Then there was (to speak in very black-and-white terms) a white audience, I would say, who were slightly further back, but also kind of going, 'Ooh . . . what is this?' And when the show finished, the place lit up – I mean, it went crazy. I know the work is good, but it was a really particular response to it in Bristol, and as I watched it, I thought, 'My God . . . this audience never watch work together . . ..' This was very clear to me.

The Eclipse audience does have regular theatre-goers, but it also has new people who are new to those spaces, so that mixture means that some jokes will land, and some people won't know what that joke is, or will feel a little uncomfortable about laughing because they know it's possibly something to do with race, 'So I shouldn't really be laughing . . . I should take this very seriously . . ..' And of course, when the Black audience laughs, the other audience goes, 'Oh, okay, we're good,' so the audience have a conversation with each other, and that's typical of an Eclipse audience – we mix audiences, and allow that conversation. In 20-odd years of directing, that's the work I've been making, that's what I care about – the mixed audience. I do not make work for an all-Black audience, I do not make work for an all-white audience; I make work for a mixed audience, because that dialogue matters.

Interview with Testament, by email, 10 May 2018

The play *Black Men Walking* is inspired by the Sheffield Black men's walking Group '100 Black Men's Walk for Health'. Could you tell us a bit more about this group?

T: The '100 Black Men's Walk for Health' was founded in 2004. It is a Sheffield-based walking group originally aimed at encouraging Black men to get out into the countryside (later expanded to invite Black women also). It was aimed at benefiting both mental as well as physical health. The group meet once a month on a Saturday, and usually walk in the Peak District. They are great guys, and walking with them, it is clear there is a sense of community among the walkers. And conversation on the walk frequently weaves in and out of the political and social, dealing with everything from current affairs, British and African politics, football, family life and everything in between. They are generally older, very well read, and have a sense of compassion and humanity about them.

Dawn Walton speaks of the creation of the play as more 'making' than 'writing'. Can you describe the process through which the script came together?

T: Dawn wanted someone to write a play inspired by the walking group, but also tying in Black British history – preferably multiple points in the Black British history, not just one narrative. Dawn also stated that it had to be for four performers. Dawn and dramaturg Ola Animashawun worked as sounding-boards and consultants, feeding back on my writing of the play. Their insight, ideas and wisdom were invaluable.

The play begins with a chant – an 'Ancestors' Prayer' shared between the three main male characters, quoted in part here:

We walk
We walk
We walk
We walk for freedom

We walk for honour
For beauty
For love
We walk out our identity
We walk for sanctuary
We walk to claim this land
We walk OUR land
We walk in the footsteps of kings

Walking plays a complex role in the play. It seems to offer the characters a means of dealing with the trauma of day-to-day racist abuse – both casual and more deliberate – of connecting with Black figures whose presence is often omitted from official historical narratives of Britain, and of asserting a sense of positive identity and belonging. How would you sum up the meaning and function of walking in the play?

T: Walking functions on multiple levels. Walking the Peak District, as well as being a communal experience, can also be a very meditative pursuit. Sinking into one's own consciousness and connecting with the landscape. Certainly, for the character of Thomas, who sees these visions of historical figures [the 'Ancestors' who appear as ghostly presences in the play], the blurring of temporal lines is something he walks through. We are passers-by with these walking historical figures. There is also walking as a political act – marching, protesting or simply asserting the right to be here, like the Kinder Scout trespass – but more than class politics, the racial and cultural barriers come into play here too.[6]

How did you go about recovering the stories of the Black British ancestors who are mentioned in the play?

T: Dawn presented me with a document which gave a brief overview of the last 500 years of Black British presence. I'd also been recommended Peter Fryer's excellent book *Staying Power*. I quickly realised I wanted to narrow the focus to Yorkshire and the Black people that may have travelled the trackways our principle characters did. So using the Internet and using the *Africans in Yorkshire* website as a jump-off point, I started to look at the cast of historical characters that might appear in the piece.[7] I also had some great conversations with historian and theatre maker Joe Williams, who runs Heritage Corner in Leeds.

You also write that the play 'is an attempt to embrace the imprint we find here in the earth, hold it in tension and grow from it'. The script reveals a strong connection with the actual earth of the Yorkshire/Derbyshire borders – 'the dales, the moors, the peaks, the vale' – and its rivers and rocks. What is the significance for you of the play's walk taking place in this landscape, and in its specific location of Padley Gorge?

T: Primarily, the route the characters take mirrors two of the walks which the real-life walking group have actually taken. The millstones that provide a very distinctive feature to those walks are also a great metaphor for human presence there. Some of the features of the landscape also make for some great dramatic locations.

In broader terms, there seems to be a lack of published 'nature writing' by British Black and minority ethnic writers – though this may be more about visibility than an actual dearth – and even a perception that BAME communities are less engaged than others with nature and landscape.[8] In relation to the US scene, Carolyn Finney recounts in *Black Faces, White Spaces: Reimagining the Relationship of African Americans to the Great Outdoors* a story in the *New York Times* where a middle-class Black woman describes her concerns about going on a vacation, driving through rural Montana. The woman quotes her teenage son saying, 'Four black folks from Oakland, California cruising the back roads of Montana. Are you nuts?'[9] Obviously, the history and ongoing complexity of race relations in the US don't necessarily map onto the British scene, but there are echoes of these kinds of issues in *Black Men Walking*, for example in Ayeesha's challenge to Thomas about what the men think they're doing in the countryside [quoted above in the interview with Dawn Walton]. Can you say a bit more about this element of the play?

T: There is a lack of Black British people getting out into the countryside, which is a shame as the benefits of being more in touch with nature is widely known. Partly, this is due to where immigrant communities settle when they first arrive in the UK – this is usually for economic reasons, jobs, industrialisation etc. And historically, my parents' generation, for example, may have experienced racism in the countryside, not making it the most attractive place to spend your leisure time.

In your introduction to the play, you say that writing it presented you with an opportunity 'to dig through the crates of history, sample, remix, cut and crash stories together'. How does your work as a hip-hop MC influence the form and style of your writing, and your treatment of the themes of *Black Men Walking* in particular?

T: For me, juxtaposing narratives, poetic form and even themes can feel very much like the process of making a hip-hop record – sonic collages of older pieces from eclectic genres, mixing with contemporary culture or elements created by the artist.

As well as blending in elements of music and poetry, the play has episodes of magic realism. Can you say a little about their function in the walk?

T: The magic realism – hearing voices from across time, unexplained weather and the gradual building to a crescendo of historical figures reaching into the contemporary world – it's all a metaphor for the much-needed unearthing of our shared history, sometimes our literal ancestors, vital for our modern-day consciousness.

Obviously, the play is called *Black Men Walking*, but it features a powerful, central female character – Ayeesha – a young Black rapper, who disrupts and challenges the masculine narratives of the group (even initially questioning the basic premise of 'walking out our identity') and also provides the perspective of a younger Black generation. Can you say something about how you deal with questions of both generational differences and gender in the play?

T: For me, as someone who is conscious of bias against minorities and women, it felt crucial that the play was not totally male-dominated and that a female presence with agency would be an important part of the story. Ayeesha is someone who really counters any pretentions the men have, and in fact it's Ayeesha who saves the day. On a macro level, it is their mutual respect and both sides' input that brings harmony. And of course, in terms of intergenerational conflict there is a simple message of how they both need each other.

You argue, very movingly and persuasively, 'In these testing times we are, I think, required, collectively and individually, to face our complex relationship to a fractured national identity.' How might walking help us to face that complexity on both a collective and individual level?

T: Walking is both physical and figurative, collective and deeply personal. By navigating landscapes and allowing other people into our spaces, conversations can be had and we can have time to reflect. Walking cityscapes is also valuable, although I think there is something special about being close to nature and being exposed to the elements. Perhaps it forces us not to walk alone.

Notes

1 https://eclipsetheatre.org.uk/; https://eclipsetheatre.org.uk/revolution-mix; Testament, *Black Men Walking* (London: Oberon Books, 2018).
2 https://eclipsetheatre.org.uk/whats-on/1452-princess-the-hustler.
3 *White Open Spaces* is a series of podcasts about race and racism in the countryside co-produced by Pentabus Rural Theatre Company and Eclipse in 2016, which combines three stories from ten years ago and three from the present day: www.pentabus.co.uk/white-open-spaces-2016.
4 http://news.bbc.co.uk/1/hi/uk/3725524.stm.

5 https://eclipsetheatre.org.uk/news/1453-the-r-word.
6 The Kinder Scout mass trespass took place in the Derbyshire Peak District on 24 April 1932 to draw attention to the lack of public walking access to areas of open countryside.
7 www.africansinyorkshireproject.com/.
8 This perception is currently being challenged in a range of ways, and there are initiatives such as *The Willowherb Review*, which 'aims to provide an initial platform to celebrate and bolster nature writing by emerging and established writers of colour': www.thewillowherbreview.com/.
9 Cited in Caroline Finney, *Black Faces, White Spaces: Reimagining the Relationship of African Americans to the Great Outdoors* (Chapel Hill, NC: University of North Caroline Press, 2014), 61.

9 The Walking Library for Women Walking

Deirdre Heddon and Misha Myers

Introduction

> But, you may say, we asked you to speak about women and fiction – what
> has that got to do with a room of one's own?
>
> (Virginia Woolf[1])

Responding to the editors' invitation to contribute an essay that explores
women, walking and landscape, we offer an account of *The Walking
Library for Women Walking* (2016–17), a recent edition of the authors'
ongoing project, *The Walking Library*. *The Walking Library for Women
Walking* strategically takes its place against a background of walking art
in which women have been rendered largely invisible. Our library, bringing
together books suggested as good to give to a woman walking, and then
inviting people to walk with them, seeks to make walking women unavoidably manifest. We might think of *The Walking Library for Women Walking*
as a feminist walking movement.

WALKING WOMEN

The Walking Library for Women Walking – hereafter abbreviated as
WLfWW – is the ninth edition of *The Walking Library*. *The Walking
Library*, launched in 2012, is an ongoing creative research project which
explores the multiple relationships between walking, literature and environment. Inspired by repeated references throughout the late eighteenth and
nineteenth centuries to books carried on long (pleasure) walks, *The Walking
Library* asks variations on the question 'What book would you take on a
walk?' to curate collections of books and then walk with them.

We initiated *The Walking Library* to accompany a month-long peripatetic arts festival, *Sideways*. *Sideways* travelled the disused, slow pathways
of the Flanders region of Belgium, aiming to inspire local publics to walk
more and drive less. We purchased a stock of nearly 100 books, each of
them suggested as good to take on this ecologically inspired walk, and we
walked and read books for some 300km, offering a mobile library service

for other artists.² *The Walking Library* project was orientated at its outset towards environmental matters: its mode of transport is foot; its pedagogy is civic, collective and horizontally distributed, with knowledge donated and circulated through the gifting and sharing of selected books; it takes place in the open; and the environments of its taking place, in combination with the materials it carries, prompt a renewed attention to and engagement with places and to our complex and mobile inter-dependencies.³

We created the *WLfWW* in 2016 for *WALKING WOMEN*, a series of events curated by London-based artists Amy Sharrocks and Clare Qualmann who sought to celebrate the work of women artists using walking in their arts practice. Sharrocks and Qualmann conceived *WALKING WOMEN* as a response to their:

> growing concern that walking is perceived as a male domain of prac-
> tice. Over a period of a year we had each experienced talks, seminars,
> and panel discussions in which the invisibility of women was being
> announced as a feature of walking – even when we pointed out that this
> is not the case. The *WALKING WOMEN* events . . . were designed to
> counter this imbalance.⁴

Publicity material for *WALKING WOMEN* drew explicitly on earlier research published by scholars and artists Deirdre Heddon and Cathy Turner.⁵ Heddon and Turner had identified a cultural landscape of walking which, they suggested, was exhausted due to the repeated recitation of certain writers and artists (including Daniel Defoe, Jean-Jacques Rousseau, Henry David Thoreau, André Breton, Guy Debord, Hamish Fulton, Richard Long and Iain Sinclair). In their view, an orthodoxy had emerged which positioned walking as almost always individualist, heroic, epic and transgressive, qualities understood predominantly in relation to a historically masculinist set of norms and challenges. Their review of existing literature revealed that walking as an aesthetic practice was framed by two enduring historical discourses: the Romantics, tramping through rural locations, and the avant-gardists, drifting through the spectacular urban streets of capitalism. Though ostensibly different 'stories', these narratives of walking shared two recurring imperatives: walking was a means to seek out adventure, danger and the new; and, through walking, one could release oneself from the relations of everyday life.

As part of their research, Heddon and Turner undertook ten walking interviews with women artists. In doing so, they revealed walking art to be much more diverse and complex than dominant discussions of it proposed. Concepts of freedom, heroism and scale were seen to be relative and contextual, or mobile, and the spatial was determined to be fully relational. Perhaps the most significant finding of their research, though, was the extent of walking work made by women, most of it unacknowledged. As they wrote in 2012:

the invisibility of women in what appears as a canon of walking is conspicuous; where they are included, it is often as an 'exception' to an unstated norm, represented by a single chapter in a book or even a footnote.[6]

Sharrocks and Qualmann reproduced this very statement in their *WALKING WOMEN* publicity, and extended it by asking:

[H]ow do we re-write a canon? How do we re-balance the perception of art, artists, and the use of walking as a creative practice? Can we not only imagine a future in which gender bias and skewed vision is destroyed, but actively build the pathway there?[7]

Like Heddon and Turner before them, Sharrocks and Qualmann insisted on the presence and diverse artistic practices of women in this landscape. More than 90 women, including the authors, shared their walking work at *WALKING WOMEN*.[8]

The Walking Library for Women Walking

As with all *Walking Library* iterations, we started this one with a question, asking:

What book would you recommend to a woman going for a walk; a book that might provide excellent company, inspiration, solace, advice, humour, information . . .?

By the date of the first walk, 16 July 2016, we had received over 75 donations, and at the time of writing have a permanent collection of 119 books and 118 suggestions. All those donating or suggesting a book were invited to give a reason for their choice, contributing to a collective 'autobibliography'. Though our library stock is rich in its diversity, a taxonomy does emerge:

- artists' books, most often donated by the artist (e.g. *Lorg-coise Footprints* by Gill Russell and *Please Watch U R Your Head* by Idit Nathan);
- factual and scholarly books about walking, many by women (e.g. *A Field Guide to Getting Lost* by Rebecca Solnit and *Why Loiter? Women and Risk on Mumbai Streets* by Shilpa Phadke, Sameera Khan and Shilpa Ranade);
- environmental writing, most of it written by women (e.g. *Silent Spring* by Rachel Carson and *H is for Hawk* by Helen Macdonald);
- published letters and journals of significant women who have some connection with walking or journeying (e.g. *Letters written in Sweden, Norway, and Denmark* by Mary Wollstonecraft);

- memoirs of women deemed inspirational, many of them related to walking (e.g. *Eight Feet in the Andes* by Dervla Murphy), but others not at all (e.g. Grace Jones' *I'll Never Write My Memoirs*);
- novels by women which feature walking (e.g. Jane Austen's *Pride and Prejudice*) alongside favourite novels (e.g. *Sacred Country* by Rose Tremain);
- books which have autobiographical significance for the donor (e.g. Simone de Beauvoir's *The Blood of Others* – 'This was almost the first feminist novel I ever read.');
- books or texts which seem to need to be walked to come fully into their own (e.g. Caryl Churchill's play *Blue Heart*: 'I wanted to find a non-naturalistic performance text, something that needed to be discovered and understood through rhythm. I think [this] needs the SPACE to work through the text in both head and body. So a combination of reading and walking seemed right.')

The *WLfWW* completed three walks as part of the *WALKING WOMEN* events, two in London and one in Edinburgh. It was also walked in Bristol, Glasgow and Newcastle, and from 22 July to 3 September 2017 was installed in the exhibition *The House that Heals the Soul* (Centre for Contemporary Art, Glasgow). A temporary library was created for *Moving Out of Doors*, an event held in Geelong, Australia in November 2017. The number of people who walked with us – mostly women – ranged from 15 to 30. The walks were free. Each walk responded to the specific combinations of place, people and books, and so was unique, though a shared structure held them together as a series. Acknowledging that space is a political matter and unevenly distributed and occupied, our walks retraced suffragette marches and actions, following in the footsteps of those who walked before us and who used space to make visible their collective power as well as their right to take up public space. Where there were no such traces to follow, we actively sought to locate women in the landscape, looking out for statues and monuments to women, or streets named after them. As the suffragettes did before us, we made place for women through our collective action and presence in space. Before each walk we displayed the full library, allowing time for browsing and then inviting participants to select a book to carry. We asked participants to stop and share a reading wherever they felt a resonance between the place and their selected book, facilitating dynamic exchanges between environments and texts. At the end of the walk, participants wrote or sketched a reflection on their experience and left suggestions for additional books we should hold. In the next section, we recite fragments from across some of the walks, aiming to reveal the *WLfWW*'s various textures, performativities and shifting relationships, alongside the interventions it conjures. References we use are taken only from library books donated.

Fragments from *The Walking Library for Women Walking*

The accounts of the various *WLfWW* events that follow are intended as 'unfinishable configurations' in the sense proposed by artist Eleanora Fabiâo in *Actions*;[9] they do not aim to present a totality, but rather to evoke the provisionality and relationality of each iteration that is the *WLfWW* to date.

16 July 2016, London: Somerset House (Embankment)–Parliament Square–Hyde Park, 6–8pm

The first walk of the *WLfWW* departed from Somerset House and retraced a suffragette 'monster march' staged on 21 June 1908, which set off from Embankment and ended in Hyde Park, joining seven other walking tributaries. The 'Women's Sunday' march, the first to be organised by the Women's Social and Political Union, sought to visibly demonstrate women's support for the vote, with more than 300,000 women gathering at Hyde Park; the largest mass demonstration London had seen. The Suffragette colour scheme of purple, white and green – symbolising dignity, purity and hope – was launched at this event. We borrowed these colours for our Walking Library rucksack patches, a gift given to anyone who donated a book or joined us for a walk.

Our first stop on the walk was just outside Somerset House, on the banks of the River Thames at Cleopatra's Needle, guarded by two large sphinxes. Here, Alison read a random page selected from *The Pennine Way: The Legs that Make Us*, a donation by dance artists Tamara Ashley and Simone Kenyon. The book documents their 2006 performance, an unfolding along the 270 miles of the long-distance Pennine Way trail, described by them as 'a choreographic pathway, a shared journey and investigation of walking as dance and dancer as traveller'.[10]

> DAY 16: Langdon Beck to Dufton 12 miles
> A gap. I am taken by Brian and Pam in their car as last night I cut my foot on a nail in the floor. Kindness. We drive around the hills to Dufton, 26 miles by road. I return to walk this leg the day after we finish the trail. I am quick on my feet this day, without my pack. It pours with rain while I recover this loss of physical distance. The gap remains.
> **Weather conditions**: overcast and humid. **Body conditions**: T – watery inside and out.[11]

That our walk in the footsteps of the suffragettes began with a story about walking interrupted, about returning so as to finish what had been started, about resilience in the face of the unexpected, about acts of kindness, about routes and the necessity to reroute and improvise, was dense with metaphorical resonances. This was just the first of such reverberations ignited across histories, geographies, lives, journeys, dreams and emotions.

Embankment was thronged with people enjoying the warm evening, and our progress was slow. Anna elected to read from Virginia Woolf's short story *Street Haunting*:

> No one perhaps has ever felt passionately towards a lead pencil. But there are circumstances in which it can become supremely desirable to possess one; moments when we are set upon having an object, an excuse for walking half across London between tea and dinner . . .. As we step out of the house on a fine evening between four and six, we shed the self our friends know us by and become part of that vast republican army of anonymous trampers, whose society is so agreeable after the solitude of one's own room.[12]

Written in 1927, the year before all women over the age of 21 were given the vote in the UK, Woolf's story offered a salient reminder of just how essential the suffragette actions had been, and just how far we have walked, figuratively speaking. But still, passing numerous statues and monuments and looking out in vain for one that might call us to a halt, we felt the overwhelming erasure of women from this teeming public space. Arriving at Parliament Square, we turned to face the Houses of Parliament, an impromptu homage to the women who walked here before us to demand the right to participate equally in democratic processes. As a sizeable group of mostly women, we did not function as Woolf's anonymous – invisible – trampers. Instead, in that moment, we created our own performative memorial and marked this in turn with a monument of books placed on the grass, swapping walking with a sit-in. Looked down on by the statues of 11 statesmen, we spotted, in the far corner of the Square, a temporary 'people's memorial', honouring the Labour MP for Batley and Spen, Jo Cox. Cox had been fatally stabbed and shot on 16 June as she arrived at Birstall Library, the venue of her weekly constituency drop-in surgery. Her murder coincided with the UK's referendum on leaving or remaining in the UK. Her attacker –Thomas Mair – was heard shouting 'Britain first!'[13] Idit shared a reading from the book she carried, *I-Spy: Religious Intolerance* by Sarah Wood:

> It was summer in London. I was in a good mood. The sun was shining. I felt expansive. I was on a busy street. Ahead of me two people were posting letters at the same post box at the same time. One was a prosperous looking white man. One was a young woman wearing a niqāb.
>
> When the man came face to face with the woman he suddenly looked furious. He said something to her that I didn't hear. I wondered if he knew her. Then he turned and looked at me and smiled. His mood seemed to have switched instantly. He looked like he was trying now to be charming. He wasn't. He turned back to the woman and with the same sudden switch of mood, thrust the letter in his hand into the space in her veil that revealed her eyes.[14]

At Wellington Arch, Amy read from the introduction to *Women Adventurers: The Lives of Madame Velazquez, Hannah Snell, Mary Anne Talbot and Mrs Christian Davies*. Amy had temporarily loaned this book to the library. Published in 1893, the book's editor is Ménie Muriel Dowie, Amy's great grandmother and author of *A Girl in the Carpathians*, a chronicle of Dowie's own adventures on horseback published two years earlier. Amy was walking not only in the footsteps of the suffragettes, but of her remarkable forebear. In 1893, Ménie Muriel Dowie wrote:

> Among the hoary, white old questions that go tottering down the avenue of time, is one of an intermittent vitality truly surprising. The Independence of Woman – is it right or wrong? – that is the tremulous, doddering head of it. Is a woman the equal of a man? May a woman engage in all that men may?[15]

The gap between then and now in this avenue of extended time seemed to us not entirely closed over yet; but in our movement and reading together, in our pulling of space and text around us into something that felt almost tangibly like a new iteration of presentness and place, there was an optimism. Sitting in Hyde Park, our destination reached, we wrote some words to add to those we had shared:

> In all this talk of walking, of what you walk on and in and who has walked before, it was wonderful to walk in the steps of hundreds of thousands of women who paved the way for our rights today.
>
> Hearing women's voices; reading women's voices; walking in women's footsteps; pausing. Marching, walking, talking, thinking, making, writing in the street.

11 August 2016, Edinburgh: Drill Hall–Leith Walk–Leith Links–Drill Hall, 12–1.30pm

In Leith there were no suffragette paths to be followed. There was rain. Hand-picked and hand-carried books were tucked proprietorially under coats from the very start. The size of our group – about 30 – buoyed us up and put a spring in our step. Serendipity beckoned. At the Podiatry Hospital, Catriona placed a perfect extract from Nan Shepherd's *The Living Mountain*:

> Walking barefoot has gone out of fashion since Jeanie Deans trudged to London, but no country child grows up without its benediction. Sensible people are revising the habit. . . . Dried mud flats, sunwarmed, have a delicious touch, cushioned and smooth; so has long grass at morning, hot in the sun, but still cool and wet when the foot sinks into it, like food melting to a new flavour in the mouth. And a flower caught by the stalk between the toes is a small enchantment.[16]

Further down Leith Walk, Louise recognised in the wind blowing across a large, muddy puddle at the side of the road the ripples on a lake described by Dorothy Wordsworth in her *Grasmere and Alfoxden Journals*. She shared the diary entry from Wordsworth's journal for 11 August 1800:

> Monday afternoon: Walked to Windy Brow.[17]

We were now on the Windy Brow of Leith Walk. Louise also carried her own artist's book, *Warnscale*, an evocative landmark-walk acknowledging infertility. *Warnscale* functions as both walking guide of an area of the Lake District and an evocative art work, made by Wilson to support rituals or rites of passage for women who have experienced involuntary childlessness. It draws on and maps a rich, literal landscape to support the mapping of an emotional one. Wilson opened her book at the photograph of Black Beck Tarn, the wind's passage marked on the surface of that water too. Her reading took us beneath the surface:

> Black Beck (oligotrophic tarn typical in cold regions) scarce in nutrients but supports aquatic flora and oligotroph organisms such as diatom flora (unicellular algae) and micro fauna.[18]

Mesmerised by the wind rippling the muddy puddle beside us, and the ripples of writing crossing time and space, we pondered what the dark water might hold, host and support, literally and symbolically.

As soon as we arrived at Leith Links, a public park with a miniature hill near the entrance, Joyce enacted Shepherd by removing her shoes and running gleefully barefoot across the grass. The books we carried placed one environment over another: here, the grass of the city park resonated with the heather on the hill; there, the muddy puddle reflected a Lake District tarn. Some of our books also drew our attention to the overlooked or taken-for-granted, including the details of different clouds and the precise, singular feel of different rains, each evoked by a different atmospheric word (dreich, drizzle, pelting). The textures, colours, scents and sights of the city were heightened, an enriched environment coming into focus through the pages of books that asked us to attend.

At the top of the park's small hill, Emma held up *messidges passing*, an artist's book made and donated by Elspeth Owen (a.k.a. 'material woman'). Emma shared with us the book's cover: a photo of a gift box tied with a red thread. Walking through Leith, Emma had traced this thread across the book's pages, and invited us now to form a circle on the top of the hill and pass an imagined red thread around it. She set this invisible red thread off on its journey, placing it carefully into the hands of the person on her left, who in turn passed it to the next person, and so on until the magic red thread had passed around the circle fully, threading us together. Though the thread was a fabrication, our actions of joining one to another were real. A group of mostly strangers, we were now bound together, like stitched leaves of a book. This threading action mirrored the artwork documented in *messidges passing, Looselink* (2005). For *Looselink*, Owen criss-crossed Britain, delivering messages on foot and building new pathways between strangers.[19] Each time a message was delivered and received, the recipient gave Owen a new message to deliver to someone else, and so on. *The Walking Library for Women Walking* is forging its own networks and pathways, treading out new and shared stories as we walk together.

16 November 2017, Geelong: The School of Lost Art, Noble Street–Mayfair Drive–Camden Road–Windmill Street–Noble Street, 12–1.30pm

In Geelong, a city southwest of Melbourne, Australia, we walked and commemorated women's labour to create paths of emancipation for women in the past and present and reflected on the challenges still to be overcome, not just for women. With every step, Misha recited the names of women from Geelong that were among the 33,000 collected by suffrage groups who went door-to-door across Victoria in 1891 to create another indomitable monster: the 260 metre-long 'Monster Petition' presented to Parliament to demand the right to vote for women.

Commissioned as the keynote for *Moving Out of Doors*, a day-long symposium and art event exploring women's artistic labour, this *WLfWW* event marked the first *Walking Library* event in the Southern Hemisphere, and it followed the announcement made the day before of Australia's vote for same-sex marriage. Lorna, Melbourne inner-city activist and elder, initiated the readings for the walk by simply holding up the spine of *The Selected Writings of Gertrude Stein* and repeating the author's name, suggesting this said it all.

Soon after departing from the walk's starting point at the artist-run studio The School of Lost Arts, the group halted and gathered at a scenic overlook of the River Barwon winding through the valley below. A group of refuse collection trucks assembled here as well, their drivers (all male) enjoying the view with their lunch. With the river before her, Devinia introduced her reading from *Dark Emu: Black Seeds Agriculture or Accident?* written by Bunurong and Melbourne-born author Bruce Pascoe. She noted its personal and wider significance by emphasising: 'as first people of this nation, although we are moving forward in a lot of ways, there are still a lot of barriers for our people in this country'. She read Pascoe's account of an encounter in 1843 at another river, the Murray, where colonial settlers misinterpreted the meaning of words shouted at them by the Aboriginal people as welcoming them to their land. She concluded with the author's thoughts on the incident:

> You have to work hard to convince yourself, or the governor, that Aboriginal people were delighted to give away their land.[20]

The view over the Barwon River enticed the group of women to linger and share an eclectic selection of readings, which continued in a kind of call-and-response to one another, with readings from Heather Rose's *The Museum of Modern Love*, Kathleen Jamie's *The Tree House*, and *The Bhagavad Gita*, which, the reader commented, is a handbook for life. The women continued walking, huddled under umbrellas protecting them from the late spring drizzle of the humid afternoon. When the awning of C. Sphinx Consulting Structural and Civil Engineers, a land development business office, offered shelter from the rain, Fiona prompted the group to assemble again for her reading from Sarah Williams Goldhagen's *Welcome to Your World: How the Built Environment Shapes Our Lives*. Later, she summarised the book's compelling argument in her comments: 'it costs no more to build something that relates to people than it does to build something that relates to economics'.

The pattern of the call-and-response continued as the women took advantage of the opportunity for shelter otherwise absent in these streets mostly filled with domestic homes set back by gated front gardens. As we were standing opposite a primary school, Kate found it a befitting place to offer a reading from Marion Molteno's *If You Can Walk, You Can Dance*, a book about a young girl, which she said she had chosen because it is about 'the creative journey and finding a true way to be oneself'.

The selected reading, a description of the sound of the vibrating strings of a cello, was interrupted by the less concordant sound of the refuse collectors honking their horns as their convoy returned to their work and passed us by. Once they had gone, a woman in the circle commented on how visible we were as a group of women in these streets, her comment reflecting how *The Walking Library* works as a kind of intervention and civic performance, but also how a group of women walking in public elicits unwanted attention from passers-by as much as a woman walking alone (though being in a group reduces feelings of vulnerability). As the circular walk turned left on Windmill Street and joined back onto Noble, this interaction prompted a small cluster of women to reflect on the courage and vulnerability of the suffragette petitioners; they speculated about how those women in the past might have been received, especially if met at the door by 'the man of the house'. This conversation continued back into the inviting doors of The School of Lost Arts, where the women wrote their reflections on the walk. Some reflected on how the walk brought the group together: 'when we left the house we were a disparate group, but when we returned we had become a coherent (united!) group'. And others expressed how the walk connected them with 'the land' even amidst the 'busy world around us'. The walk prompted many questions about the complexity of the political matters of space encountered throughout all instances of the WLfWW: who has the rights to own it, to be in it and to make it their own and the distance still to go.

Conclusion

The *WLfWW* was inspired by *WALKING WOMEN*. The political motivation which prompted *WALKING WOMEN* is explicit in its curators' aims of revealing as misperception and presumption walking as a male domain of artistic practice. Sharrocks' and Qualmann's tactical approach to re-balancing the perceptions of walking art at this time – what it is and who makes it – was to focus singularly on female artists and their work, making them visible and enacting an interruption in the repetition that is so crucial to canon formation and its persistence. At the launch of the event, Sharrocks and Qualmann suggested that *WALKING WOMEN* would be a success if there was no longer a need for such a singularly gendered platform.

The *WLfWW* functioned as another tool for rewriting the walking canon. Most obviously, *The Walking Library* is an ongoing walking project created by two women artists. That the *WLfWW* solicited and carried books considered good to give to a *woman walking* offered another means of challenging directly the walking canon. Its invitation explicitly foregrounded women who walk. The *WLfWW* also held a collection of donated books which moved well beyond Heddon and Turner's cited 'fraternity'. In contrast to the first *Walking Library* (2012), where approximately 85% of the books suggested were written by men, here 77% of the donated books were written by women. Viewed in relation to the first *Walking Library*, we consider this a radical act of re-balancing. This recent collection is diverse, and books *about* women and walking, including those by women artists, predominate. The *WLfWW* literally provides a place for women artists to have their walking work displayed, browsed, circulated, shared and discussed. As this collection has been donated onwards to another library – Glasgow Women's Library – the documented work of these artists is offered a future. The cards attached to each book, recording the personal reason for its donation, diversify the library's – and walking's – stories even further.

As the fragments we have shared here reveal, each iteration of the *WLfWW* is as different as the women, books and places that make it and the complex constellations that emerge from their interrelation. Walking as a group of mostly women, we physically take up space, creating a mobile, gendered place as we move along city streets, perhaps in our very collectivity standing in for those absent monuments of and to women.[21] Our *Walking Library*, activated by those who carry and walk it, intervenes in and makes anew a place in the world for women through sharing authored ideas with those which emerge from our embodied knowledges and memories of place. As we stand together on Embankment, listening closely to the words of Virginia Woolf, we add ourselves to her story, seeing ourselves there as – and with – her, just as she now features in the stories we tell of this event. In this, we accompany and make more complex Rebecca Solnit's insight that 'landscapes, urban and rural, gestate the stories, and the stories bring us back to the sites of this history'.[22] Sometimes, the stories we carry 'gestate' the landscapes, creating new paths and 'senses of place', 'shaping cities and parks'. We make literal Solnit's reference to 'a vast library of walking stories and poems, of pilgrimages, . . ., meanders, and summer picnics'.[23] As we perform a cartography of suffragettes' labours, we join our bodies and contemporary landscapes to their monstrous geographies, the march and petition, and ensure their efforts persist against those obstacles to human equality that remain. Our *Walking Library*, the stories it holds, relays and conjures, reminds us that sometimes we do not walk in the footsteps of those who went before us, but rather we walk beside them – and each other – and must continue to do so.

The Walking Library functions as a convivial and collective space. The books, the women, the environment and the temporal location perform as a call-and-response, in complex but attentive replies and continuations of the conversation. As a feminist walking movement, the *WLfWW* creates a relational and temporary architectural space for women to gather and move together, united and empowered beyond the solitude of the room of one's own or those masculinist norms of walking which Heddon and Turner identified (individualist, heroic, epic). The act of bringing women, walking, books and environment together might be considered transgressive still. This account of the *WLfWW* is offered as another chapter, another step towards the inscription and re-inscription of women's practices of walking into history. Whether it pursues and performs memorial-scapes, crosses paths with or follows in the footsteps of spectral women (suffragettes, scholars, artists, authors), forges new paths or retraces familiar and familial meshworks, the *WLfWW* is a collective and ongoing hunt for Woolf's lead pencil. Where Woolf's pencil offered her 'an excuse for walking half across London between tea and dinner', the *WLfWW* is a stratagem to write a place that is of and for women walking, and that is produced with and by women walking. We are here. We have always been here.

Notes

1 Virginia Woolf, *A Room of One's Own* (London: Penguin Books, 2004 [1928]), 3.
2 Deirdre Heddon and Misha Myers, "Stories from the walking library", *Cultural Geographies* 21(4) (2014): 639–55.
3 Deirdre Heddon and Misha Myers, "The walking library: mobilising books, places, readers and reading", *Performance Research* 22(1) (2017): 32–48.
4 Amy Sharrocks and Clare Qualmann, *WALKING WOMEN: A Study Room Guide on Women Using Walking in Their Practice* (London: Live Art Development Agency, 2017), 1, www.scribd.com/document/346143517/WALKING-WOMEN-A-Study-Room-Guide-on-women-using-walking-in-their-practice.
5 Deirdre Heddon and Cathy Turner, "Walking women: interviews with artists on the move", *Performance Research* 15(4) (2010): 14–22; Deirdre Heddon

and Cathy Turner, "Walking women: shifting the tales and scales of mobility", *Contemporary Theatre Review* 22(2) (2012): 224–36.

 6 Ibid., 225.
 7 Amy Sharrocks and Clare Qualmann, "WALKING WOMEN", www.liveartuk. org/blog/walking-women/.
 8 For information on participants, see Sharrocks and Qualmann, *WALKING WOMEN*.
 9 Eleanora Fabiâo, *Actions* (Rio de Janeiro, Brazil: Tamanduá, 2015), 5.
10 Tamara Ashley and Simone Kenyon, *The Pennine Way: The Legs that Make Us* (Oxford, UK: Brief Magnetics, 2007).
11 Ibid.
12 Virginia Woolf, *Street Haunting* (London: Penguin Books, 2005 [1927]), 1.
13 BBC News, 23 November 2016, www.bbc.co.uk/news/uk-38079594.
14 Sarah Wood, *I-Spy: Religious Intolerance* (self-published, 2015), 12.
15 Ménie Muriel Dowie, ed., *Women Adventurers: The Lives of Madame Valazquez, Hannah Snell, Mary Anne Talbot and Mrs Christian Davies* (London: T.F. Unwin, 1893), v.
16 Nan Shepherd, *The Living Mountain* (Edinburgh, UK: Canongate Books, 2011 [1977]), 103–4.
17 Dorothy Wordsworth, *Grasmere and Alfoxden Journals* (Oxford, UK: Oxford University Press, 2008), 17.
18 Louise Ann Wilson, *Warnscale: A Land Mark Walk Reflecting on In/Fertility And Childlessness* (Leeds, UK: Louise Ann Wilson, 2015).
19 Heddon and Turner, "Walking women: interviews with artists on the move".
20 Bruce Pascoe, *Dark Emu: Black Seeds Agriculture or Accident?* (Broome, Australia: Magabala Books, 2014), 2.
21 Though the publicity for *The Walking Library for Women Walking* walks indicated that they were open to all participants, it is unsurprising, given the name, that it was mostly women who joined the walks.
22 Rebecca Solnit, *Wanderlust: A History of Walking* (London: Granta Books, 2014), 4.
23 Ibid.

Works cited

Ashley, Tamara, and Simone Kenyon. *The Pennine Way: The Legs that Make Us* (Oxford, UK: Brief Magnetics, 2007).
Dowie, Ménie Muriel, ed. *Women Adventurers: The Lives of Madame Velazquez, Hannah Snell, Mary Anne Talbot and Mrs Christian Davies* (London: T.F. Unwin, 1893).
Fabiâo, Eleanora. *Actions* (Rio de Janeiro, Brazil: Tamanduá, 2015)
Heddon, Deirdre, and Cathy Turner. "Walking women: interviews with artists on the move." *Performance Research* 15(4) (2010): 14–22.
Heddon, Deirdre, and Cathy Turner. "Walking women: shifting the tales and scales of mobility." *Contemporary Theatre Review* 22(2) (2012): 224–36.
Heddon, Deirdre, and Misha Myers. "Stories from the walking library." *Cultural Geographies* 21(4) (2014): 639–55.
Heddon, Deirdre, and Misha Myers. "The walking library: mobilising books, places, readers and reading." *Performance Research* 22(1) (2017): 32–48.
Pascoe, Bruce. *Dark Emu: Black Seeds Agriculture or Accident?* (Broome, Australia: Magabala Books, 2014).

Sharrocks, Amy, and Clare Qualmann. "WALKING WOMEN", www.liveartuk. org/blog/walking-women/

Sharrocks, Amy, and Clare Qualmann. *WALKING WOMEN: A Study Room Guide on Women Using Walking in Their Practice*. London: Live Art Development Agency, 2017. www.scribd.com/document/346143517/WALKING-WOMEN-A-Study-Room-Guide-on-women-using-walking-in-their-practice

Shepherd, Nan. *The Living Mountain* (Edinburgh, UK: Canongate Books, 2011).

Solnit, Rebecca. *Wanderlust: A History of Walking* (London: Granta Books, 2014).

Wilson, Louise Ann. *Warnscale: A Land Mark Walk Reflecting On In/Fertility And Childlessness* (Leeds, UK: Louise Ann Wilson, 2015).

Wood. Sarah. *I-Spy: Religious Intolerance* (Self-published, 2015).

Woolf, Virginia. *A Room of One's Own* (London: Penguin Books, 2004 [1928]).

Woolf, Virginia. *Street Haunting* (London: Penguin Books, 2005 [1927]).

Wordsworth, Dorothy. *Grasmere and Alfoxden Journals* (Oxford, UK: Oxford University Press, 2008).

10 Walking backwards

Art between places in twenty-first-century Britain

Judith Tucker

This chapter will offer a series of close readings of art practices that engage with walking. My purpose is to demonstrate the diverse ways in which walking finds a critical place in contemporary British art. Through offering an interpretation of selected works, I will consider both the diversity of practices and the differences between selected practices and explore the key issue of power relations, or rather, bring a sensitivity to the socio-economic and cultural experience of difference in contemporary Britain that requires attention to these walking practices at several levels simultaneously. This sensitivity involves, in particular, attention to what the material conditions of doing the work *qua* walking involve that inscribe socio-economic factors into the work and hinge the aesthetics of walking to major cultural issues such as ecocriticism, sustainability and human impact on "nature". To do so, I will explore the ways in which artistic walking practices in Britain have moved beyond what I suggest is the binary set up by Richard Long (born 1945) and Hamish Fulton (born 1946) between process-driven and conceptual walking practices and the kind of art that privileged the aesthetic object.[1]

Long and Fulton were certainly brave when they began their walking as art. These were times when formalism and media-specificity were the order of the day. As Andrea Phillips notes, "Walking, in this sense, is one marker of an economy of art in which the desire for process-based, participatory, embedded experience has replaced ideals of abstracted contemplation for reasons that compound a schism between ethical engagement and aesthetic representation."[2] The London which, as young art students, Long and Fulton walked around was *still* in the long shadow of World War II. Linked to nationalism, the practice of landscape painting was at this time perceived by the young environmental artists as part of the reactionary, atavistic, commodified London art scene. As we near the end of the second decade of the twenty-first century, immaterial, readymade performance and relational works, including those that involve walking, have become mainstream in artistic practice and valorised in and by high-profile international exhibitions. For example, in 2017 walking was key for *Documenta 14*: the curators invited prospective visitors on walks where "Paths, routes, and parcours cross and intertwine, as visitors consider the pathways taken by peripatetic thinkers as a point of departure for a reflection on the act of walking."[3]

Paradoxically, object-based art practices, even painting, sculpture and drawing in their respective expanded fields, acquire as a result an unexpectedly radical status. The proliferation of walking as an element of artistic practice might imply a shared walking aesthetic; I will argue that this is belied by the extraordinary variety of works available about an embodied and shifting experience of place. Iain Biggs (born 1950), an artist/academic for whom walking has long been a key aspect of practice, draws attention to this in a recent email, where he writes that he is:

> puzzled, and challenged, by the way the relationship between walking and art practice has been fragmented by very literal notions of process. As a result, it's much harder to think about a painter like Eamon Colman[4] in relation to, say, Hamish Fulton than it ought to be. (Colman's two most recent exhibitions were called *Walking at Three Miles an Hour*, 2015 – which I take to be a reference to Rebecca Solnit – and *Thinking-in-movement*, 2017.) Since 1972 all Fulton's work has, like Colman's, been based on the experience of walks. But while Colman translates his experience of walks into the highly condensed form of paintings, Fulton translates his into a wide variety of media. This process of *translating* what is experienced through walking is, however, central to both men's work and also an important aspect of my own deep mapping work.[5]

In the opening section of his book *Landscape Painting and Maps*, the phenomenologist Edward Casey asks, "Why take the trouble to represent [. . .] what we now see with our eyes and what we now feel with our feet? [. . .] Why re-present what is already effectively and thoroughly in ordinary direct experience?"[6] Perhaps there is just an indication here of how Long and Fulton's works go some way to addressing, complicating and challenging the relation between walking and documenting, and this is one of the ways in which their works remain pertinent today. There are artists who walk and walking artists. What a viewer might find in a gallery is that there are artworks that are produced through walking as some kind of a record of those walks and those that are experienced by walking. Ultimately, though, how most of us experience the work of "walking artists" of all kinds is what remains as documentation or representation of the walk in the gallery, in a catalogue or online. Veronica Sekules makes this point in relation to Long and Fulton: "It is within the art gallery that their expression finds form in maps, words, photographs and drawings, as well as, in Long's case, physical works of sculpture."[7] The relation between walking, fieldwork, studio and gallery, of the places of production and of consumption, which was once so disrupted by artists such as Long and Fulton, has come full circle.

With this in mind, why shouldn't contemporary, abstracted, landscape painting, as exemplified by the works of the Irish painter Eamon Colman and others mentioned in this chapter, be seen in relation to ethics as well as aesthetics and other critical and ecocritical theory any less or more than obviously performative walking practices, for example those of Alison Lloyd and Edwina Fitzpatrick, who are also discussed herein? In this chapter, therefore, I am seeking to reconsolidate what has become fragmented. I also seek to interrogate and expose the power relations that have become naturalised in ideas of "nature" and the British countryside in ways that are consistent with the intentions of ecocriticism. Power relations, for instance, are already implicit in the cost and quality of the material paraphernalia required for walking and the documentation of walking – clothing, maps and equipment of various kinds. These both ground the practice and, at the same time, bring considerations of privilege, geopolitics and environmental cost into play.

The touring exhibition and its accompanying catalogue essays for *Walk On: From Richard Long to Janet Cardiff* in 2013 provide meaningful points of departure for this move to consolidate diverse artistic walking practices.[8] This exhibition brought together forty artists to whose practice walking is crucial. In his introductory essay, Alistair Robinson writes that *Walk On* "attempts to gently challenge the orthodox distinctions through which artists' work created by walking has been understood".[9] The range of media on show in *Walk On* began to put this consolidation into practice. The selected walking artists under discussion in this chapter are also representative of such different approaches: for example, Lloyd and Fitzpatrick are largely performative, while Ruth Philo walks in order to be able to make objects. Artists might walk to make work, or the walk might be the work. Either way, we usually find that further artworks or documentation have been produced as a record of those walks, and these are exhibited as objects in galleries. Thus, the works of these artists, alongside Ingrid Pollard, Iain Biggs, Rebecca Thomas and Elizabeth-Jane Burnett, all complicate the boundaries of document, artefact and performance. While these artists who walk certainly benefit from the legacy of Long and Fulton, they are as much indebted to the related ideas of deep mapping, the resurgence in popularity of psychogeography and the recent re-evaluation of the neo-romantic artists.

As important an influence for many contemporary walking artists as Long and Fulton is W.G. Sebald. While he never actually used the term "deep mapping", his work has much in common with this approach. "Deep mapping" is a term which emerged from cultural geography that has been revived for new usages by contemporary artists to aid with these processes and their conceptualisation. We might for instance consider "deep mapping" as described by Pearson and Shanks as "attempts to record and represent the grain and patina of place through juxtapositions and interpenetrations of the historical and the contemporary, the political and the poetic, the factual and the fictional".[10] It is the way in which it is believed he conducted his artistic walks that has inspired writers of psychogeography and nature writing, and walking artists alike, especially those who are interested in coastal geographies. As Veronica Sekules argues, his writing method:

of weaving in and out of observation, memory and association as he traced his path, both in the present and through history, in real space and time, as well as in imaginary realms, recalling distant histories, has been enormously influential.[11]

I suggest that Sebald's walking practice, as outlined in the 1998 English translation of *Die Ringe des Saturn: Eine Englische Wallfahrt,*[12] is congruent with both psychogeographic and deep mapping approaches to place, and Sekules is absolutely right that his work reinvigorated creative walking practices in the UK in terms of narratives, fictions and stories.

From the inception of the Ramblers' Association, walking in convivial groups has been important, as many contemporary walking artists now attest. Some of these artists walk alone, some with others, either in collaboration or through chance meetings. Some extend the notion of guided walks, acting as facilitators between people and places and between ecology and culture. The collaborative way in which Dee Heddon has worked with Misha Myers, as discussed in Chapter 9, "*The Walking Library for Women Walking*", in this volume, is a prime example of this sort of facilitation. In this collaborative spirit, I have spoken with many of the artists mentioned here, incorporating their original comments into my discussion while also drawing on my own collaborative walking practice with the radical landscape poet Harriet Tarlo.

Contemporary British walking art

In terms of an overtly and consciously embodied approach to drawing and walking in the landscape, let us first consider the artist Rebecca Thomas' drawings made while actually hillwalking. Unlike most drawings made on walks, they are not executed during pauses in the walks, but instead while moving through the landscape. Thomas has produced an extensive collection of these hectic, raw, raucous mixed-media drawings both in notebooks and on loose-leaf papers. They are not to be reworked in the studio, but act as works in their own right, "forming a record of the phenomenological engagement with the environment and raising thoughts about perception, documentation and visual translation".[13] She has presented these in juxtaposition with a juddering video piece in which a viewer becomes more and more aware of the alterations in her breathing and her breathlessness as the topography changes. She notes that the works comprise "a complex of accumulated marks which echo in their frenzied overlay the arrhythmic movement of the artist's body as it engages with the uncertainty of the terrain".[14]

Thomas' work reflects the kind of corporeal relationship we have with place that John Wylie describes in his article "On Ascending Glastonbury Tor", when "[t]he act of walking takes over, becomes more serious in a way, and the only purpose is the walking".[15] The lie of the land affects the way we walk: we feel the landscape in our muscles, and the "habitual ambient resonance of depths and surfaces distils into knees, hips and shoulder-blades".[16] While walking and landscape are equally crucial for the work of painter Ruth Philo, for her it is more about the parallels between drawing, painting and walking rather than an indexical relation. Philo's paintings are not at all concerned with any direct representation of landscape. Nonetheless, she draws clear comparisons between the two activities of walking and painting, considering both to be immersive: "To start a work, I have to immerse myself, usually by walking. It is a sensory process mixing seeing, feeling, thinking, hearing, tasting, touching, moving. I notice aspects of terrain, light, weather, temperature, smell and sound."[17] There is a surprising resonance with Wylie. However abstract they seem, her paintings clearly emerge out of an understanding of place. In common with other painters, analogies can be drawn with the palimpsestic nature of the surface of a place and of a painted surface. Philo terms this "condensed histories".[18] We can see this in her works in the way she scratches, wipes and rubs through to previous layers. The thickness of paint at the very edges of her canvas reveals the multiple re-workings of her surfaces.

While Thomas' drawings directly index her body's movements as she walks and Philo's studio paintings could not be made without a prior walking practice, other artists' works remind us rather more overtly that our perception of landscape through walking is, of course, deeply affected by whose body it is that walks. All knowledge is situated, to draw on Donna Haraway.[19] In what follows, I will also attend to what these bodies might be wearing to explore this idea further.

Our understanding of where we are depends on who we are, both being determined by social, economic and political relations. The curator and artist Mike Collier notes that "walking is (and has been) politically and socially value laden".[20] Ingrid Pollard's well-known 1992 photographic piece *Wordsworth's Heritage* remains as unsettling today as when it was made. She presents images of groups of waterproofed, walking-booted, rucksack-carrying hikers, sitting on rocks, among trees and standing among tumbledown stone walls. The figures strike poses reminiscent of advertisements for outdoor clothing, as much as the landscapes in which they sit reference Turner's paintings or Wordsworth's poetry. The works are produced as postcards (to be sent home) and billboards presented in various cities. One bears the text "After reaching several peaks, Ms Pollard's party stops to ponder on matters of History and Heritage". What has not yet been mentioned is that all the walkers are black. So, against the background of images of the Lake District, an area deeply associated with a Romantic vision of wild Britain, she places a group of walkers of Caribbean birth or descent. That they walk, and love doing so, claims a place in this landscape, and so this practice is asserted to interrupt the normalised assumptions of who belongs in this freighted British landscape. Pollard invites considerations as to who might be excluded from outdoor leisure pursuits, sublime landscapes and their representations. In addition, she both collapses and draws attention to the UK urban/rural divide with this project:

it's as if the Black experience is only lived within an urban environment. I thought I liked the Lake District where I wandered lonely as a Black face in a sea of white. A visit to the countryside is always accompanied by a feeling of unease, dread . . ..[21]

This work reminds those who need reminding that rambling through the British countryside is fraught not only with uncertain terrain, but also with a colonial history.

Another reading of Pollard's work might consider the walking gear of the walkers. Peer at the 1992 image carefully, and it's clear the walkers are fully kitted up in the everyday, practical rugged walking clothes of the era – walking boots, heavy socks, some in over-trousers, and all of them in large, even oversized, waterproof jackets, their maps sensibly in plastic covers. While we might walk to feel attuned to our bodies' movements through a connection with the landscape, there is a paradox, at least in Britain, that in order to do this, we also need to protect, even defend, our bodies from the very place itself. How to know what to wear in Utopia? Here I borrow the artist Tania Kovats' phrase from her playful and ironic piece written in 1997 entitled "100% Waterproof: Gore-Tex – What to Wear in Utopia". "I can't recommend Gore-Tex highly enough," writes Kovats. "My two-way front zipped with raingutter flaps, rugged windproof nylon shell, Velcro closure cuffs, and fully breathable layer. Gore-Tex waterproofs have to be the ideal choice for what to wear in Utopia."[22] Her language suggests outdoor clothing advertisements, themselves drawing on the aesthetic of the sublime also referenced in Pollard's images. Both artists draw attention to the complexities of walking clothing linked with wealth, class, status, consumerism and privilege, and reflecting the latest textile technological breakthroughs with, of course, their own environmental and human costs.

In Pollard's photographs, no labels are actually revealed; it is certainly not designer wear. Rather, the clothing is practical, looks well-used and perhaps harks back to the radical beginnings of the Ramblers' Association. This reflects Catherine Horwood's argument that during the interwar period and "unlike tennis, activities such as hiking, cycling and rambling were not seen as opportunities for sartorial statements or social advancement".[23] Only five years later, however, Kovats plays with manufacturers' names and gestures towards what follows in terms of the expansion of specialist, designer walking gear in the last twenty years. The walking artist Alison Lloyd, whose photo-essay features as Chapter 3 in this book, also works occasionally in an outdoor clothing store and has noticed that people are beginning to ask for vegan walking boots.[24] The altruistic desire to have vegan shoes might actually encourage people to choose synthetic materials with hazardous poly-fluorinated chemicals that are environmentally harmful. In contrast, other walkers have perhaps realised that much popular outdoor clothing and other gear is made with such chemicals and are seeking more "natural" alternatives. Walkers and walking artists alike are beginning to take this dilemma into consideration. In recognition of the role of embodied knowledge and bodily risks in walking, artists include images of themselves walking, either as casual or formal documentation or, as with Alison Lloyd and Edwina Fitzpatrick, as an intrinsic part of the artwork itself. In this more performative work, the clothing can become significant.

Twenty years after Pollard's walking party, the photographs documenting Alison Lloyd's "walks" demonstrate that this walking artist owns a stylish selection of contemporary outdoor wear, suitably high-tech and specialist. The complementary colours of her favourite red top and green rucksack show she is aware of how they might appear in the images she takes to document her walks. This was not intentional to begin with – at first, her choices were entirely practical, based on lightness and ensuring a garment had a multitude of pockets. As the documentation developed, she became attuned to what worked in terms of colour with the places she was working in.[25]

Lloyd is an artist who appears at first to be entirely performative in her approach to her practice, but who on closer examination turns out to be as interested in the photographic object as the walk. This is demonstrated in her photo-essay in this volume. True, she appears in some of the images as a conventionally upright figure, fully clad in protective gear, but in others she appears off kilter, perhaps clinging onto a tree for support, or perhaps crouching very low to the ground behind boulders or between walls. In yet others, she is framed by the detritus of walking gear, plastic buckles or maps close to hand and slightly out of focus. Sometimes, it's just the rucksack or thermos that both simultaneously stand in for and displace the romantic figure in the landscape. Lloyd calls these solo, off-path walks "contouring". This term expresses a close relationship with the terrain – when she moves, it is sometimes more like dancing than walking, and her movement involves an unusual form of embodied and proximate mapping. This relation between walk as performance and its documentation resonates with the ways in which earlier walking artists recorded their walks. I am thinking especially of Long's way of drawing his walked lines on maps.[26] In terms of her group contouring walks, Lloyd writes:

> Contouring is used to navigate around a hill following a contour ring. Altimeters determine which ring a person is on; timing is based on William W. Naismith rule of thumb for walkers in fair conditions: allow 1 hour for every 5 km walking forwards; add 1 hour for every 600m ascent. By learning their own pace, a walker is able to estimate their location.[27]

Since most of these contourings are, however, undertaken as solo activities, the photographs taken often have a wire trailing through the heather, almost like an umbilical cord, leading our eye along where her feet once walked, forming a visual connection between the viewer and the artist. What is also interesting from an environmental outlook is that since the camera is usually balanced on a rock or nestling among grasses, most of the images have a very low perspective, almost the imagined viewpoint of an animal, insect or even perhaps the land itself.

Figure 10.1 Edwina Fitzpatrick: *The Lost Tour Guide*

In Edwina Fitzpatrick's work, walking as performance and her costume are paramount. Although in one of the photographs documenting the work *The Lost Tour Guide* (2014) she is standing alone near a rocky outcrop, unlike Lloyd's "selfies", it is clear this image has been taken by someone else. She is almost planted among bilberries and heather, with forest in the middle distance and paler higher ground just visible in the far distance. Fitzpatrick is certainly not wearing the kind of rugged outdoor wear that we have come to expect from a walking artist. The photographic documentation of the event (made for the Lake District's Grizedale Forest) shows *The Lost Tour Guide* to be wearing a light-coloured two-piece skirt suit, calf-length wellington boots, bare legs, sunglasses, and clasping a clip board. Closer examination reveals the suit to be made out of a map-print fabric. The artist explains:

> I made a uniform consisting of a blazer and A-line skirt printed with the Ordinance Survey (OS) map of the south-eastern area of The English Lakes. It referenced the official city tour guides of English cities such as Exeter, who wear semi-formal uniforms and tote folding umbrellas and large bags.[28]

In another photograph, our lost guide is studiously making notes on her clipboard, standing at the foot of a crag atop of which is a trig point. While the creases and patches of green forest in the map-suit find a curious visual equivalence in the striations and lichen patches on the rocks, the actual forest represented by the green stretches away behind the path along which she walks, the Lakeland hills visible in the far distance. Perhaps she is asking for advice from the well-shod resting rambler, perched on the rocks, who points the way on confidently. The absurdity, incongruity and unsuitability of the uniform is all part of a deliberate strategy: "an unravelling of a map's functionality".[29] She calculatingly placed the area of Grizedale in which she was conducting her walks on the back of her jacket, so she couldn't refer to it unless she took it off, such that it would be easier for others to help her out. The same applies to the miniature compass buttons on the sleeves: "In effect, the Lost Tour Guide is beholden to others. She can assist them in orientating themselves but can't orientate herself without assistance from them."[30]

Thus, Fitzpatrick engages with others as she walks in an entirely unscripted way in a process she terms "interactive fieldwork". Through interviews, she collects anecdotes and tales, and links topography with fragments of narrative about the places themselves. Fitzpatrick's accumulation of facts, fictions, poetics and geologies helps her to deal with complex issues in relation to creating an archive of all the artworks made in Grizedale since 1977, her task in *The Lost Tour Guide*. She plays with the idea of "getting lost" both in terms of actually getting lost in the forest and of lost artworks, creating the *Lost and Found* (2014) digital archive and the *Missing Persons Files* (2014). *The Lost Tour Guide* also addresses wider-scale and more-than-human losses, offering us an interpretation of landscape-as-archive in the Anthropocene. She deals with these important issues without the earnestness of some of her walking predecessors, who have a predisposition to appear rather worthy at times. Her sense of the ridiculous and the absurd combined with the lightness of touch that we see, for example, in the impractical garb of her lost guide, prevent this work going anywhere near being didactic.

Although they do not cite deep mapping as a methodology, both Pollard's and Fitzpatrick's works have aspects of this approach, coalescing the invented, the imaginative, the factual and the poetic, along with the past and present, into their walking works. Iain Biggs has long engaged with the idea of walking and deep mapping explicitly, and he is now working with a new and nuanced version of this. In his recent series entitled *Notitia* – a hybrid form of collage and painted construction – he draws heavily on walking and photographic documentation in the English/Scottish Borders, where he has been working for more than twenty years. Biggs refers to this walking as "ground work" rather than fieldwork.[31] These pieces combine multiple ways of visually representing place, an approach to deep mapping that Biggs has described elsewhere as "polyvocal".[32] They are playful, experimenting not only with ideas of landscape and environment, but also

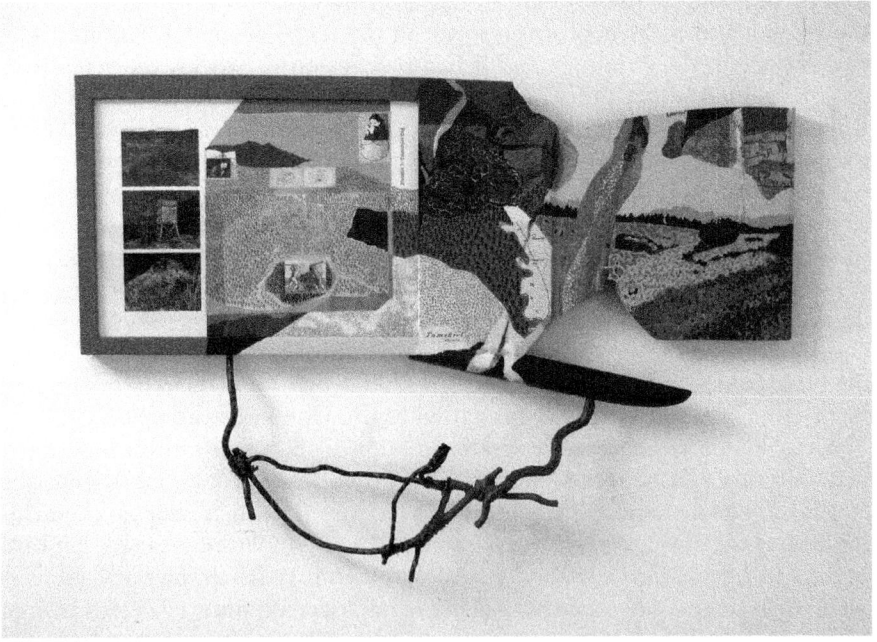

Figure 10.2 Iain Biggs *Notitia 7, Tamshiel Rig* (2018, 88.5 × 62 cm), acrylic on wood, including the frame, with a mixed-media, collaged "inset" which includes digitally printed photos

with painterly ideas and notions of representation, using an extraordinary range of materials and categories of sign.

In this series of Biggs' works, the painting and imagery burst out of the picture plane and include embedded old and new photographs as well as realist and codified signs for trees. There are aspects of autobiography or of direct experience: small black-and-white photographs, photographs from walks, images of bird hides. Some sections appear to be of observed landscapes, while others seem to be painted representations of maps. Painted wires and other found objects are "a shameless borrowing of Polynesian stick charts".[33] Biggs has long seen these as a tactile form of mapping.[34] This focus on the haptic, the phenomenological relations between vision and touch, and his long interest in sound and music point to the idea of "mapping" as being far more than a visual experience. Like walking, it is a much fuller, embodied form of understanding, a point I will return to in relation to viewing.

Biggs describes works such as his series *Notitia* as "trying to convert my experience of deep mapping into a lyrical 'micro-mapping' that evokes a condensed sense of the richness of place".[35] What happens when we view Biggs' painted, collaged constructions is that there is the kind of levelling out, or lack of hierarchy of visual experience, that also occurs when walking. As when walking, it is up to us to consider what we are presented with. What is the relative significance of a discarded wrapper, a stony outcrop, a rare plant, a dank smell, the sound of birdsong, of traffic or silence?

There are considerations in this series, too, of the relation between species. For example, in *Notitia 3, Birch Moss* (2017) there is something very poignant in the juxtaposition of an oversized image of a greenfinch, clearly taken from an identification chart or book, overlapping and touching on a greyscale image of a thoughtful, troubled-looking boy. There are all sorts of confusions of scale, of micro and macro: which of the green-painted marks represent moss, and which trees? What is key in terms of environmental thinking is that Biggs is neither privileging the human view, nor is he writing himself out of the place. There is an acknowledgement of the very impossibility of the latter that is an intrinsic element of this work. This kind of composite work with its constellation of viewpoints, montage, collage and bricolage does not allow any fixed reading of the landscape that is referenced. It is at times as if we are mapping from the inside of the land out.

This idea of working and thinking with what is underneath our feet as we walk and giving soil and microbes credence in relation to family history, memory and geology was key for visual artist Rebecca Thomas and poet Elizabeth-Jane Burnett in a recent collaboration. The artist book they produced after working together in the field in Devon was just such a micromap. It is a long-format landscape-shaped *leporello* or concertina book, with Burnett's text at times superimposed over Thomas' images. In other places, the text finds its own space, with Thomas' lines dancing across the page.

Field, past tense of feel: to have felt like an eel slipping

Slipping, from sleeping: to dream of being flat like an image or spread like felt

Felt, from pelt: a hide of buttercups

Whip or stroke the field, use its diminutive, whippet: a brisk, nimble woman, trembling

Fieldet: a list of small things trembling (a dither, a dodder, a quiver)

Figure 10.3 Elizabeth-Jane Burnett and Rebecca Thomas, page from artist book, 2017

For Burnett, I suggest there are parallels with Biggs in terms of working from a long-term family history with a place. Burnett and Thomas took as their point of departure three fields in Devon, a sketch map of which appeared in a book written by Burnett's father, whose family have farmed the fields for several generations. Burnett has known and walked on these fields since childhood. Like Biggs, while she acknowledges the other-than-human view, she values the personal and autobiographical as being an essential part of her work:

> My family on my father's side have worked and walked on these fields in past centuries and I was interested in how my own movements through the fields might connect me to theirs. My father's etymological research into the field names in his *History* (connecting "Drewshill" with "the fields of the Druid") also suggested that there might be a spiritual legacy in these fields. I wondered whether this legacy was something that could be accessed.[36]

This notion of a spiritual legacy in the material and space of a field resonates with the geographer Karen Till's interest in mapping what she has termed "spectral traces", in that both would map or encounter the unseen.[37] Till considers how we may come into "contact with past lives through objects, natures, and remnants that haunt the contemporary landscape".[38] Burnett does not necessarily expect to find anything physical, but a "spiritual" trace. Nonetheless, in common with other British walking artists, she seeks to discover and interpret via her experiences in the field. Her writing and poetry reflect on the relation between social history and geology with an explicitly environmental agenda:

> I was interested in both the present life to be found there, predominantly the invertebrates in and under the field, and the past life that had moved through it. For my book *The Grassling: A Geological Memoir* I had taken soil samples and done site-specific writing on worms, which had brought me to an engagement with worm linguistics. Just as the fields hold millions of hidden organisms below the ground, I wondered if they might hold human traces, perhaps in the form of memories.[39]

This resonated with Thomas. When she met with Burnett to work in the fields, she too felt drawn to what might be under the ground:

> My own investigations into these fields have led to me thinking about how one might literally unearth something from this deep and unrefined area of land, roll back the surface and examine its literally deep, dark depths, what is hidden under the grass and the centuries of accumulated soil – a whole ecosystem of tiny creatures, secreted but essential to the continuing life of this subterranean world and its rough and ready, unspoilt surface formation.[40]

This statement has a contemporary and ecological resonance, suggesting an embodied, phenomenological approach that really does take account of the non-human world. In my own collaborative walking fieldwork with the poet Harriet Tarlo:

> we attempt to extend our engagement beyond the purely human perspective, however polyphonic. Moving through landscape is shared not only with people: "[M]otion is the natural mode of human and animal vision: 'We must perceive in order to move *but we must also move in order to perceive*'" writes Pierre Joris in his *Nomad Poetics*.[41] This is a matter of perception in which we shift from dwelling on our *difference* from animals (which Solnit locates in our bipedal relationship to walking as much as to our consciousness), but on our *sameness*.[42] Thus our conceptions of walking and placing change. As Massey argues in her book, *For Space*, "if everything is moving, where is here?"[43] She notes that, when we walk, we join in the mobile processes of the non-human world in which continents, seas, animals, birds and plants are all migrating, moving in small and big scale ways.[44]

As Thomas walked and wandered apparently aimlessly through the field making small, sharp coloured marks in her sketch book, responding to the colours, light and textures of the grass covered, or at times uncovered earth, she suddenly noticed Burnett get closer to the field, swimming and rolling in the grass. It is interesting that Burnett starts doing what might be considered the "wrong thing": swimming in grass. This playful and slightly ridiculous activity echoes the absurdity of Fitzpatrick's *Lost Tour Guide* – there is a surreal self-mockery here that undoes any notion of the lyrical sublime. But perhaps she's not the first person to try to swim on grass; this full-bodied manner of experiencing landscape is what the environmental philosopher Arnold Berleant refers to as an immersive environmental experience, a fuller and more haptic aesthetic experience in the landscape, a:

> dynamic interplay between viewer and landscape as we extend ourselves into the landscape, looking not *at* but from *within* the landscape, feeling its physical magnetism as it works with our bodies from every direction, and a kinaesthetic sense of the landscape as something to be entered, engaged with and worked through, embraced physically, perhaps rather like swimming in the landscape.[45]

Walking backwards and between

Some years ago, I was on the Isle of Mull with a group of artist/researchers for an experimental, exploratory week of fieldwork as part of LAND2 research network activities.[46] As might be expected, much walking, clambering, collecting and recording ensued as we introduced each other to different ways of working in place. Iain Biggs was among our number. He suggested that we should spend a day doing a collective project: a creative transect, what was essentially a very long, slow walk with regular pauses. The site ran from a river bed over rough, scrubby land and up to a rocky outcrop. It was a line selected as being characteristic of the environmental diversity found everywhere on Mull. Some people made and recorded performances by stepping, lying and creeping flat on the ground; other people sketched, photographed, recorded sounds; somebody strung beads together, carefully matching colours they found. At the very end of the day, there were two of us left, the slowest walkers/workers of the group: one, an artist fascinated with raw geology who dug holes to a certain depth and collected the materials, the other, myself, making a very, very long and thin watercolour with written notes on the reverse. Although, our processes and products could not have been more different, we bonded in our shared relation to the place and watched the land change into darkness.

Later that evening, when we discussed the day's work, we realised that we had begun a kind of communal deep map. Why am I recounting this tale? Well, firstly the way in which I selected the artists for consideration in this chapter is analogous to the way that we might sample a place: they are the ones who intersected with the path of my imaginary transect. Secondly, in a parallel way to the walking artists discussed earlier, the range of conceptual approaches and media in both cases was extraordinarily varied: from the performative to the representational, from a direct

Figure 10.4 Elizabeth-Jane Burnett, photo by Rebecca Thomas

engagement with the rawest of materials of earth itself, to a consideration of the digital. Yet what every artist shared is that the work is grounded in phenomenological experience of being in place and there was collaborative experience of working and "walking with". All of the walking artists whose work I have discussed have environmental perspectives that emerge from a phenomenological, embodied approach. There are pitfalls to this approach, of course, in terms of repeating in a new form the Romantic approach to walking, with a focus on the experience of the individual and troubling implicit assumptions about gender and untrammelled nature. Many artists have sought to counteract this or subvert this in some way, through the absurd, the humorous, or by working with and collaborating with others, attempting a subversion of the lyric "I", or at the very least to convey an understanding of the limitations of their own experience.

One final question remains: how might such an embodied methodology, which in some ways inevitably privileges the (able-bodied) human body, remain open to considerations of the post-human or more-than-human, including inter- or trans-species communication? In our article "'Off Path, Counter Path': Contemporary Walking Collaborations in Landscape, Art and Poetry" published in 2017, Harriet Tarlo and I consider our work not only in the context of contemporary critical walking practices, but also within the context of the ecocritical turn, via the phenomenological, towards New Materialist thinking:

> we might offer a more entangled interpretation of this activity, moving through landscape, the interaction between the physical materiality of the body of the artists, the material of making and the material of place. We might re-imagine the practice in terms of the material of the place being in collaboration with the materiality of mark-making in words and lines and of paint via that material constellation that is a body.[47]

This way of thinking certainly applies to many of the artists discussed – Thomas, Philo and Biggs in particular, perhaps. In their recent article, Springgay and Truman expand on this idea, recognising the significance of embodiment and corporeality in walking research but taking up this challenge of how bodies might relate to "larger more-than-human networks and events".[48] They offer some further insights, arguing that "embodiment needs to move beyond an individual and sensuous account of the body in space towards a different ethico-political engagement".[49] Drawing on Haraway, Barad (and her New Materialist thinking in terms of intra-actions and assemblage), and on Stacy Alaimo's trans-corporeality, they develop an idea of trans-materiality which does not place the human at the centre: "Whereas some theories of embodiment propose an understanding of an individual and undivided self (Ingold, 2011), transcorporeality posits humans and non-humans as enmeshed with each other in a messy, shifting ontology."[50]

With reference to this kind of messy enmeshment, and to remind ourselves of the wide range of academic discourses considered from the start of this chapter in relation to walking from geographies, ecocriticism, anthropology and art histories, I will conclude by drawing on the geo-humanities scholar Harriet Hawkins. This is by way of a reminder that these discourses need to remain in conversation with each other, as so often they are discovering different elements of the same thing. Hawkins points out that it's many years since:

> [i]n the mid 1980s Cosgrove described a geography based on the "Argument of the Eye". Since then geography, like the humanities more broadly, has seen the decline of vision's hegemony with embodied accounts of vision taking the place of the detached Cartesian observer.[51]

What is important here is that this approach has not only opened more nuanced ways of considering a contemporary reading of landscape or site through performance or walking, but has also developed understanding of the importance of an embodied approach to viewing as well as making artworks. Hawkins summarises this as an understanding of the experience of art not as grasped by a solely intellectual act, but by the complex perception of the body as a whole. As the examples we have explored suggest, this means the displacement of the notion of a separated gaze on nature by the acknowledgement that looking is always embodied and particular to the artist/walker. Other concepts come into play as we also experience nature differently now in terms of notions such as equally valuable co-existent forms of life even down to microbic activities. I would like to suggest a parallel move from the embodied to an even more complex entangled and messy relation for the viewer in the gallery. For, after all, it is there in the gallery that most of us are likely to encounter walking artists, apart from those few people who are fortunate enough to "walk with" other artists. Encountering the walking work in this way does substantially erode the binary between the process-driven conceptual walking art and the kind of art which appeared to privilege the aesthetic object set up at the beginning of this chapter. Perhaps as audiences for art, it is more important that we understand artists who walk and walking artists by considering them as walking not just between places, between past and present, but operating between human and more-than-human, however varied and ambivalent their approaches. In this way, they offer us an understanding of place and subjectivity as fluid and symbiotic, and a desire to explore how walking might be a way to begin to respond to some of the urgent environmental challenges of our times.

Notes

1 While both Long and Fulton have been critiqued for perpetuating the Romantic tradition, Alistair Robinson considers that Long has often been misrepresented as "rugged or wholesome or worse, merely anodyne", and argues, "by contrast, that Long's decision to base his practice on walking was an audacious, even astonishing one for his time"; in Mike Collier, Cynthia Morrison-Bell and Alistair Robinson, *Walk On: From Richard Long to Janet Cardiff – 40 Years of Art Walking* (Sunderland, UK: Art Editions North, 2013), p. 13.
2 Andrea Phillips, Cultural Geographies in Practice: Walking and Looking. *Cultural Geographies*, 12(4), (2005), 508.

3 This is taken from the *Documenta 14* website, www.documenta14.de/en/walks.
4 Eamon Colman is an Irish landscape painter with whom Biggs has been corresponding for ten years.
5 Iain Biggs, personal communication, 2018. Chapter 2 of Rebecca Solnit's, *Wanderlust: A History of Walking* (New York: Penguin Books, 2001) is entitled "The Mind at Three Miles an Hour".
6 Edward S. Casey, *Representing Place: Landscape Painting and Maps* (Minneapolis, MN: University of Minnesota Press, 2002), p. xiii.
7 Veronica Sekules, *Cultures of the Countryside: Art, Museum, Heritage, and Environment, 1970–2015* (London: Taylor & Francis, 2017), p. 187.
8 Collier, Morrison-Bell and Robinson, *Walk On.*
9 Ibid., 15.
10 Michael Pearson and Michael Shanks, *Theatre/Archaeology* (London: Routledge 2001), p. 64.
11 Sekules, *Cultures of the Countryside*, p 192.
12 W.G. Sebald and Michael Hulse, *The Rings of Saturn* (New York: New Directions, 1998).
13 Rebecca Thomas, personal communication, 2013.
14 Ibid.
15 In John Wylie, An Essay on Ascending Glastonbury Tor. *Geoforum*, 33(4) (November 2002), 441–454.
16 Ibid., 449.
17 Ruth Philo, personal communication, 2018.
18 Ibid.
19 Donna Haraway, Situated Knowledges: The Science Question in Feminism and the Privilege of Partial Perspective. *Feminist Studies*, 14(3) (Autumn 1988), 575–599. For Haraway, "situated" means knowledge situated socially that then moves to a socialised subjectivity embodied. In this chapter, I explore how artists drawing on this deal with phenomenological body experience of place and space.
20 Collier, Morrison-Bell and Robinson, *Walk On*, p. 74.
21 Ingrid Pollard, *Pastoral Interlude* (1987) [text within artwork], http://collections.vam.ac.uk/item/O107865/pastoral-interludeits-as-if-the-photograph-pollard-ingrid/.
22 Tania Kovats, 100% Waterproof: Gore-Tex – What to Wear in Utopia, in: Victoria Walsh, ed., *Arcadia Revisited: The Place of Landscape* (London: Black Dog, 1997), p. 102.
23 Catherine Horwood, *Keeping Up Appearances: Fashion and Class between the Wars* (Stroud, UK: Sutton Publishing, 2003), pp. 86–95.
24 Alison Lloyd, personal communication, 2018.
25 Ibid.
26 There are many examples of this in Long's works: for example, see Richard Long, *A Hundred Mile Walk* (1971–72), www.tate.org.uk/art/artworks/long-a-hundred-mile-walk-t01720.
27 Alison Lloyd, personal communication, 2018.
28 Edwina Fitzpatrick, personal communication, 2018.
29 Ibid.
30 Ibid.
31 Iain Biggs, personal communication, 2018.
32 Iain Biggs and Jane Bailey, "Either Side of Delphy Bridge": A Deep Mapping Project Evoking and Engaging the Lives of Older Adults in Rural North Cornwall. *Journal of Rural Studies*, 28(4) (October 2012), 318–328.
33 These were "maps" made by Polynesian seafarers to help with navigation. They remained in use until the end of World War II. They are three-dimensional grids of bamboo sticks which represent routes, currents and wind directions, with cowrie shells denoting islands.

34 Iain Biggs, personal communication, 2018.
35 Ibid.
36 Elizabeth-Jane Burnett, personal communication, 2018.
37 Karen Till and Julian Jonker, Mapping and Excavating Spectral Traces in Post-Apartheid Cape Town. *Memory Studies*, 2(3) (September 2009), 303–335.
38 Spectral traces are also discussed in the exhibition catalogue by Karen Till, *Mapping Spectral Traces* (Blacksburg, VA: Virginia Tech College of Architecture and Urban Studies, 2010).
39 Elizabeth-Jane Burnett, personal communication, 2018.
40 Rebecca Thomas, personal communication, 2018.
41 Pierre Joris, *A Nomad Poetics: Essays* (Middletown, CT: Wesleyan University Press, 2003), p. 40.
42 Rebecca Solnit, *Wanderlust: A History of Walking* (New York: Penguin Books, 2001), pp. 32–33.
43 Doreen Massey, *For Space* (London: SAGE, 2005), p. 138.
44 Harriet Tarlo and Judith Tucker, "Off Path, Counter Path": Contemporary Walking Collaborations in Landscape, Art and Poetry. *Critical Survey*, 29(1) (Spring 2017), 121.
45 Arnold Berleant, The Art in Knowing a Landscape. *Diogenes*, 59(1–2) (February 2012), 56.
46 The creative practice-led research network LAND2 ("land squared") was started in 2002 by Iain Biggs and Judith Tucker as a national network of artist/lecturers and research students with an interest in landscape/place-oriented art practice. Following the expansion of the network, they invited Mary Modeen to join the coordination group. See http://land2.leeds.ac.uk/.
47 Tarlo and Tucker "Off Path", pp. 112–113.
48 Stephanie Springgay and Sarah Truman, A Transmaterial Approach to Walking Methodologies: Embodiment, Affect, and a Sonic Art Performance. *Body and Society*, 23(4) (October 2017), 35.
49 Ibid., 30.
50 Ibid., 29, referencing Tim Ingold, *Being Alive: Essays on Movement, Knowledge, and Description* (London: Routledge, 2011).
51 Harriet Hawkins, "The Argument of the Eye"? The Cultural Geographies of Installation Art. *Cultural Geographies*, 17(3) (July 2010), 321.

Works cited

Berleant, Arnold, The Art in Knowing a Landscape. *Diogenes*, 59(1–2) (February 2012), 52–62.

Biggs, Iain and Bailey, Jane, "Either Side of Delphy Bridge": A deep mapping project evoking and engaging the lives of older adults in rural North Cornwall. *Journal of Rural Studies*, 28(4) (October 2012), 318–328.

Casey, Edward S., *Representing Place: Landscape Painting and Maps* (Minneapolis, MN: University of Minnesota Press, 2002).

Collier, Mike, Morrison-Bell, Cynthia and Robinson, Alistair, *Walk On: From Richard Long to Janet Cardiff – 40 Years of Art Walking*. Sunderland, UK: Art Editions North, 2013.

Haraway, Donna, Situated Knowledges: The Science Question in Feminism and the Privilege of Partial Perspective. *Feminist Studies*, 14(3) (Autumn 1988), 575–599.

Hawkins, Harriet, "The Argument of the Eye"? The Cultural Geographies of Installation Art. *Cultural Geographies*, 17(3) (July 2010), 321–340.

Heddon, Deirdre and Turner, Cathy, 2012. Walking Women: Shifting the Tales and Scales of Mobility. *Contemporary Theatre Review*, 2(22), 224–236.

Horwood, Catherine, *Keeping Up Appearances: Fashion and Class between the Wars*. Stroud, UK: Sutton Publishing, 2003.

Ingold, Tim, *Being Alive: Essays on Movement, Knowledge, and Description*. London: Routledge, 2011.

Joris, Pierre, *A Nomad Poetics: Essays*. Middletown, CT: Wesleyan University Press. 2003.

Kovats, Tania, 100% Waterproof: Gore-Tex – What to Wear in Utopia, in: Walsh, Victoria, ed., *Arcadia Revisited: The Place of Landscape*. London: Black Dog, 1997.

Maclagen, David, Reframing Aesthetic Experience: Iconographic and Embodied Responses to Painting. *Journal of Visual Art Practice*, 1(1) (2001), 37–45.

Massey, Doreen, *For Space*. London: SAGE, 2005

Pearson, Michael and Shanks, Michael, *Theatre/Archaeology*. London: Routledge, 2001.

Phillips, Andrea, Cultural Geographies in Practice: Walking and Looking. *Cultural Geographies*, 12(4) (2005), 507–513.

Sekules, Veronica, *Cultures of the Countryside: Art, Museum, Heritage, and Environment, 1970–2015*. London: Taylor & Francis, 2017.

Sebald, W.G. and Hulse, Michael, *The Rings of Saturn*. New York: New Directions, 1998.

Solnit, Rebecca, *Wanderlust: A History of Walking*. New York: Penguin Books, 2001.

Springgay, Stephanie and Truman, Stephanie, A Transmaterial Approach to Walking Methodologies: Embodiment, Affect, and a Sonic Art Performance. *Body and Society*, 23(4) (October 2017), 27–58.

Tarlo, Harriet and Tucker, Judith, "Off Path, Counter Path": Contemporary Walking Collaborations in Landscape, Art and Poetry. *Critical Survey*, 29(1) (Spring 2017), 105–132.

Till, Karen, *Mapping Spectral Traces*, Blacksburg, VA: Virginia Tech College of Architecture and Urban Studies, 2010.

Till, Karen and Jonker, Julian, Mapping and Excavating Spectral Traces in Post-Apartheid Cape Town. *Memory Studies*, 2(3) (September 2009), 303–335.

Wylie, John. An Essay on Ascending Glastonbury Tor. *Geoforum*, 33(4) (November 2002), 441–454.

Part III

Walking on

Routes, directions, steps

11 Autism and cognitive embodiment

Steps towards a non-ableist walking literature

Anna Stenning

Introduction

How can environmental writing and ecocriticism embrace the perspective of neurodiversity?[1] Two recent autism memoirs, read in the light of earlier works in environmental humanities and critical disability studies, suggest ways this can be achieved. Temple Grandin's *Animals in Translation* and Chris Packham's *Fingers in the Sparkle Jar* both unsettle the ideology of human exceptionalism, by describing their narrators' cognitive embodiment as autistic individuals.[2] Packham's and Grandin's cross-species identification described in these works shows how supposedly 'abnormal' forms of experience and perception, when removed from their stigmatised position in culture, can alter our engagement and empathy with other species. It is only once we move beyond dominant conceptions of human subjectivity and agency that we can comprehend the extent of human interdependence and vulnerability in line with ecological thinking. I will argue that this movement may begin to offer a framework within which to critique the perspectives of those with different abilities in environmentally oriented literature. This is particularly necessary for walking literature, nature writing and wilderness literature, which often involve the presupposition of a hyper-fit body and mind that are represented as attaining a problematic spiritual purity by performing a series of physical and mental tasks.

This chapter ultimately argues for an ethics based on relationality – including relations between disabled and non-disabled people, those with impairments and chronic illnesses, as well as with other species. It is also the aim of this work to show that certain forms of experience and knowledge are devalued by ideologies that celebrate human physical and mental perfection and supposed self-sufficiency. Grandin's and Packham's narratives pose challenges for both the 'ableism' of environmental writing and medical literature, and the presupposition of human exceptionalism that still dominates cultural and scientific representations of other species. In orienting themselves towards a neurodiverse subjectivity, Grandin and Packham suggest what a non-ableist walking narrative, involving human and animal encounters, might look like.

This chapter does not aim to represent all autistic experiences nor suggest that Grandin and Packham stand for all autistic people. It is hoped readers will not assume that all autistic people experience cross-species affinities to the extent that Grandin or Packham do. It just so happens that there is a growth in autism memoirs that simultaneously present a marginalised subjective identity, contribute to a burgeoning autism culture, and describe different forms of human embodiment. These texts make explicit their privilege, dependency on the environment and non-human others, and vulnerability to different types of pain and to mortality and loss. It is argued that the outsider status of writers who identify as autistic provides opportunities to challenge the ideologies of human uniqueness and ableism. These ideologies are perpetuated by environmentalist texts that posit self-sufficiency and bodily and intellectual perfection as the unique indicators of human worth. These memoirs have, in turn, the potential to extend the range of individuals who are able to participate in environmental movements.[3] Yet it seems that the valorisation of subjective autonomy and rationality are deeply embedded in Western culture, well beyond environmental literature.

Cary Wolfe is a critic of liberal humanism who believes that the humanities and social sciences are still deeply implicated in perpetuating anthropocentrism. In *What Is Posthumanism?* he suggests that many have failed to distinguish critical 'posthumanism' or the posthumanist stance from the myth of posthuman as 'being "after" our embodiment has been transcended'. Instead, understanding our true role in a continuum of technological and biological systems, we discover that it 'opposes the fantasies of disembodiment and autonomy, inherited from humanism itself'.[4] The objects of Wolfe's critique are humanist conceptions of agency, autonomy and subjecthood, which are often linked to narrow conceptions of rationality and communication.

A case can be made that this critical stance is itself inherent to humanism, which has always been by definition 'critical', and does not require the supposition of a posthumanist condition. For the sake of developing a model which may de-centre (if only temporarily) the human from its centrality in the social sciences, a concern for cognitive embodiment in the form of a neurodiverse perspective will allow us to question assumptions about ideal cognitive functioning, rationality, communication and, eventually, anthropocentrism, as we discover alternative cultural valuations of the non-human. It offers a unique role for situated experiences by those with neurobiological differences.

It is hoped that the neurodiverse perspective will become a helpful tool for disability studies scholars and the environmental humanities alike. Those working within the field of disability studies question the ways that particular bodies and minds are valorised by society. They explore the ideology of ability, or ableism, which is the paradoxical position whereby two contradictory positions are held: the body is unimportant compared to the realm of the mind and its attributes, and at the same time, the physical body must be perfected. These contradictory values impede our recognition of ordinary experiences of embodiment, and result in our belief that individual bodily and mental ability – such as overcoming, self-reliance and willpower – are the exclusive markers of human value.[5] Within this ideology, 'ability is the ideological baseline by which humanness is determined' – 'the lesser the ability, the lesser the human being'.[6]

Critical disability theory seeks both to critique ableism and the notion that disability resides exclusively in the individual, rather than being composed, at least in part, by the society that values certain types of bodies and minds. One way to critique ableism is to stress the positive knowledge that people possess by way of their embodiment as biological, historical and social beings. The position known as complex embodiment was first articulated by Tobin Siebers in *Disability Theory*. He explains how 'many embodiments are each crucial to the understanding of humanity and its variations, whether physical, mental, social, or historical'.[7] Stories of embodiment – including the visibly and invisibly disabled – along with the marginalised and the poor, may help us to understand 'ability' as a temporary and occasional state.[8]

This chapter focuses, however, on what has been called 'non-normative cognition', which is a parallel materialist position by David Mitchell and Sharon Snyder that attempts to understand 'the way alternative cognitions/corporealities allow us to inhabit the world as vulnerable, constrained, yet innovative embodied beings rather than merely as devalued social constructs or victims of oppression'.[9] While acknowledging the reality of neurological difference in people with autism, attention deficit hyperactivity disorder and dyslexia (as in 'the medical model'), non-normative cognition tackles normative ideas – which are based on national and cultural ideologies – about what counts as correct or 'normal' bodily and mental functioning. Non-normative cognition offers potential for critiquing medical and social discourses about what it is to be human. It proposes that situated (or embodied) experiences of neurological difference have a particular epistemic power within the critique. The neurodiverse perspective allows for those who consider themselves cognitively and bodily 'typical' to ally themselves with this position. This perspective informs my own analysis of *Fingers in the Sparkle Jar* (henceforth referred to as *Sparkle Jar*).

This chapter will begin to consider whether memoirs that present complex embodiment and non-normative cognition are capable of challenging some of the ideals of ableism and anthropocentrism. It considers, in doing so, what they might teach us about what Cary Wolfe has called 'the necessity of an ethics based not on ability, activity, agency, and empowerment, but on a *compassion* that is rooted in our vulnerability and passivity'.[10] While my argument is focused on Chris Packham's memoir, it was inspired by observations that Wolfe has made on an earlier autism memoir, *Animals in Translation* by Temple Grandin. Professor Grandin's memoir recounted the knowledge she had gained about her own complex embodiment as a result of interactions with farm animals and horses. Diagnosed with autism early in her life due to apparent communicative and behavioural differences, Grandin was given behavioural therapy to develop her verbal skills, but this did little to reduce her feelings of anxiety or alienation. After being bullied at a normal school, she was moved to one for 'emotionally disturbed teenagers', where she discovered she had an intense affinity with 'disturbed horses'; this, in turn, led to an interest in the behaviour of farm animals. The depth of her interest, and her uncanny ability to perceive the world as though from the position of farm animals, inspired first the development of unique 'tools' to aid anxious animals and autistic teenagers, and later, her distinguished career as a writer and speaker on both animal behaviour and autism. For Wolfe, this is an example of Grandin's autism, or her disability, being a 'pre-requisite for a particular experience'.[11]

In *Sparkle Jar*, the highly accomplished British naturalist and TV presenter Chris Packham narrated his childhood devotion to wildlife and his discovery of his unusual preference for interacting with the non-human world, rather than fellow humans. Drawing on his ability to discern visual patterns, and his willingness to create tools from everyday objects such as jam jars, library books, binoculars and paper, he learned to map and record the comings and goings of wild animals and birds and, in doing so, develop an understanding of their, and his own, complex embodiment.

In the case of Packham's memoir, walking is prominent, but it is always walking in search of another species, or to get to school or home, rather than the retreat from, and return to, civilisation that informs much pastoral walking literature and nature writing. In this, it is closer to the 'new nature writing' than to either classic memoirs or nature writing. Like Robert Macfarlane's *The Wild Places*, inner experience and outer nature are addressed; in Packham's memoir, however, inner experience is much more deeply entangled with his perception of non-human lives. His adolescent walks into the wilder areas around his suburban home demonstrate both his isolation from human and familial activities and his hunger for interaction with other types of life. In *Sparkle Jar*, and unlike classic pastoral narratives, walking out of the limits of the urban is movement towards the social, rather than a retreat from it. Although the narrative shares some formal features with the new nature writing (where the search for something external parallels the inner quest for knowledge or transformation), in Packham's treatment, walking is almost free from the dominant cultural constraints of the genre, including high-cultural references and the elevated or spiritualised tone.

Packham's encounters with other species suggest new forms of solidarity and affinity between different forms of life, human and otherwise. In line with material ecocriticism, which affirms the co-creation of all the various forms of life, and the neurodiverse perspective described above, the memoir shows that the most interesting stories develop our understanding of what it is to be human. My reflections on Packham's narrative will be used to produce a series of initial suggestions for how ecocriticism and environmental writing might become more attuned to neurodiversity by addressing cognitive embodiment, ableist assumptions, and chauvinism towards new forms of writing and cultural movements. In my conclusion, I propose some ideas for what a non-ableist walking literature might look like.

Autism, perception and cross-species identification

As Wolfe explains in a 2008 article, if we are able to overcome the illusion of a stable human subject, and understand our dependence and vulnerability, we can create the possibility that: 'new lines of empathy, affinity and respect between different forms of life, both human and non-human, may be realised in ways not accountable, either philosophically or ethically, by the basic coordinates of liberal humanism'.[12] Wolfe describes how Temple Grandin had recognised the rarity of her visual thinking and heightened tactile sense as a result of her work with cattle in the livestock industry. Grandin, who is Professor of Animal Studies at Colorado State University, explained in *Animals in Translation* how other animals, including cattle, are visual creatures to a greater extent than humans. She believes that her own neurological difference – which she attributes to autism – has provided her with the tendency to think in pictures. By this, she explains:

> I don't just mean that I am good at making architectural drawings and designs, or that I can design my cattle-restraining systems in my head. I actually think in pictures. During my thinking process I have no words in my head at all, just pictures.[13]

Grandin does not assert that all autistic people are visual thinkers. In her later book, *The Autistic Brain* (2014), she identifies two other thinking styles of autistic individuals: mathematical/pattern thinkers and word thinkers. In this earlier work, however, she confirms her belief – following the research of John Mitchell and Alan Snyder – that 'autistic people don't process what they see and hear into unified wholes, or concepts, rapidly the way normal people do'.[14] She continues: 'autistic people are stuck in the *pieces* stage of perception to a greater or lesser degree, depending on the person'.[15]

Grandin's *Thinking in Pictures* shows how her own visual thinking and tactile sensitivity provided her with the ability to understand, and hence to empathise with, the suffering of animals in so-called 'livestock processing facilities'. Freed from 'inattention blindness' caused by verbal processing (which is where an individual fails to respond to an unexpected stimulus in plain sight because it does not conform to linguistic expectations), Grandin believes that her experiences of her surroundings are more akin to those of other species.[16] According to Wolfe, as Grandin narrates her experiences of using the restraining chutes of the cattle processing facility in *Thinking in Pictures*, 'disability becomes the positive, indeed necessary condition for a powerful experience by Grandin that crosses not only the lines of species difference, but also of the organic and inorganic, the biological and mechanical, as well'.[17]

Whatever we think of the ethics of Grandin's involvement in the livestock industry and whether it is meaningful to talk of such an encounter as a crossing of species lines, her writing sheds light on experiences that are widely described in autistic life writing, but could not be accounted for by the existing medical literature on autism. The medical understanding is sustained by the widely used diagnostic criteria for an Autism Spectrum Disorder, which are contained in the *Diagnostic and Statistical Manual of Mental Disorders, Volume 5* (DSM-5).[18] Grandin's focus on the unique perceptual differences she attributes to autism is supported by recent research, produced in partnership with autistic researchers, into the nature of autistic experience. In the first decade of the millennium, Laurent Mottron and Michelle Dawson developed the 'enhanced perceptual functioning' theory of autism:

> We suggested that the operations that are superior among autistic persons can be encompassed under the term 'perception', as understood in the 1990s cognitive neuropsychology literature . . .. This broader view of perception ranges from feature detection up to and including pattern recognition.[19]

Perceptual performance was demonstrated across the visual and auditory fields, and was accompanied by 'greater autonomy of discrimination processes from the top-down influence of categorization'.[20] And yet, according to anecdotal sources within the autism community, the sensory and perceptual experiences of people with autism can be sources of the greatest areas of discomfort, as well as of joy. These experiences are seldom taken into account in medical and social interventions for autism, which focus on curing or eliminating autism rather than improving the day-to-day lives of autistic people.

In *Sparkle Jar*, naturalist and TV presenter Chris Packham emphasised, among other things, the unusual perceptual experiences that resulted from his encounters with non-human nature. As he explained in a National Autistic Society (NAS) interview about his latest book, what may be described as deficits in filtering perceptual information – his fascination with 'light, patterns, sounds and smells' – actually meant he was able to 'see things which others couldn't in nature'.[21] He does not automatically locate the ability in himself, but suggests that this knowledge is embedded between the 'sensory qualities' of animals and 'his ability to engage'.[22] He does, however, believe that he is 'uniquely visual':

> I am more visual, so my pattern recognition is good. It's not that I conjure the image in my mind, because when I see something, it's a matrix and everything is interconnected and forms a pattern. I can remember

the pattern. If a branch falls off a tree, I can tell because I remember that pattern. When you take a piece out, it no longer fits. I tried to infuse the book with those things to get the reader to try and feel it too.[23]

Although he does not explicitly state this, Packham's teenage walks to locate nesting kestrels – which are an important component of the narrative – depend on his enhanced perception of his surroundings.

The following section argues that *Sparkle Jar* presents neurodiversity, with its emphasis on atypical visual perception. It considers what Packham's text offers to supplement our knowledge, understanding and empathy with other species. In presenting his complex embodiment as a positive identity that brings with it a degree of vulnerability, Packham challenges the ideology of nature writing narratives that focus on self-improvement and self-reliance. However, even as he makes explicit his views on the positivity of autistic identities, he risks having his words subsumed into an ableist culture that regards disability as something to be overcome at the individual level.

Fingers in the Sparkle Jar and Animals in Translation as autism-biographies

Sparkle Jar is Chris Packham's first published memoir. It describes his early and teenage years growing up with a passion for non-human nature, the pain of losing a beloved companion, his relationships with family and neighbours, his first love interests and his intense social alienation from his peers. It is told through a non-linear series of flash-backs, in a broad range of grammatical persons and tenses, but with Packham as the focaliser. The book does not once mention autism, but it is popularly understood as a memoir about autism in the form of Asperger's Syndrome, which Packham spoke about in the BBC documentary entitled *Asperger's and Me* in 2017, which is the same year the book was published.

In this sense, *Sparkle Jar* is not classic 'autism-biography' in the sense of providing a description of autism for autistic or non-autistic readers, or of the process of seeking diagnosis. Packham's search for a diagnosis happens after the events narrated in the text. However, the author is 'an autistic subject who writes about his/her autistic experience or identity'.[24] In recent autism-biography texts, the work is increasingly motivated by 'a sociocultural disability perspective and education and raising awareness'.[25] In an announcement about his role as an NAS ambassador, Packham states his intention to develop what people know about how young autistic people see the world.[26] In the NAS interview about his book, he says he wishes to 'facilitate an environment where autistic people don't have to suffer'.[27]

The radical potential for 'autism-biography' comes from the fact that, until recently, autistic people were seen as unreliable informants about their own condition due to the nature of autism itself. However, as I will argue, both Packham and Grandin demonstrate both greater sensitivity to (and willingness to share) their feelings in a general sense than is typically present in much (although not all) nature writing, and if we require ethics to be founded on moral sentiment, then there is potential in this writing to encourage readers to widen the scope of their moral concern. It becomes clear in what follows that it is necessary to explore how atypical sensory and emotional experiences challenge ableist assumptions about 'correct functioning'.

Packham's memoir fulfils the social function of autism-biography by contributing a narrative that challenges ableist discourses. As I explain below, Packham contradicts stereotypes that deny autistic people an inner world, and he encourages the self-identification and social validation of autistic and Asperger's individuals. By focusing on the knowledge his unusual perceptual faculties afford, Packham suggests that his autism is not an abject social identity. In these ways, Packham takes on the role of representing autism as a cultural identity with positive aspects.[28]

The subsequently stated aim of *Sparkle Jar* is to contribute to greater understandings of autism. The equally radical second narrative thread of the book is also of interest. This story presents the author coming to terms with the death of his pet kestrel and subsequent realisation of mortality and vulnerability. The two narrative threads are intertwined: Packham's validation of autistic self-knowledge provides support for his claims to experience empathy with other species, and hence we understand his despair at losing his beloved companion. However, Packham's emotional attachment to these other lives raises questions that belong to broader considerations than autism studies.

The focus on autistic experience within the book in the NAS interviews deflects from the presentation of Packham's radical identification with other species in the text itself. The narrator's intense reaction to the death of the kestrel and description of his depression after losing two of his dogs suggests both his personal vulnerability and high valuation of non-human lives. The story of cross-species identification, and the narrative of self-understanding and acceptance, provide a new direction in the 'new nature writing'. *Sparkle Jar* does not focus on the recuperation of an able body and mind – it is a story about survival in spite of, and perhaps because of, awareness of vulnerability across all species.

Grandin's arguments about cross-species identifications and changing our attitudes to autism are much more explicit in *Animals in Translation: The Woman Who Thinks Like a Cow*. While her earlier memoirs *Emergence: Labelled Autistic* and *Thinking in Pictures: My Life with Autism* dealt more overtly with the validity of autistic self-presentation, *Animals in Translation* addresses how autism has informed her work in animal studies. She argues that the predominantly visual nature of her inner life provides her with a unique perspective on the ways that animals respond to their environments. She determines that animals possess far more sophisticated perceptual and sensory processes, and hence more thought and consciousness, than is commonly understood. Grandin concludes that animals and humans share a capacity for non-verbal thought that is overlooked by human exceptionalism. A secondary narrative is akin to Packham's *bildungsroman*, although less prominent in this text. Grandin found herself alienated from her peers during her teenage years, and found social contact with animals provided her with the opportunity for happiness and self-knowledge.

This chapter will begin to explore how far both texts go to offering an alternative ethics based on cross-species identifications, but it is worth asking how far both authors perpetuate ableist discourse with their combination of personal and nature memoirs. Do they speak directly to non-autistic audiences about what it is to be human, or merely operate at the level of social curiosity? Do Packham and Grandin represent their efforts to overcome their disabilities to serve as useful members of society, providing able-bodied readers with curious information about other species? To create what Cary Wolfe calls 'new lines of empathy, affinity and respect' between all types of lives, it is important that Packham and Grandin don't just describe their bonds with the non-human world, but that they are able to show us what these bonds feel like. To be able to do so, however, they need to persuade readers that they are reliable informants about their own mental states. It is perhaps unfair to expect that two authors may overcome the discourses that would position autistic writers as incapable of recognising their emotional states and to challenge readers to rethink ideologically loaded narratives about human independence and invulnerability. The wide popularity of both texts suggests that they are able to do this.

Fingers in the Sparkle Jar

Chris Packham's memoir may be mined for a portrait of autism that emphasises the 'triad' of impairments, including difficulties with back-and-forth conversation, deficits in developing, maintaining and understanding relationships (with humans) and an intense, unstinting, interest – this time in the natural world. These characteristics are identified in the diagnostic criteria for Autism Spectrum Disorder.[29] In the language of DSM-5, autism is described in terms of deviance from a supposed cognitive 'norm' and by the failure to achieve a socially acceptable identity:

- Highly restricted, fixated interests that are abnormal in intensity or focus.
- Hyper- or hyporeactivity to sensory input or unusual interest in sensory aspects of the environment (e.g., apparent indifference to pain/temperature, adverse response to specific sounds or textures, excessive smelling or touching of objects, visual fascination with lights or movement).
- Deficits in developing, maintaining, and understanding relationships.
- Deficits in social-emotional reciprocity, ranging, for example, from abnormal social approach and failure of normal back-and-forth conversation to reduced sharing of interests, emotions or affect, to failure to initiate or respond to social interactions.

Packham employs various literary techniques to illuminate both how his childhood and adolescence may be defined by these supposed impairments, but asks us to reconsider their accuracy at describing the subject's inner world once we know more about the context. The opening chapter of the book, 'The Collector', presents a 'lonely' 'ladybird boy' who may be regarded as struggling with 'social-emotional reciprocity' and seems to have 'highly restricted, fixated interests'. There is a symbolic transaction with an 'amiable' ice-cream van driver who occupies the place of the benevolent diagnostician and humours the child's attempts to offer dioramas in jam jars in exchange for lollies. Without knowing how to proceed, the narrator asks:

> What do you say to a weird kid with dinosaurs in jam jars who never speaks, who only ever points, who buys your cheapest ice lollies and seems to think that bartering with various bugs is a viable currency for exchange?[30]

The unnamed narrator apparently regards the child as eccentric, yet it becomes clear that the boy is the author's younger self. We soon learn that the boy isn't lonely; or, at least, he does not consider himself lacking in company or connections. It is apparent that the boy's assumed deficits in the range of his interests and in his lack of (human) social reciprocity may obscure our awareness of his other qualities, which include his heightened focus and assumed connection with his chosen interlocutors. Yet his enthusiasm for wildlife combines with the DSM's 'unusual interest in sensory aspects of the environment', as demonstrated by the description of his experience of the back garden:

> He lay back and whistled, the bird spluttered on, he wet his lips and whistled again adding a flourish and the bird whistled back mimicking his notes, he waited, the bird rambled through its repetitive repertoire, then he whistled again and the bird replied. The duet went on until the mimic vanished and then he whistled and answered himself, stroking the polka dotting of daisies with sweeping arcs of his arms, in synchrony and symmetry.[31]

In whistling to the bird, the boy shows an awareness of its reciprocity, and his own urge to the more thoroughly equal relationship of 'symmetry', an extreme form of cross-species sociability. This encounter foreshadows encounters with more exotic animals and birds that are presented later on. The dioramas, or sparkle jars, of the title evoke the boy-naturalist's urge to comprehend a diverse natural world through a process of joyful close study and familiarity; they also stand for the process of abstracting knowledge from lived experience, based on incomplete samples, that is common to autistic and non-autistic alike.

The first-person narrator doesn't appear until the third section of the first chapter, 'Brand New Savage', which is set a few months later than the opening section in September 1966. In this way, both the narrator's experiences and his surroundings are revealed in more detail. From this point on, the story moves out of chronological or thematic sequence, with many switches in perspective. The flash forwards to the present day – which is the sort of device we might expect to find in a celebrity memoir – does not occur until page 42, and it is written from the perspective of an omniscient spectator. Chapters often begin with no clues as to who is talking and from where: this must be pieced together through details. The reader finds herself in the middle of an intensely detailed sensory landscape. What prevents this from becoming overwhelming is that the more recent events are presented in italics.

While the text focuses on the boy's interest in the natural world, the descriptions of his surroundings include many references to popular culture and people. A behavioural psychologist examining these circumstances might take the boy's actions as signs of narrowness of interest and a failure to engage socially; yet the narration of the boy's thoughts and feelings conjures up a sense of pleasure gained from the enormous variety of sensory stimuli, including visual, tactile, auditory and olfactory information from many different sources. As Packham reveals later on, it's not so much that he wanted to be alone with animals, but that 'it was the only time when I could feel comfortable'.[32]

Packham describes a search for social relationships based on shared interests. By comparison with the popular interests of the majority of his peers, the range of his interests in the natural world is enormous in scope. In the DSM criteria, reciprocity is presented as a positive social exchange, although it is deprived of any significant qualitative description. In his interactions with his peers, the narrator finds little reciprocation in terms of his interests or the emotions he conveys them with. On the other hand, in the description of his relationship with the kestrel the narrator suggests emotional reciprocity:

> he was still there, whispering to his bird. His face was really close to it and it was bending forward and playfully pecking at his nose and, although she could only see his silhouette in profile, she could tell he was smiling.[33]

When Packham describes his local environment and the creatures found in it, the sentence structure and syntax sometimes require an effort on the part of the reader. The environments of ponds, trees, copses, fields, houses and even shops are drenched in adjectives and adverbs, neologisms and pronouns. The subject is at first obscure and heavy with detail. However, despite the potential for the reader to become overwhelmed, the reader is rewarded when the subject of the paragraph or sentence is finally revealed in its precise rendering. Another jarring factor is the scarcity of proper names for people and animals (although brands and cultural references are named) apart from the confusing use of 'Kestrel' and 'Tyrannosaurus' for both individuals and the species.

Together, these features hint at both the rich sensory world that the narrator experiences as well as a focus on beloved individual creatures that are constantly changing.

Walking is one of the ways in which the young Chris Packham traces the movements, sound, smells and tracks of the creatures he is interested in, including foxes, badgers, toads, grass snakes, minnows and sticklebacks, and even the elderly soldier he is fascinated by. He does not always walk along paths, and he is as likely to crawl, scramble, run, stagger or perch as he is to walk. Movement is never a monotonous act, but it punctuates the visual descriptions with a kinetic rhythm of its own:

> he turned and smacked his soles down on the pavement, zigzagging in staggers and bounds to avoid stepping on the cracks, skipping along the kerb by dropping his left foot in the gutter, dodging dog shit and curling round the lamp post [. . .].

Musical effects such as these help to unify the diverse array of information. Packham also incorporates many kinds of reported speech, which provides stylistic variation and, in the case of the conversation with his therapist, allows the narrator to speak at greater length about his emotions. These features reveal a rich and nuanced emotional life, and contradict the 'robotic' stereotype of autism. The shifts between perspectives demonstrate an emotional life that differs in quality, but not kind, from the 'neurotypical' norm.

These complex representations of sensory and perceptual detail, alongside the disorienting structural features that confuse the perception of space and time, intimate Packham's 'complex embodiment'. As he explains in response to a question about the 'sensory description' he uses in the book:

> Those passages you mention in the book are deliberately intense. My purpose was to try and get the reader to visualise and feel that cascade of sensory in out that happens at a rapid pace. Too much information is one of [the National Autistic Society's] catchphrases; I think it's actually too much information, too quickly.

The narrator of the text is apparently aware that other people don't see the world in the same way as he does – suggesting he understands the perspective of his neighbours and readers. He has presumably gained awareness of how his ways of perceiving and responding to the world differ to the supposed 'norm'.

The secondary narrative about Packham's relationships with particular species emerges in part out of, but also inseparably entwined with, the discovery of his unusual perceptual and sensory awareness. It is through frequent and solitary explorations on foot that Packham first encounters the kestrel. Walking thus contributes to the central narrative arc, since it enables the bird's acquisition, its taming and eventual semi-'domestication'.

His heightened visual perception, combined with the ability to explore the countryside on foot, allow the narrator to locate a nesting kestrel when he is just 14 years old:

> I sat up and breathed and, mildly calmed, gave the second whole page over to a neatly drawn map of a tiny patch of Hampshire. It showed individual trees and there was a scale and a legend that illustrated the symbols for fencing, a bog and a wet ditch, and at its centre a great ballooning oak labelled 'nest tree'.[34]

The narrator's attachment to the kestrel he rears from a chick becomes so intense that he is devastated when it inevitably dies some years later. Only as an adult does he find the language to describe the paradox of attachments that are so intense that they both endanger him and make his life possible: 'I was on my own with the dogs. I couldn't leave them. They loved me. I hated that though, at that point I hated them for loving me . . . pure love, immaculate, perfect love.'[35]

As the adolescent boy develops his love of the kestrel, he simultaneously fails to experience reciprocal relations with his human companions. To the narrator, the deficit in feeling lies in the part of his apparently 'normal' peers who seem to have no source values that are not based on fashion or hierarchy. As the narrative proceeds, it becomes clear that Packham still finds more meaning and beauty in his relationship with individual animals than in any status he has in the world of humans. His inclusion of a reported dialogue with the therapist provides a perspective through which this can be examined alongside more 'typical' emotional challenges. This indirect characterisation – even in its third-person form – may even be a way to persuade readers of the validity of the narrator's claims about his own mental states. His 'unreliability' is mediated by the perspective of the therapist.

While Packham emphasises his intellectual abilities, there is little in the text that supports ableist assumptions about the importance of individual will and endurance in overcoming disability. In fact, while adolescent Packham refers to his drive to outdo his peers in typical language about motivation and willpower, he later states that he turned to the therapist to find a 'framework' to deal with death.[36] The experiences the memoir celebrates – 'empathy, affinity and respect' – are enhanced by the author's awareness of his own and others' vulnerability and mortality. In the NAS interviews, Packham acknowledges that he is both lucky to have had the type of childhood where he was allowed to collect and obtain such a wide variety of pets, and an adult life where he can afford to pay for help with his mental health.[37] This acknowledgement of privilege is absent from most examples of nature writing.

Describing himself from the point of view of others, including those of a shell-shocked former soldier and a struggling single dad, suggests that adult narrator *does* have a great deal of empathy with other people, and this does not support Simon Baron-Cohen's 'extreme male brain' theory of autism. There are, in fact, more representations of empathic experience in *Sparkle Jar* than in many other nature memoirs: however, they focus on non-normative subjects rather than dominant cultural figures or family, and risk being discounted. Being labelled 'queer' by his peers suggests that Packham's adolescent behaviour challenged hegemonic identities, but offered him little cultural recognition at the time. His subsequent adoption of the punk culture he describes in Chapter 7 offered a more empowering alternative to a mainstream masculinity.

Towards an ethics of shared vulnerability

Packham and Grandin show us valuable things about autism, and suggest that if we question the importance of linguistic reciprocity, it will lead us to regard other species in a new light. This has far-reaching consequences for how we *should* behave towards other species, some of which are explicitly stated by Grandin in her text. For Grandin, this does not mean that we should treat other species as we treat humans, but that we need to re-think the suffering we cause them.

There are also key differences between the texts. Grandin reports the experiences that had led to her empathy for other species as a scientist; Packham shows us the processes that led to his stance towards the natural world and its basis in unfolding conjunctions of material dependency and embodiment. Walking is just one of several ways in which Packham develops skills that attune him to the perceptions of other occupants of the ecosystem. While the narrative emphasises Packham's unusual visual perception, *Fingers in the Sparkle Jar* demonstrates how atypical corporeal and cognitive embodiment may lead us to feel empathy for other lives. Perhaps it is precisely this sort of empathy that is needed to dispel Wolfe's target 'fantasies of disembodiment and autonomy'.[38]

Lessons from *Fingers in the Sparkle Jar* and *Animals in Translation*: what might we learn as ecocritics?

What do we learn from both Packham's and Grandin's memoirs that may help us develop forms of environmental literature and criticism? What do we gain from thinking about the role of walking in *Sparkle Jar* in comparison to other works of nature writing or memoir? While it is far from comprehensive, this final section predicts what non-ableist environmental literature might look like, based on the readings of these two memoirs. It is hoped that this will help establish future links between ecocriticism and critical disability studies. The neurodiversity perspective described earlier offers a starting point from which to spot the most salient parallels. Both critical practices ask us to question the cultural basis for the marginalisation of certain forms of life. As a consequence, this type of intersectional ecocriticism:

- Is aware of how dominant social identities reinforce ableist social mechanisms. For instance, ecocriticism has not yet addressed the way that much (although not all) published nature writing is both produced and consumed by able-bodied, middle class professionals.
- Is conscious of how bodily and mental ability are fleeting and occasional states for humans and other species, produced by complex material and social processes beyond the individual. A related question might be: why are disability and vulnerability so often elided in nature writing?
- Will consider other forms of kinship and 'sym-collaborations' in addition to nuclear human families.[39]
- Questions why narratives involving nature so often focus on the white, male, young, able, educated, middle-class individual alone in the wilderness or in communion with more charismatic and endangered mammalian or avian species.
- Continues to question why technology, adaptations, medication and prostheses of different types are considered impediments to meaningful contact with nature.
- Explores how the myths of bodily and spiritual purity in nature are historically dependent on the perceived threats to the elite that originated in the Industrial Revolution. A fully intersectional ecocriticism will explore how social and democratic changes such as the improved status of women, healthcare, labour movements and migration, combined with elitism and social Darwinism, informed the various strands of the 'back to nature' movements and risk cultures upon which British nature writing is based.

With respect to walking narratives, in particular, such literature will:

- Acknowledge privileged material and social positions are often the basis for solitary walking encounters in remote and sublime places.
- Explore how the Romantic foundations of environmental culture in Britain during the Industrial Revolution and subsequent capitalism inspired a walking literature that is distinctly ableist, elitist, Eurocentric and anthroparchic.
- Seek out a new aesthetic paradigm that does not require superior physical or mental abilities, but addresses embodiment in all its complexity and entanglement with organic and material prostheses.
- Supplement linguistic mastery over landscape with imaginative, kinetic, visual, tactile and auditory forms of environmental knowledge and experience.
- Notice other walkers, wayfarers and inhabitants encountered along the path, including those who do not look or sound like us, who are 'uncanny' or 'unfamiliar', who are less able and fit than us, and

where relevant, treat them with empathy and compassion – or at least kindness.[40]

- Acknowledge that feelings of vulnerability and dependency are more likely to be part of our experiences of walking than not. Such literature will address what Elizabeth A. Wheeler asks of environmentally oriented literature: 'How can the vulnerability of disabled people be perceived as a part of our shared vulnerability on the planet itself, rather than a unique and separate kind of weakness?'[41]

Acknowledgement

With thanks to Dr Nick Chown for the helpful discussion of an early draft of this chapter.

Notes

1 Judy Singer, a sociologist who is autistic, used the term 'neurodiversity' to describe conditions including attention deficit hyperactivity disorder, autism and dyslexia. It was hoped that this term would focus on the different ways of thinking and learning that are associated with these conditions, rather than on the litany of deficits that are more typically described. See Judy Singer, '"Why Can't You Be Normal for Once in Your Life?" From a "Problem with No Name" to the Emergence of a New Category of Difference', in Marian Corker and Sally French (eds), *Disability and Discourse* (Buckingham, UK: Open University Press, 1999), pp. 59–67. The term has since been applied to other conditions that aren't associated with autism, such as bipolar disorder, schizophrenia and speech difficulties.

2 The definition of autism used in this chapter is as follows: 'autism is a developmental (social learning) disability, not an intellectual learning disability or a mental health issue. However, it may be accompanied by an intellectual learning disability and/or mental health issues'; Chown et al., 'Improving Research about Us, with Us: A Framework for Inclusive Autism Research'. *Disability and Society*, 32.5 (2017), endnote 3.

3 As Sarah Jaquette Ray explains with respect to American wilderness culture: 'The myths of the individual, genetically superior body, and the wilderness plot all powerfully shape contemporary adventure culture in ways that are at odds with any vision of an inclusive environmental movement'; Sarah Jaquette Ray, 'Risking Bodies in the Wild: The "Corporeal Unconscious" of American Adventure Culture', in Sara Jaquette Ray and Ray Sibara (eds), *Disability Studies and the Environmental Humanities: Towards an Eco-crip Theory* (Lincoln, NB: University of Nebraska Press, 2017), p. 62.

4 Cary Wolfe, *What Is Posthumanism?* (Minneapolis, MN: University of Minnesota Press, 2010), p. xv.

5 Opposing the rhetoric of ableism does not entail denigrating all human efforts and achievements and obliterating the notion of individuality – it is about questioning the *a priori* superiority of actions according to dominant cultural ideas of human worth.

6 Tobin Siebers, *Disability Theory* (Ann Arbor, MI: University of Michigan Press, 2008), p. 10.

7 Ibid., p. 271.

8 Ibid., p. 278.

9 David T. Mitchell and Sharon Snyder, 'Precarity and Cross-species Identification: Autism, the Critique of Normative Cognition, and Nonspeciesism', in Sara Jaquette Ray and Ray Sibara (eds), *Disability Studies and the Environmental Humanities: Towards an Eco-crip Theory* (Lincoln, NB: University of Nebraska Press, 2017), p. 570.

10 Wolfe, *What Is Posthumanism?*, p. 141.

11 Cary Wolfe, 'Learning from Temple Grandin, or, Animal Studies, Disability Studies, and Who Comes after the Subject', *New Formations*, 64 (Summer 2008), p. 117.

12 Ibid., p. 110.

13 Temple Grandin and Catherine Johnson, *Animals in Translation: The Woman who Thinks Like a Cow* (London: Bloomsbury, 2005), p. 17.

14 Temple Grandin and Richard Panek, *The Autistic Brain* (London: Rider, 2014), p. 299.

15 Ibid.

16 Temple Grandin, *Thinking in Pictures* (London: Bloomsbury, 2006), p. 25.

17 Wolfe, 'Learning from Temple Grandin', p. 117.

18 Clarity about autism is certainly not increased by the fact that by its inclusion in the DSM it appears to be a form of mental illness, when in fact it is generally understood by the same clinicians who use the DSM as a form of developmental disorder. DSM-5 was published by the American Psychiatric Association in 2013.

19 Laurent Mottron et al., 'Enhanced Perceptual Functioning in Autism: An Update, and Eight Principles of Autistic Perception', *Journal of Autism and Developmental Disorders*, 36.1 (January 2006), p. 28.

20 The research Grandin referred to concerned autistic access to typical low-level perceptual processes, rather than the extent and role of such enhanced perception in a range of complex tasks, which is examined by Mottron et al. (ibid.).

21 National Autistic Society, 'Chris Packham, About *Fingers in the Sparkle Jar*', *Your Autism* magazine, n.d., www.autism.org.uk/chrispackham.

22 Ibid.

23 Ibid.

24 L. van Goidsenhoven, '"Autie-biographies": Life Writing Genres and Strategies from an Autistic Perspective', *Journal of Language, Literature and Culture*, 64.2 (2017), p. 82.

25 Ibid.

26 National Autistic Society, 'Chris Packham, Television Presenter and Naturalist, Is Our Charity's New Ambassador', 16 October 2017, www.autism.org.uk/get-involved/media-centre/news/2017-10-16-chris-packham-ambassador.asp.

27 O'Connor, 'Chris Packham Opens Up on Asperger's Syndrome'.

28 In suggesting that autism may contribute to a positive cultural identity, I also acknowledge that autism may be accompanied by 'impairment effects', which are disabling things that are not a result of societal attitudes and barriers; see Carol Thomas, *Female Forms: Experiencing and Understanding Disability* (Buckingham, UK: Open University Press, 1999). This is consistent with the social-relational model of disability as defined by Carol Thomas and others, which conceptualises disability as 'forms of oppressive social reaction visited upon people with impairments'; see Carol Thomas, 'Rescuing a Social Relational Understanding of Disability', *Scandinavian Journal of Disability Research*, 6.1 (2004), pp. 8–21.

29 The terms Asperger's Syndrome, High Functioning Autism and Autism Spectrum Disorder (ASD) are rejected by some neurodiversity activists in favour of the term 'autism' because of their associations with ableist rhetoric and because they are so generally misunderstood. Further, DSM-5, published in 2013, removed Asperger's Syndrome as a separate diagnosis and included it under the umbrella term ASD. The term 'Asperger's' was formerly used to

refer to an autistic individual with a supposedly higher-than-average or average IQ and no delays with speech acquisition in childhood. It is the term used by Packham, but Grandin refers to herself as 'autistic'.

30 Packham, *Fingers in the Sparkle Jar*, p. 7.
31 Ibid., p. 10.
32 Ibid., p. 273.
33 Ibid., p. 73.
34 Ibid., p. 19.
35 Ibid., p. 368.
36 National Autistic Society, 'Chris Packham, About *Fingers in the Sparkle Jar*'.
37 Packham, *Fingers in the Sparkle Jar*, p. 371, National Autistic Society, 'Chris Packham, About *Fingers in the Sparkle Jar*'.
38 Cary Wolfe, *What Is Posthumanism?* (Minneapolis, MN: University of Minnesota Press, 2010), p. xv; see also p. 2.
39 Donna Haraway, 'Anthropocene, Capitalocene, Plantationocene, Chthulucene: Making Kin', *Environmental Humanities*, 6 (2015), pp. 161–162.
40 Ibid., p. 165.
41 Elizabeth A. Wheeler, 'Moving Together Side by Side: Human-animal Comparisons in Picture Books', in Sara Jaquette Ray and Ray Sibara (eds), *Disability Studies and the Environmental Humanities: Towards an Eco-crip Theory* (Lincoln, NB: University of Nebraska Press, 2017), p. 595.

Works cited

Chown, Nick, Jackie Robinson, Luke Beardon et al. 'Improving Research about Us, with Us: A Framework for Inclusive Autism Research'. *Disability and Society*, 32.5 (2017), 720–734.

Grandin, Temple. *Thinking in Pictures*. London: Bloomsbury, 2006.

Grandin, Temple and Catherine Johnson. *Animals in Translation: The Woman Who Thinks Like a Cow*. London: Bloomsbury, 2005.

Grandin, Temple and Richard Panek. *The Autistic Brain*. London: Rider, 2014.

Grandin, Temple and Margaret M. Scariano. *Emergence – Labelled Autistic: A True Story*. New York: Grand Central Publishing, 1996.

Haraway, Donna, 'Anthropocene, Capitalocene, Plantationocene, Chthulucene: Making Kin'. *Environmental Humanities*, 6 (2015), 159–165.

Mitchell, David T. and Sharon Snyder. *The Biopolitics of Disability: Neoliberalism, Ablenationalism, and Peripheral Embodiment*. Ann Arbor, MI: University of Michigan Press, 2015.

Mitchell, David T. and Sharon Snyder. 'Precarity and Cross-species Identification: Autism, the Critique of Normative Cognition, and Nonspeciesism', in Sara Jaquette Ray and Ray Sibara (eds), *Disability Studies and the Environmental Humanities: Towards an Eco-crip Theory*, pp. 553–572. Lincoln, NB: University of Nebraska Press, 2017.

Mottron, Laurent, Michelle Dawson, Isabelle Soulieres et al. 'Enhanced Perceptual Functioning in Autism: An Update, and Eight Principles of Autistic Perception'. *Journal of Autism and Developmental Disorders*, 36.1 (January 2006), 27–43.

National Autistic Society. 'Chris Packham, About *Fingers in the Sparkle Jar*'. *Your Autism* magazine, n.d., www.autism.org.uk/chrispackham

National Autistic Society. 'Chris Packham, Television Presenter and Naturalist, Is Our Charity's New Ambassador', 16 October 2017, www.autism.org.uk/get-involved/media-centre/news/2017-10-16-chris-packham-ambassador.asp

O'Connor, Rory. 'Chris Packham Opens Up on Asperger's Syndrome: "Autistic People Don't Have to Suffer"'. *Daily Express*, 17 July 2017. www.express.co.uk/showbiz/tv-radio/829755/Chris-Packham-Aspergers-Syndrome-Earth-Live-Nat-Geo-Springwatch-Autumnwatch-BBC

Packham, Chris. *Fingers in the Sparkle Jar: Lessons in Life and Death*. London: Ebury Press, 2016.

Ray, Sara Jaquette. 'Risking Bodies in the Wild: The "Corporeal Unconscious" of American Adventure Culture', in Sara Jaquette Ray and Ray Sibara (eds), *Disability Studies and the Environmental Humanities: Towards an Eco-crip Theory*, pp. 29–72. Lincoln, NB: University of Nebraska Press, 2017.

Ray, Sara Jaquette and Ray Sibara (eds). *Disability Studies and the Environmental Humanities: Towards an Eco-crip Theory*. Lincoln, NB: University of Nebraska Press, 2017.

Russell, Charlie (director). *Chris Packham: Asperger's and Me*. Raw TV, 2017.

Siebers, Tobin. *Disability Theory*. Ann Arbor, MI: University of Michigan Press, 2008.

Siebers, Tobin. 'Disability and the Theory of Complex Embodiment', in Lennard J. Davis (ed.), *The Disability Studies Reader*, pp. 272–291. New York: Routledge, 2013.

Singer, Judy. '"Why Can't You Be Normal for Once in Your Life?" From a "Problem with No Name" to the Emergence of a New Category of Difference', in Marian Corker and Sally French (eds), *Disability and Discourse*, pp. 59–67. Buckingham, UK: Open University Press, 1999.

Thomas, Carol. *Female Forms: Experiencing and Understanding Disability*. Buckingham, UK: Open University Press, 1999.

Thomas, Carol. 'Rescuing a Social Relational Understanding of Disability'. *Scandinavian Journal of Disability Research*, 6.1 (2004), 8–21.

van Goidsenhoven, Leni. '"Autie-biographies": Life Writing Genres and Strategies from an Autistic Perspective'. *Journal of Language, Literature and Culture*, 64.2 (2017), 79–95.

Wheeler, Elizabeth A. 'Moving Together Side by Side: Human-animal Comparisons in Picture Books', in Sara Jaquette Ray and Ray Sibara (eds), *Disability Studies and the Environmental Humanities: Towards an Eco-crip Theory*, pp. 594–622. Lincoln, NB: University of Nebraska Press, 2017.

Wolfe, Cary. 'Learning from Temple Grandin, or, Animal Studies, Disability Studies, and Who Comes after the Subject'. *New Formations*, 64 (Summer 2008), 10–123.

Wolfe, Cary. *What Is Posthumanism?* Minneapolis, MN: University of Minnesota Press, 2010.

12 Walking with the digital

Heartlands – 'Ere Be Dragons and A Conversation Between Trees

Rachel Jacobs, Pippa Marland and Steve Benford

Introduction

An increasing reliance on technologically mediated forms of experience is an aspect of Western modernity that has been heavily criticised in environmental discourse. Jerry Mander, writing in 1978, suggested that as we have moved into 'artificial environments', particularly in our viewing of the world through the medium of television, 'our direct contact with and knowledge of the planet has been snapped'.[1] This critical stance has been perpetuated in responses to the development of more recent digital technologies. Richard Louv, for example, argues in *Last Child in the Woods* that those who have grown up in the digital age have traded the richness of sensory life for a 'daily immersion in indirect, technological experience' leaving them susceptible to a 'nature deficit disorder'.[2] These concerns have also permeated other forms of environmentally oriented literature, especially those whose primary mode of exploration is walking. In *Common Ground*, the nature writer Rob Cowen contrasts the practice of walking out into the rural edges of an urban environment to experience 'the rhythms of land and nature' with an ever-more indoor-based participation in a technologically produced and mediated world:

> Clouds [i.e. 'cloud' data storage], hyper-real TV shows, 3D films, multiplayer games, online stores and social media networks – these are today's areas of common ground [. . .]. Ours is a world growing yet shrinking, connected yet isolated, all-knowing but without knowledge.[3]

Perspectives such as these perpetuate a long-standing binary division between nature and 'technology' (a term often used as an indiscriminate catch-all for the vast range of different applications of technology in contemporary society). As Sid Dobrin notes, 'technology writ large is cast as a primary origin of environmental crisis, the very kind of situation against which much ecocritical research works'.[4] However, he argues that maintaining 'reductive binaries in our current cultural, economic, environmental, and technological situation is no longer realistic'.[5] At the same time, there is a concern among ecocritics that existing cultural forms such as literature lack the capacity to respond adequately to the spatial and temporal scales involved in the growing environmental crisis, to the extent that Timothy Clark questions whether 'certain limits of the human imagination, artistic representation and the capacity of understanding [are] now being reached'.[6] It is, at least in part, as a result of this anxiety that ecocriticism is showing an increasing interest in digital technologies and applications, particularly in their potential to offer new ways to engage with the cognitive and imaginative challenges of the Anthropocene. A field of 'digital environmental humanities' is emerging, as evidenced, for example, by special issues of the journals *Green Letters* and *Ecozon@*, focused, respectively, on 'Digital Environments' and 'Green Computer and Video Games'. While expressing understandable caution around the materiality of technological equipment in terms of its sources and disposal, and thus an awareness of the ways in which 'games and gamers may be complicit in, or at least uncomfortably close to, legitimating unsustainable practices at a political or sociological level',[7] these studies have begun to explore the potential of digital environments for fostering ecologically oriented sensibilities. Alenda Chang suggests that, while no substitute for direct experience, game environments 'can offer a compelling way to reconcile a deep connection to nature and the nonhuman world with an equally important connection to technology and the virtual', and John Parham argues that computer games can assist in 'constituting or shaping environmental or ecological awareness'.[8]

This engagement with the environment through digital technologies has not been restricted to game design. Recent developments include an array of mobile, wearable and even implanted technologies that allow us to envisage a wider range of relationships between the ecological and the digital and the embodied and the virtual. In terms of the latter in particular, the notion of the virtual as separate from the physical environment is perhaps being replaced by understandings of more complex relationships, where the two are interwoven and juxtaposed in various ways. Sensing and geo-spatial (satellite and locative) technologies and complex climate modelling systems provide us with the opportunity to capture the data that underpins our scientific understanding of contemporary climate change.[9] Increasingly these technologies are being developed within citizen science contexts and in collaboration with environmentally engaged artists. In this way, they can be used to engage non-scientists in ecological discourse and in participatory and community sensing activities, for example helping communities to capture data on local water quality and pollution levels. Artists such as Active Ingredient, Duncan Speakman, Proboscis, Christian Nold, Wapke Feenstra and Andrea Polli all look to digital, interactive and data-driven technologies to explore environmental questions in new ways, often linking their explorations with walking, and producing works that confront, inhabit and disrupt the kind of binaries surrounding nature and technology that are prevalent in existing environmental discourse.[10] What, then, are the specific ways in which digital artworks such as these might assist in the development of greater ecological awareness?

This chapter presents a case study of two artworks created by Active Ingredient – the game-based *Heartlands – 'Ere Be Dragons* and, in a fuller discussion, the multi-stranded artwork *A Conversation Between Trees* – assessing their potential for engaging and extending the ecological imagination. Active Ingredient is an arts collective founded in 1996 by Rachel Jacobs, Matt Watkins, Gareth Howell and Zini Pandya. The artists came from a background of interdisciplinary performance, visual and participatory art, at a time when the Internet was just beginning to influence the contemporary arts world.[11] In parallel, notions of sci-art and interactive art provided the impetus for increasing opportunities for collaborations between artists, scientists and technologists.[12] In 2005, Active Ingredient began a long-term collaboration with computer scientists from the Mixed Reality Lab at the University of Nottingham. Their first collaboration involved creating an early example of a locative mobile phone game – *Heartlands* – exploring how interactive and networked technologies can help us make sense of our bodies as we walk and explore different environments. The game was played in a range of locations, on urban streets in cities around the world, including Nottingham, Cambridge, Paris, São Paulo, Singapore and Yokohama (as well as a forest in Finland), and used mobile and sensor technology – GPS (Global Positioning System) and heart rate monitors – to mediate the players' sensory experience of the world around them. This process ultimately provided the creators of the game with a more complex understanding of how these technologies might be used in their subsequent multi-faceted piece *A Conversation Between Trees (ACBT)* (2011–12), in order to initiate an ecological discourse around forest environments and climate change. *ACBT* combined using environmental sensors placed in geographically distant forests, gallery-based projected visualisations of this live sensor data, a 'climate machine' that created images of historical global CO_2 levels, and a forest walk taken by participants carrying mobile technologies. Where *ACBT* in particular differed from other mixed-reality, locative, networked experiences such as Blast Theory's locative artwork *Uncle Roy All Around You* or the commercial augmented reality game *Pokémon GO* was in its attempt to point back to an ecological, emotional and aesthetic understanding of the physical environment – in this case, of forests.[13]

The ecocritics Stefanie Posthumus and Stéfan Sinclair point out that the initial logo for the Association for the Study of Literature and Environment featured a person sitting at the foot of a tree, reading a book, and they comment: 'The idea behind the image is that by going outdoors to read, the literary scholar can begin closing the gap between the written word and the physical world.'[14] They compare this image with the Kindle logo, and question whether the acts of reading a text in a book or on an electronic tablet while sitting under a tree 'represent different digital ecologies'.[15] At the heart of this chapter are the following questions: What happens when our 'text' becomes a mediated, technological experience we take on a walk with us, combining it with more 'direct' sensory experience of the world? What kinds of 'ecologies' emerge from such an activity? Our investigation is augmented and enhanced by the inclusion of audience/participant responses to *ACBT*.

Heartlands – 'Ere Be Dragons

Heartlands invited participants carrying smart mobile phones to go on a 60-minute walk through an urban environment without thinking about a destination. It focused specifically on the players' individual and collective responses to walking through a city, capturing their heart rate and overlaying this data onto a map of the external landscape they were navigating. The game was instantiated by four forms of technology: an early smart phone with an embedded screen that showed the game interface, the player's heart rate captured using a heart rate monitor attached to the phone, a GPS unit also attached to the phone that tracked the player's locations as they walked, and networked play – using GPRS (General Packet Radio Service Internet) on the phone – to enable different players to track each other's locations. A visualisation of all the players' locations and heart rates was also overlaid onto a map of the city that was projected at a central venue so that spectators could watch as the multi-player game unfolded.

The aim of the game was to maintain a 'healthy' heart rate while exploring as much of the environment as possible over one hour in order to create a digitally rendered abstract map of the player's 'world' on the screen of the phone. The target heart rate for individual players was established through an equation, suggested by health scientists with whom Active Ingredient collaborated at the planning stage, which calculated the optimum average heart rate based on the age of the player. As the player walked, a path appeared on the screen that followed the direction in which the player was walking in the real world. When the player's heart rate was at an optimum level, this path appeared as a green meadow with flowers; when their heart rate was too high, it turned into a forest of dark, shadowy trees; and when it went too low, it turned to desert, complete with skulls and cactus. Players scored points based on whether the heart rate was at an optimum level for their age and on the distance they had walked, represented by the amount of 'meadowed' path they had created. Additionally, the multi-player element revealed the paths the other players had created, which appeared on the screen as small white 'ghost' trails. If a player followed the ghost paths of the other players – by following them in the real world – they could 'steal' the virtual world of the player, turning the ghost path into their own path and taking points from the other player at the same time.

Central to *Heartlands* is the concept of *paidia* – freeform, exuberant play – which contrasts with the more rule-based and structured forms of play often found in digital games, particularly those focused on health

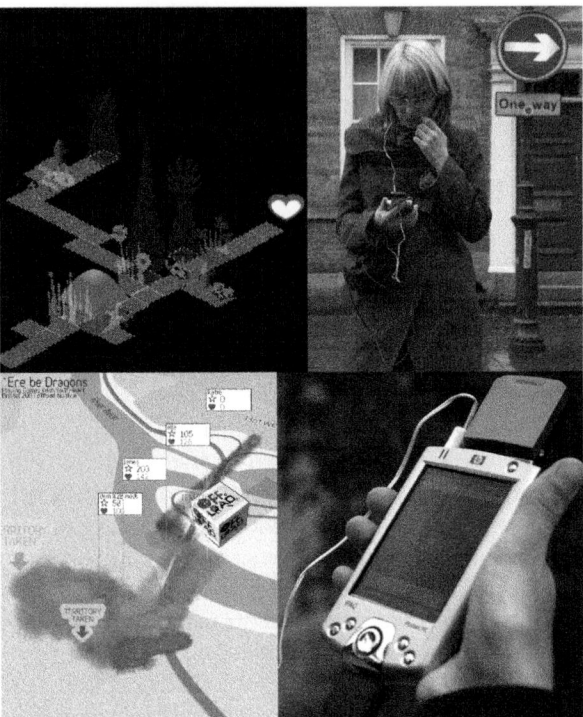

Figure 12.1 Heartlands

and well-being.[16] These features of 'open play', or 'ludic design', aim to encourage curiosity, exploration, reflection and ambiguity, all of which might help to foster a greater attentiveness in the players to both the physical and the virtual environments and to the embodied interactions between the two.[17] The game also involves elements of 'rhetorical play', a form that involves three modes of interaction based on Aristotle's modes of persuasion – logos (logic), ethos (credibility) and pathos (empathy) – modes that can potentially help to shape how the players think about their beliefs, behaviours and identities.[18] By designing a game that allows the players to explore freely – to choose whether to compete with others or simply to reflect on the landscape, their heart rate, and the map they are creating – opportunities are generated for discourse across these modes of interaction. It is not only through the strand of possible empathy (pathos) involved in the decision-making process about whether or not to behave competitively that the affective dimension of *Heartlands* emerges: the heart rate sensors reveal in the virtual space the physiological effects of both the players' level of exertion *and* the landscape's impact upon them, with their heart rate rising as they enter particular areas. This establishes a deep and multi-faceted level of connection between player and environment (ethos). Feedback from the participants showed many of them beginning to weave their own situated narratives (logos) around why their heart rate was rising in certain places. One participant noted, 'I tried to make a mental connection to the world I was creating (with the heart rate data) and the real world around me. It was a new and interesting experience,' while another commented, 'I found it interesting to see a world being mapped out based on my physical movements.'

The combination of these different modes of engagement suggests that the game can be viewed in terms of Gordon Calleja's concept of 'incorporation' – a term he uses to move beyond notions of player 'immersion' in order to denote 'intensified and internalised blends' of experiential phenomena.[19] He outlines six dimensions to this model: kinaesthetic involvement, spatial involvement, shared involvement, narrative involvement, affective involvement and ludic involvement.[20] *Heartlands* is notable for the way in which it deploys all of these elements simultaneously in ways that cross between the virtual and the real, blurring the distinction between the two (for example, the way in which the kinaesthetic, affective and narrative involvement are experienced by the participants as they walk through the city streets while at the same time these elements are visualised on their mobile screens and woven into the narrative of the game by means of their heart rate monitors and GPS trackers). Dobrin argues that 'virtual worlds and *digital environments* exceed the representational; they are themselves natures and environments in and with which humans and non-humans forge relationships', and that exploring these worlds and environments presents ecocriticism with a new kind of artefact – one that is 'simultaneously virtual and real'.[21] *Heartlands* perhaps presents a further new kind of artefact for ecocriticism – one that is simultaneously virtual and real, not just in terms of the game world itself, but in terms of the juxtaposition and interleaving of the game world with a material environment in a manner that generates a complex awareness of interconnection that might be seen as intrinsically ecological. The game experience was described by one participant as creating a feeling of being 'happy and stimulated at the end. It was curious, but somehow it made me sort of feel love for everything and everybody around!'

That said, *Heartlands* is not overtly environmentalist; it does not engage with questions of environmental risk and anthropogenic environmental effects. But, as Eugénie Shinkle points out: 'It is not simply as didactic tools or ideological vehicles that digital games can foster political change, but in the way that they open up a space for the emergence of new relations between body, mind and technology.'[22] The imagery for *Heartlands* relies, albeit playfully, on relatively simple environmental tropes – pastoral, meadow landscapes as benign, forests as fearful, and deserts as barren – and as such cannot necessarily be said to disrupt existing (restrictive) cultural constructions of nature. Nevertheless, through its kinaesthetic, spatial, shared, narrative, affective and ludic elements, all of which are linked to its central mode of engagement – walking – and its focus on rendering visible the invisible processes of the human body in terms of fluctuations in heart rate, it does potentially foster a powerful sense of complex embodied relationship between the players and their physical environment in a manner that might not be available to players immersed in a purely virtual game environment nor, arguably, a walker simply passing through the city streets.

A Conversation Between Trees

In *ACBT*, the artists extended their collaboration to look beyond the urban space – to forests, and to the atmosphere, weather and climate that bind human and non-human together in these often-threatened environments. The work was motivated by the recognition that 'the global and long-term nature of climate change data defies easy or immediate comprehension' and by the conviction that 'by engaging the public in emotional experiences on a human scale, artists may open up new opportunities for analysis and debate'.[23] During a presentation of *Heartlands* at *Mobilefest 2009* in São Paulo, Brazil, Active Ingredient began a discussion with the festival organisers, Marcelo Godoy and Paulo Hartmann. They discussed how similar sensing and mobile technologies might be used to encourage an awareness of deforestation in Brazil. After some consideration, the British artists felt that they were uncomfortable responding to forests on the other side of the world from where they lived. This position became an important starting point for a dialogue about local and global deforestation and climate change, and the potential for locative, mobile technologies to act as bridges between forests in different parts of the world. Instead of arriving in the Amazon 'armed' with mobile sensing technologies, the artists suggested these technologies might enable different communities in Brazil and the UK to connect to local forests and share the data captured with each other. In doing so, they hoped they could begin to deepen the conversation about deforestation and reveal some of the often invisible environmental changes occurring on local and global scales.

The team initially looked to the Mata Atlântica surrounding São Paulo. This Brazilian forest stretches along the coast, but according to SOS Mata Atlântica, has decreased by approximately 93 per cent since the 16th century.[24] In England, Active Ingredient focused on Sherwood Forest, which had once surrounded Nottingham where they were based, and of which now, also, only small pockets remain.[25] Together the artists visited the forests, walked, talked, collected data and stories, conducted workshops, and initiated dialogues with local communities and schools, deepening their relationships with both forests and investigating how learning about science, technology and local and global environments could be combined.[26] As the project evolved, the team was augmented by the addition of the Brazilian artist Silvia Leal, a senior climate scientist working at the UK

Met Office, and a botanist at Rio de Janeiro Botanical Gardens. The *ACBT* project was thus cumulatively developed through conversations between the artists, technologists, scientists, forest managers and school children in the UK and Brazil, ultimately evolving into a touring exhibition in which the artists explored ways of 'performing' scientific processes in order to explore meaning-making around the scientific data. The exhibition was presented at Museo da Imagem e de Som in São Paulo and Sherwood, Rockingham and Haldon forests in the UK, alongside an exchange programme between schools in Nottingham and Rio de Janeiro and community workshops.

The *ACBT* exhibition was made up of four parts. Firstly, temperature, humidity, sound, light, colour, atmospheric pressure and carbon dioxide sensors were connected to a networked mobile phone with a camera, placed on a branch of a tree in the Mata Atlântica and on a tree in whichever UK forest the exhibition was centred on in each of its different iterations. Secondly, two projection screens were set up on either side of an exhibition space, showing an animated visualisation of the live data captured from the two trees, respectively, as if they were in conversation with each other. The artists programmed a set of ranges that were applied to each dataset (for example, deciding ranges for freezing, cold, warm and hot temperatures) and made some decisions about how these data ranges might influence the visual interface in terms of colour, form, narrative and metaphor (e.g. cold temperatures of 0–10 degrees Centigrade meant small blue dots appeared). Both visualisations appeared as rotating spheres with fronds reminiscent of sea anemones, bromeliad leaves or unfurling ferns that changed colour, height, diameter, 'wateriness' and movement in response to the live data that was being sent every 60 seconds from the forests. The rotating spheres were formed from the photographs that were taken by a camera on the back of the mobile phone attached to the sensors in the trees. The photograph was turned into a grid that separated the image into squares, and the data coming from the sensors then influenced the way the pixels that made up each square of the photograph appeared within the grid. While testing an early version of the visualisation, the artists watched the data (and the programmed rules that applied the ranges and effects to the abstracted image) with no idea how it would respond. Suddenly the grid became alive: the light extruded the pixels in each square of the grid so that they appeared like a strange life form that jumped in response to the songs of the birds and the sounds of monkeys in the trees, and glimmered and unfurled in response to the temperature, light and carbon dioxide levels.

The third element of the exhibition worked with global and historical data rather than contemporary, localised environmental data. It involved an intriguing wooden 'climate machine' which stood in the centre of the gallery and plotted out circular graphs onto large discs of recycled paper using a soldering iron to scorch the graphs into the paper. This continued for the whole duration of the exhibition. Each disc represented the carbon dioxide levels in the global atmosphere for each year between 1959 and 2011, using data

Figure 12.2 ACBT exhibitions, guided and interactive walks

from the Mauna Loa Observatory in Hawaii which has been monitoring and collecting data relating to atmospheric change since the 1950s.[27] Once complete, each disc was hung from the ceiling of the gallery, creating a pathway of 53 discs. Visitors could walk along and search through the circular graphs, which increased in diameter as they moved towards the present day, forming ever-increasing circles which reflected increasing rates of CO_2.

Finally, in an element of the experience reminiscent of *Heartlands*, visitors were invited to take a mobile phone out into the forest where the exhibition they were attending was being staged, to take part in a guided interactive walk. The phone screen displayed a smaller version of the abstract visualisation projected in the gallery, this time showing only one visualisation, a 'mobile' representation of the data from the forest the visitor was exploring. The photographs were captured by the walkers themselves using the cameras on the back of the phones they were carrying which were programmed to take a photograph every 10 seconds. As with *Heartlands*, there was no pre-determined destination for this walk and visitors could go in any direction. A soundtrack played out a narrative written and voiced by the artists Jacobs and Leal, describing their own sensory and reflective journeys in Sherwood Forest and the Mata Atlântica. As the walkers explored the forest, they were invited to make links between the nature of the forest, any changes or deforestation they might encounter, and the data visualisations presented on the mobile phone screen and in the gallery exhibition. At the end of the 60-minute walk, the visitors were invited to stop where they were in the forest and answer a set of questions that appeared on the screen of the mobile phone. They were asked to decide on a scale of 1–10 what humidity, light, sound and air quality they felt in the forest, with 1 being the lowest level and 10 the highest, capturing these experiential, subjective measurements using their own bodies. For example, for humidity the question prompts suggested that people felt their skin, dug a hole in the ground, and touched the soil and bark of the tree – prompts partly influenced by the artists' interest in notions of sensory geography.[28]

Visualising data, 'the aesthetics of ecology' and visitor responses

The four elements of *ACBT* – the networked environmental sensors, the projected visualisations of this live sensor data, the climate machine that scorched the recorded global CO_2 data, and the mobile technologies taken on a forest walk – enabled the artists to explore different ways of interpreting and presenting the data. Active Ingredient have previously stated in an account of the work that 'artists are triggered by the value of a piece of data to frame it in a way that suits their poetic process' which in turn encourages them 'to draw up new futures where we can situate ourselves at the centre of the data,' and in doing so to 'present another way into the aesthetics of ecology'.[29] The visualisations of the data captured in the forests were not truly scientific, despite their use of scientific data. Instead they were shaped by the artists' subjective and 'poetic' interpretations. The artists chose to place the sensors in specific trees that suited their aesthetic and personal relationships to the forest, and at times the data captured in the forest was not live (due to issues with the Internet signal deep in the forest). In these cases, data from another day was replayed through the visualisations that appeared in the gallery in order to maintain the 'suspension of disbelief'.

From studies of the visitors' engagement with the scientific data embedded across each element of the exhibition, it became clear that the details and accuracy of the data, as long as it was in an expected range, were less important than the ideas and emotions the artwork provoked.[30] One visitor stated:

> I think you were trying to make visual some scientific data that's usually inaccessible to normal people [. . .]. I look at figures and graphs and things and I just have a shut-down [. . .]. I do go on the visual impact first of all and start to investigate any ideas further from that and it is intriguing to see the imagery, [to] get in to the ideas through the imagery.

This response suggests that for some people, formal graphic displays of scientific data are less meaningful or accessible than when the data is mediated through more aesthetic, sometimes metaphoric forms. Likewise, too didactic an approach can also shut down rather than stimulate further engagement with environmental issues. As another visitor noted:

> there is an environmental point, there is a message [. . .] how the climate data has changed over the years, over the past 20 years, for the worst [. . .]. I certainly don't feel like that the message was the overriding [element], was rammed down my throat at all.

The gallery-based visualisations that had so surprised and delighted the artists when trialling the technology also worked powerfully on the audiences. The visualisation of the tropical forest in Brazil often had more movement, which was connected to higher decibel levels in the forest, and often appeared to show brighter colours and more light, while moments of intense 'wateriness' reflected the tropical rainfall. In contrast, the images generated by the deciduous forests in England were often smaller in scale, with slower movements and more muted colours (these trees were oaks, an ancient ash and a silver birch). A large number of the visitors said that they could sense the nature of each forest and the differences between the climates, bio-diversity and locations simply from watching the visualisations, expressing their feeling that the forests were revealing themselves through these technological, data driven mediations. Others remarked on the similarities, recognising a 'sort of commonality between forests [. . .] and the fact that their [. . .] ecosystems are generative natural systems'. The process of gaining insight was described by one visitor as being 'like when [you haven't] got [your] glasses on and everything's blurred and you realise that you're actually looking at trees in a different form'. Many visitors said that the visualisation representing the Brazilian tree looked like it was dancing. These comments are a testament to the power of the work to recalibrate ways of seeing, enabling visitors to experience the trees as vibrant, living beings, each forest distinctive in different ways, but brought conceptually together in a manner that helped imaginatively to bridge the great physical distance between the forest locations.

One of the key criticisms of modern society's use of interactive technologies is the way that they speed up our engagement with information and the world.[31] Heather Houser has levelled this critique insightfully and specifically at forms of 'infovis' – artistic visualisations that 'act as an interface between the individual and data sets that are too large, complicated, inaccessible, or tedious for him or her to comprehend' – suggesting that these visualisations typically rely upon speed for their impact.[32] In Houser's view, this element of rapidity tends to allow the infovis to 'slough off' any accompanying literature that might render more nuanced and more political understandings, constructing an audience of 'vessels for input'.[33] The aesthetic treatments of the data in *ACBT*, though they can be regarded as forms of infovis, saw the artists playing with the theme of temporality, both in relation to the speeds at which the information was delivered through the medium of the artworks and in terms of representing the multiple timescales at which environmental processes occur. Sometimes the data was revealed immediately, and at other times more slowly (at least relative to the length of a visit to the exhibition): for example, while the visualisations on the gallery screens relayed (mostly) live data, the guided walk asked visitors to take time to reflect in the forest, and the climate machine was scaled to slowly reveal 53 years of data over the course of the two-week exhibition. The effect of the latter was described by one visitor as 'allow[ing] you to condense time and see what is happening in the real world [. . .] across years [. . .] past or future' – an effect they found 'a bit scary' – and by another as 'a really good visual way to see the changes over time'.

The artists also thought deeply about the ways in which the materials used in the exhibition might draw out both physical and metaphorical resonances that could further augment the affective impact of the work. The construction of the climate machine in wood, and the way in which it scorched the circular graphs onto paper, which also produced a burning smell, proved particularly effective in this respect: one visitor commented that 'the elements of the wood are really key [. . .] there's a visual kind of rhyme; it also reminds you that you are within a forest'. The hanging paper discs created by the climate machine also appeared to be a crucial element of the work's impact. Another visitor described the paper as 'a very tactile medium' and recounted wanting to touch it 'because it's so circular [. . .] measured and in order' and enjoying 'seeing into the centre of the circles'; others suggested that the graphs reminded them of tree rings. Again, this element of the work could be seen to be extending the visitors' imaginations, enabling them to make connections between the visualisations of rising CO_2 levels and the materiality and long lives of trees. This was certainly an element that the climate scientist involved in the project found to be particularly effective, commenting: 'The fact that you made the CO_2 trend from Mauna Loa so evident in something people can relate to, I think was really exciting.' These material and metaphorical 'rhymes' – that reflected the 'poetic process' of the artists – added to the sense of a narrative emerging from the cumulative effect of the gallery elements, and encouraged visitors to create their own narratives as they walked. Some searched out the CO_2 levels for their year of birth and discussed why a particular year's circle might have increased more than the other years, or in the case of a group of children, re-interpreting the narrative through their own performative response: one of the gallery staff at Rufford Country Park observed how 'a group of young boys pretended to do a presentation of the data in front of their parents, saying what they had found out, pointing at the projection while the parents sat on the bench'. Their re-working of the data reflected an embodied learning experience, in which the exhibition, while avoiding overt didacticism, had proved to be both informative and meaningful for these children.

The walk in the actual forest was the culmination of the exhibition, focusing the affective and cognitive impacts of the gallery-based pieces back onto the physical environment and pushing the walkers to experience 'what data feels like in the forest'.[34] Visitors went on their walk with an already stimulated sense of the animacy of the trees, the distinctive qualities of the geographically separated forests, and an awareness of rising levels of CO_2 in the atmosphere. While a few participants felt that the artists' audio commentary disrupted their sensory experience of walking in the forest, particularly those who walked together in a group, responses from others suggested that the walking element as a whole augmented their experience of the forest, allowing them to notice elements that they did not normally perceive, such as moisture and temperature. They commented that this phenomenon 'encouraged [them] to open [their] eyes more, be more susceptible to the details around [them]'. The cumulative effect of the exhibition also helped visitors to bridge the imaginative gap between different areas of the world. One described how this induced 'the feeling that I haven't just been to Haldon today, I've experienced another forest, a very long way away'.

Further thoughts on ACBT

There were some issues involved in the creation and reception of *ACBT* that perhaps merit further attention in future projects. The artists felt that 'delivering an emotional engagement while remaining "true" to the authenticity of the scientific data is not a simple matter', though it is undoubtedly a crucial one.[35] Houser notes, in relation to infovis, that 'though artists may not themselves generate the data they use, their images must retain a degree of facticity at the same time as they engage audiences affectively, cognitively and ethically'.[36] How great that 'degree of facticity' should be is perhaps debatable. For the artists of *ACBT*, the notion that the data could not always be strictly 'live' (for example, when the Internet signal was poor in the forest), was not in itself a major issue as long as the data displayed remained within an expected range. But, for the climate scientist, this particular form of artistic licence compromised the accuracy of the information encapsulated in the project: he stated, 'from my personal view it's absolutely fundamental the data is live'.[37] There is a danger that if the scientific data is perceived as having been manipulated for artistic or 'poetic effect', it may lose credibility or even inadvertently play into the discourse of climate change denial.

Having said this, as Houser again argues, too certain a sense of 'transparency' in relation to data – the assumption that 'raw data' is 'inscrutable and affectively neutral' unless visualised – may shut down valuable processes of enquiry into the 'making' of that data itself, rendering its consumers passive, uncritical and distanced from its source.[38] As already noted, the manifestations of data throughout *ACBT* were deliberately ambiguous in multiple ways, from delivering artistic impressions rather than charts to burning what looked like scientific graphs onto paper. These were strategies designed to foster questions rather than give answers, and for the artists created an interesting tension around the authenticity of the data, particularly in reference to controversies around veracity and uncertainty in climate science and the spread of misinformation through digital communications. *ACBT* deliberately played with these issues of authenticity in order to stimulate questions around, and focus visitors' attention on, the 'live' experience of being in the forest. In this respect, the element of the walk in which participants were themselves asked to become sensors and enact the process of data capture was a valuable addition to the gallery displays: while the photographic element inevitably drove the visitors' attention towards their mobile phone screen every 10 seconds, it did so with the effect of getting them to re-appraise the environment through the lens of their own focused sensory perceptions. This experience appeared to situate the walkers 'within' the data, so that they could connect emotionally and viscerally to what the scientific data itself might reveal about the forest. There was some evidence for the success of this approach: as one visitor noted: 'In some ways the artist is trying to make people who come to see it make their own judgment, make their own interpretation of what they see.'

It is a moot point whether this openness to interpretation drove participants to consider their own implication and culpability in relation to the climate change data they encountered – another criticism Houser levels at infovis, which often fails to 'invite the viewer to see him- or herself as complicit in the real-world processes under investigation'.[39] However, for one visitor the lack of didacticism here was a positive aspect:

> I don't think you've touched on how our behaviour might affect climate change and I think in a way that's quite a good thing because people don't necessarily come and engage in these type of exhibitions and then be [. . .] 'guilted' into changing behaviour.

The inference here is perhaps that the immersive and affective elements might function more effectively to cause participants to reflect on their own behaviours than externally imposed feelings of responsibility. While not all of those participants who responded were positive about the exhibition or fully understanding of issues of climate change, several, as we have seen, attested to the ways in which the experience of *ACBT* expanded their opportunities to have conversations about climate change and develop an emotional engagement with and awareness of environmental questions.[40]

Conclusion

Both of the case studies described in this chapter – Active Ingredient's *Heartlands* and *ACBT*– enabled the participants to engage in a playful, exploratory, technologically mediated experience of walking through the 'outdoor' environment, the latter also providing the means to directly explore issues of environmental change. The artists' approaches encouraged responses to environmental issues that were embodied and questioning, fostering an emotional engagement with data rather than it taking on an explicitly persuasive or informative role. To return to the anxieties around technological and digital media cited at the beginning of the chapter, neither of these works invites us to withdraw into artificial environments as Mander might have it. Nor is the experience they offer 'indirect' in the terms Louv posits, but instead it is one that intrinsically involves a sensory dimension. Rather than removing us from the rhythms of nature, as Cowen fears, they bring to light our involvement in those rhythms, and indeed make those rhythms themselves more evident through their visualisations.

Perhaps it is not the use of digital technologies *per se* that is the problem here, but the way in which early generations of Internet technologies chained us to our desks and consoles and so encouraged our retreat from the wider environment outside. After all, our non-digital experiences of the environment are often mediated by technologies – we travel on paths, we wear shoes, we carry a map or even a walking stick. Perhaps what is significant about the digital technologies in *Heartlands* and *ACBT*, then, is that they are examples of digital technologies that bring us into, connect us to and remediate our experience of the landscape – they are our paths and shoes, or perhaps better, they serve to transform the perceptions through which we experience the natural world in a manner that may assist rather than detract from environmental and ecological awareness. Walking is central to both works – a kinetic act that brings home to the participants a valuably embodied sense of what data 'feels like' both in an urban landscape and among the trees of a beleaguered forest. As such, hybrid forms like *Heartlands* and *ACBT* that benefit from the complex interweaving of virtual and real environments offer the potential to contribute new cultural forms able to engage with the cognitive and imaginative challenges of environmental crisis and climate change.

Notes

1 Jerry Mander, *Four Arguments for the Elimination of Television* (New York: HarperCollins, 2002 [1978]), 51.
2 Richard Louv, *Last Child in the Woods: Saving Our Children from Nature-Deficit Disorder* (Chapel Hill, NC: Algonquin Books, 2008), 36.
3 Rob Cowen, *Common Ground* (London: Penguin Books, 2015), 12.
4 Sid Dobrin, "Introduction: Frontier 2.0", *Green Letters*, 18(3) (2014), 203.
5 Ibid.
6 Timothy Clark, *Ecocriticism on the Edge: The Anthropocene as a Threshold Concept* (London: Bloomsbury, 2015), 24.
7 Alenda Chang and John Parham, "Green Computer and Video Games: An Introduction", *Ecozon@*, 8(2) (2017), 1.
8 Alenda Chang, "Games as Environmental Texts", *Qui Parle*, 19(2) (Spring/Summer 2011), 57; John Parham, *Green Media and Popular Culture: An Introduction* (London: Palgrave, 2016), 205.
9 See Peter John Robinson and Ann Henderson-Sellers, *Contemporary Climatology* (London: Routledge, 1999), and Greg O'Hare et al., *Weather, Climate and Climate Change: Human Perspectives* (London: Routledge, 2013).
10 See www.i-am-ai.net; https://duncanspeakman.net; http://proboscis.org.uk/projects/2000-2005/urban-tapestries/; www.christiannold.com/#11; www.wapke.nl/wapke.php; https://sites.google.com/andreapolli.com/main/andrea-polli.
11 See Gabriella Giannachi, *Virtual Theatres: An Introduction* (London: Routledge, 2004).
12 For a discussion of sci-art, see Bergit Arends and Devina Thackara, *Experiment: Conversations in Art and Science* (London: Wellcome Trust, 2003). For interactive art, see Stephen Wilson, *Information Arts: Intersections of Art, Science, and Technology* (Cambridge, MA: MIT Press, 2002).
13 For discussion of *Uncle Roy*, see Martin Flintham et al., "Uncle Roy All Around You: Mixing Games and Theatre on the City Streets", in *DiGRA '03: Proceedings of the 2003 DiGRA International Conference: Level Up* (Tampere, Finland: DiGRA, 2003); for *Pokémon GO*, see Janne Paavilainen et al., "The Pokémon GO Experience: A Location-based Augmented Reality Mobile Game Goes Mainstream", in *Proceedings of the 2017 CHI Conference on Human Factors in Computing Systems* (New York: ACM, 2017), 2493–2498; for the argument that future iterations of the game could increase awareness of, and interaction with, real-world nature, see Leejiah, J. Dorward et al., "Pokémon Go: Benefits, Costs and Lessons for the Conservation Movement", *Conservation Letters*, 10(1) (2016), 160–165.
14 Stephanie Posthumus and Stéfan Sinclair, "Reading Environment(s): Digital Humanities Meets Ecocriticism", *Green Letters: Studies in Ecocriticism*, 18(3) (2014), 254.
15 Ibid., 256.
16 For further discussion of the 'open play' elements of *Heartlands*, see Stephen Boyd Davis et al., "'Ere Be Dragons: Heartfelt Gaming", *Digital Creativity*, 17(3) (2006), 157–162.
17 For 'ludic design', see William Gaver et al., "Cultural Probes and the Value of Uncertainty", *Interactions*, 11(5) (2004), 53–56.
18 For 'rhetorical play', see Paul Coulton et al., "Designing Data Driven Persuasive Games to Address Wicked Problems Such as Climate Change", in *Proceedings of the 18th International Academic MindTrek Conference: Media Business, Management, Content & Services* (New York: ACM, 2014), 185–191.
19 Gordon Calleja, *In-game: From Immersion to Incorporation* (Cambridge, MA: MIT Press, 2011), 3.

20 Ibid., 4.
21 Dobrin, "Introduction: Frontier 2.0", 205.
22 Eugénie Shinkle, "Corporealis Ergo Sum: Affective Response in Digital Games", in Nate Garrelts (ed.), *Digital Gameplay: Essays on the Nexus of Game and Gamer* (Jefferson, NC: McFarland, 2005), 33.
23 Rachel Jacobs et al., "A Conversation Between Trees: What Data Feels Like in the Forest", in *CHI'13: Proceedings of the SIGCHI Conference on Human Factors in Computing Systems* (New York: SIGCHI, 2013).
24 See www.sosma.org.br/nossa-causa/a-mata-atlantica/.
25 See http://sherwoodforest.org.uk/.
26 The workshops involved secondary school children capturing scientific data from their local forest and using Internet technologies to share information with the children in the country on the other side of the world. For a more detailed account see Rachel Jacobs and Silvia Leal, "Digital Participation through Artistic Interventions", in Michael Dezuanni et al. (eds), *Digital Participation through Social Living Labs* (Cambridge, UK: Chandos Publishing, 2017), 37–54.
27 Mauna Loa Series, trends in CO_2, www.esrl.noaa.gov/gmd/ccgg/trends/.
28 In which 'the sensuous – the experience of the senses – is the ground base on which a wider geographical understanding can be constructed'; Paul Rodaway, *Sensuous Geographies: Body, Sense and Place* (London: Routledge, 2002), 3.
29 Steven Rimmer (ed.), *Paralelo – Unfolding Narratives: In Art, Technology and Environment* (São Paulo, Brazil: MIS and Imprensaoficial, 2009), https://issuu.com/virtueelplatform/docs/qaf.
30 The artists surveyed the audience perspective through conducting 20 semi-structured interviews that took place immediately after the experience, and through feedback questionnaires that were also made available to all visitors.
31 See, for example, Nicholas Gane, "Speed Up or Slow Down? Social Theory in the Information Age", *Information, Communication and Society*, 9(1) (2006), 20–38.
32 Heather Houser, "The Aesthetics of Environmental Visualizations: More than Information Ecstasy?", *Public Culture*, 26(2) (2014), 319.
33 Ibid., 326–328 and 334.
34 Jacobs et al., "A Conversation Between Trees".
35 Ibid.
36 Houser, "The Aesthetics of Environmental Visualizations", 320.
37 Jacobs et al., "A Conversation Between Trees".
38 Houser, "The Aesthetics of Environmental Visualizations",
39 Ibid.
40 For a more detailed and substantial account of audience response, see Jacobs et al., "A Conversation Between Trees". For example, one visitor wrote in the questionnaire: 'as soon as I walked in, it just, I couldn't see the reasoning behind it, it did nothing for me visually . . . I couldn't see what it was all about.'

Works cited

Arends, Bergit and Devina Thackara. *Experiment: Conversations in Art and Science.* London: Wellcome Trust, 2003.
Calleja, Gordon. *In-game: From Immersion to Incorporation.* Cambridge, MA: MIT Press, 2011.
Chang, Alenda. "Games as Environmental Texts". *Qui Parle*, 19(2) (Spring/Summer 2011): 57–84.
Chang, Alenda and John Parham. "Green Computer and Video Games: An Introduction". *Ecozon@*, 8(2) (2017): 1–17.

Clark, Timothy. *Ecocriticism on the Edge: The Anthropocene as a Threshold Concept.* London: Bloomsbury, 2015.

Coulton, Paul, Rachel Jacobs, Dan Burnett, Adrian Gradinar, Matt Watkins, and Candice Howarth. "Designing Data Driven Persuasive Games to Address Wicked Problems Such as Climate Change". In *Proceedings of the 18th International Academic MindTrek Conference: Media Business, Management, Content and Services*, pp. 185–191. New York: ACM, 2014.

Cowen, Rob. *Common Ground.* London: Penguin Books, 2015.

Davis, Stephen Boyd, Magnus Moar, Rachel Jacobs, Matt Watkins, Chris Riddoch, and Karl Cooke. "'Ere Be Dragons: Heartfelt Gaming". *Digital Creativity*, 17(3) (2006): 157–162.

Dobrin, Sid. "Introduction: Frontier 2.0". *Green Letters: Studies in Ecocriticism*, 18(3) (November 2014): 203–208.

Dorward, Leejiah J., John C. Mittermeier, Chris Sandbrook, and Fiona Spooner. "Pokémon Go: Benefits, Costs, and Lessons for the Conservation Movement". *Conservation Letters*, 10(1) (January/February 2017): 160–165.

Flintham, Martin, Rob Anastasi, Steve Benford, Adam Drozd, James Mathrick, Duncan Rowland, Amanda Oldroyd et al. "Uncle Roy All Around You: Mixing Games and Theatre on the City Streets". In *DiGRA '03: Proceedings of the 2003 DiGRA International Conference: Level Up.* Tampere, Finland: DiGRA, 2003.

Gane, Nicholas. "Speed Up or Slow Down? Social Theory in the Information Age". *Information, Communication and Society*, 9(1) (2006): 20–38.

Gaver, William W., Andrew Boucher, Sarah Pennington, and Brendan Walker. "Cultural Probes and the Value of Uncertainty". *Interactions*, 11(5) (2004): 53–56.

Giannachi, Gabriella. *Virtual Theatres: An Introduction.* London: Routledge, 2004.

Houser, Heather. "The Aesthetics of Environmental Visualizations: More than Information Ecstacy?". *Public Culture*, 26(2) (2014): 319–337.

Jacobs, Rachel and Silvia Leal. "Digital Participation through Artistic Interventions". In Michael Dezuanni, Marcus Foth, Kerry Mallan and Hilary Hughes (eds), *Digital Participation through Social Living Labs*, pp. 37–54. Cambridge, UK: Chandos Publishing, 2017.

Jacobs, Rachel, Steve Benford, Mark Selby, Mike Golembewski, Dominic Price, and Gabriella Giannachi. "A Conversation Between Trees: What Data Feels Like in the Forest". In *CHI'13: Proceedings of the SIGCHI Conference on Human Factors in Computing Systems.* New York: SIGCHI, 2013.

Louv, Richard. *Last Child in the Woods: Saving Our Children from Nature-Deficit Disorder.* Chapel Hill, NC: Algonquin Books, 2008.

Mander, Jerry. *Four Arguments for the Elimination of Television.* New York: HarperCollins, 2002 [1978].

O'Hare, Greg, John Sweeney, and Rob Wilby. *Weather, Climate and Climate Change: Human Perspectives.* London: Routledge, 2013.

Paavilainen, Janne, Hannu Korhonen, Kati Alha, Jaakko Stenros, Elina Koskinen, and Frans Mayra. "The Pokémon GO Experience: A Location-based Augmented Reality Mobile Game Goes Mainstream". In *Proceedings of the 2017 CHI Conference on Human Factors in Computing Systems*, pp. 2493–2498. New York: ACM, 2017.

Parham, John. *Green Media and Popular Culture: An Introduction.* London: Palgrave, 2016.

Posthumus, Stephanie and Stéfan Sinclair. "Reading Environment(s): Digital Humanities Meets Ecocriticism". *Green Letters: Studies in Ecocriticism*, 18(3): 254–273.

Rimmer, Steven (ed.). *Paralelo – Unfolding Narratives: In Art, Technology and Environment*. São Paulo, Brazil: MIS and Imprensaoficial, 2009, https://issuu.com/virtueelplatform/docs/qaf.

Robinson, Peter John and Ann Henderson-Sellers. *Contemporary Climatology*. London: Routledge, 1999.

Rodaway, Paul. *Sensuous Geographies: Body, Sense and Place*. London: Routledge, 2002.

Shinkle, Eugénie. "Corporealis Ergo Sum: Affective Response in Digital Games". In Nate Garrelts (ed.), *Digital Gameplay: Essays on the Nexus of Game and Gamer*, pp. 21–33. Jefferson, NC: McFarland, 2005.

Wilson, Stephen. *Information Arts: Intersections of Art, Science, and Technology*. Cambridge, MA: MIT Press, 2002.

13 The crisis in psychogeographical walking

From paranoia to diversity, ecology and salvage

Phil Smith

In 1987, Stephen Poliakoff's movie *Hidden City* was released, and has rarely been seen since. It received very limited exposure on TV, and is not presently (2018) available on DVD. It is perhaps appropriate that such an esoteric work, with its detailed double-layering – both geographical and informational – should so precisely and unintentionally reflect the complexities of a hinge point for psychogeography in the UK, marking the beginning of a declining influence for a particular London-based version. In this chapter, I will attempt to sketch out how a confident, if marginal, metropolitan psychogeographical discourse has become more dispersed, disoriented and diversified, shifting between urban streets and countryside, via edgelands, as a result of multiple forces including internal contradictions, climate change, academic critique, activism and practical feminism.

In the 1980s and 1990s, Manchester, Nottingham, Glasgow and Newcastle all had small psychogeographical associations, their activities documented in *Transgressions*, a Newcastle-based journal edited by Alistair Bonnett. Nevertheless, most other accounts, such as Merlin Coverley's widely read *Psychogeography* (2006), represent UK-based psychogeography as a metropolitan avant-garde literary and art (or anti-art) practice with an occult tinge. They focus on London authors like Iain Sinclair and Will Self, on the situationist fringes of punk, nodding to magazines/groups like King Mob and Vague and micro-collaborations like Spontaneous Combustion, The Pleasure Tendency, Hapt, BM Chronos, and Here and Now,[1] Patrick Keiller's films, and the arch misrepresentations of the London Psychogeographical Association (a *ludibrium*: publications of fable-documentations intended to provoke others to realise their fictions for real).

The London vividly portrayed in *Hidden City*, with its tunnels, bunkers, rubbish dumps, incinerators, abandoned medical facilities and crumbling archives, and its evidence of covert establishment projects and abuses, is wholly consistent with the prevailing default-paranoia of urban-centric occult-psychogeographical method dominant in the 1980s, with an assumption of profound significance (hidden supernatural force or state activity) in the everyday patterns of the city. Even more apposite to this essay is how the movie depicts this London as one that is disappearing, eluding attempts at intervention, and as more hospitable to contemplation than engagement.

The paranoid pleasures of *Hidden City*'s storyline (scraps of footage tacked onto Public Information films reassembled to reveal an illegal government project) extinguish any erotic spark between its main characters, a statistician and a film editor. Like the sound artist heroine of Neil Jordan's thriller *The Brave One* (2007), these characters are driven by psychogeography as much as psychology. Yet the sphinx-like melancholic urban terrain, the primary object of their desire, is being snuffed out. Semi-covert storehouses are emptied, piles of celluloid information are transferred to VHS tape (prefiguring its eventual evaporation into digital form), cans of film thrown into incinerators. The mysterious voids of the city are briefly exposed to public view just prior to their swallowing up in the aggressive redevelopment of central London. This marks the disappearance of spaces crucial to a subversive re-mapping of the city by political psychogeographers which recorded such voids as the base elements of a "'non-city' or 'urban chaos'. . . spaces that inhabit the city in a nomadic way . . . difficult to control . . . urban amnesias . . . [ready] to be filled with meanings".[2]

Many of Poliakoff's shooting locations no longer exist in any way recognisable from the film. The paranoid well-spring of the city – the possibility of access by exploratory means to a city's real, but secret meaning – crucial to the literary product of UK psychogeography, marked at its beginnings by the publication of Iain Sinclair's *Lud Heat* in 1975, vanishes before the viewer's eyes.

By the end of *Hidden City*, a more reparative spirit (healing, but retaining difference, as in Deleuze and Guattari's "plane of consistency") is at work.[3] The reconstructed footage renders a coherent narrative of government malfeasance. Yet the main characters do not discuss sharing this information publicly; instead, they vow to continue their own privately mutual exploration. Unlike the familiar paranoid-style narrative of hunch, research, justification and, finally, intervention (as in, say, Alan J. Pakula's *All the President's Men* [1976]), in *Hidden City* the protagonists retain for themselves the recovered surplus of pleasure from their exploration and assemblage of fragments, rather than share the outcomes for a public good.

Such pleasure has a value in itself, without the need for an end product, whether activist or literary. Breaking from a default paranoid style, the outcome consists in the rolling out of further performativities of exploration, reparation and assemblage. This models a change of direction for UK psychogeography during the years either side of the millennium, characterised partly by a series of shifts; by a move towards live art and performance and away from literary production; by a popularisation and democratisation through activity rather than consumption; by an output more likely to consist of practical and accessible handbooks than the "self-hating commodity"[4] of post-Dada deconstructed art; by a radical expansion in the kinds of space where psychogeography is practised.

The challenge to the old psychogeography

Around the turn of the millennium, the old psychogeography of small low-profile groups and mainstream literary practitioners was caught by the full force of social change. A decline in the global fortunes of the Left had already undermined many of the smaller psychogeographical associations. The competitive attrition of the literary and art "worlds" did nothing to connect the more well-known and productive of the psychogeographically inclined artists and writers to the growing numbers of new, less demonstrative and differently oriented, radical walkers, many of whom communicated via social media rather than print or gallery. This was exacerbated when leading figures denied any connection to "psychogeography" (Patrick Keiller, Peter Ackroyd) or expressed derisive animosity, ironic or otherwise, to what Iain Sinclair called "this whole walking fetish. Now everywhere you go, you find people doing strange conceptual walks, taking photographs of road signs and trying to get arrested in the car park of IKEA."[5]

Where works by Iain Sinclair, like *Lights Out for the Territory* (1997), were often cited as inspirational for radical walkers, his later works were cited less often (and sometimes with hostility). Sinclair and Andrew Kotting's 2012 *Swandown* project, for which well-known figures from live art, radical comedy and psychogeography piloted a swan-shaped pedalo from Hastings beach to Hackney, suggested this branch of psychogeography had lost its way in whimsical backwaters: "a jokey stunt . . . a vanity project".[6] The works of Sinclair, Will Self, Alan Moore and more conventional writers like Robert Macfarlane continued to serve as gateways to radical walking, but the gap between the public figures (whose numbers and identities were unchanging) and a growing grassroots movement of walkers whose numbers grew, but whose cultural capital remained almost non-existent, widened. Although, in 2010 the Walking Institute of Deveron Projects at Huntly, Aberdeenshire could organise for Hamish Fulton to create two slow walks with the general public as part of his *21 Days in the Cairngorms*, there has been little equivalent collaboration between an older generation of psychogeographers and the new movement of walkers. The outstanding exception being Will Self's psychogeography module at Brunel University.[7]

At the same time, the published literature on the origins and earliest practices of psychogeography has increased in quantity and quality. This includes McKenzie Wark's trilogy (2008, 2011 and 2013) with key ideas and practices contextualised for the first time (for English readers, at least); Jean-Michel Mension's autobiographical account (2002) of the Parisian Situationist International (SI); and *Expect Anything, Fear Nothing* (Rasmussen & Jakobsen, 2011), which illuminates the situationists in Scandinavia. Now, the contemporary walker's understanding of psychogeography is as likely to be influenced by accounts of (or even from) its original practitioners in 1950s Paris rather than relying on versions of them defined by more recent re-inventors. Significantly, this has provoked very little in the way of a return to an "authentic" *dérive*; instead, increased access to the historical narrative has added an extra dimension, and authority, to the multiplicity of styles, practices and intentions characterising what Tina Richardson calls "the new psychogeography . . . [as] first and foremost, one of heterogeneity . . . not exclusive, snobbish or protectionist".[8]

The more dispersive and de-materialised quality of the new psychogeography (informed by tendencies in performance, conceptual art summarised by Lucy Lippard as the "dematerialisation of the art object"[9] and the emergence of social media) has challenged the reliance of the older psychogeography upon a particular urban architecture. Through old buildings and street plans, Sinclair, Ackroyd and Moore had channelled an urban equivalent of "earth mysteries"; at the same time, through (mostly) modernist literary devices, they had mapped and brandished an ancient rottenness at the heart of the capital's neo-liberal transformation. For them, arcane patterns such as those based on the churches of sinister (possibly satanic) designers had come to represent a fundamental explanation for the modern city and its corruption; just as for John Michell (1973) and others in the 1960s the lines of the "old straight track" discerned by Alfred Watkins (1925/1978) became a spiritual map of energy maintaining a largely hidden, but more essential, rural Britain.

Post-industrial redevelopment has increasingly secured, sanitised and monetised many of the sclerotic or ruined metropolitan spaces lauded and mapped by the older psychogeography. At the same time, an unintended result of early online postings by "urban-explorers" or "place-hackers",[10] who often shared a wonder and respect for the city's hidden spaces with psychogeographers, was the pioneering of party or rave sites that often left sublime spaces trashed. Immersive and site specific theatre performances in unusual, redundant or derelict sites were often precursors to demolition or development, and subject to an economy of unique experience and immersion. Many of the last resorts for "aura" in the city were popularised or neutralised – from the sanitisation of sleazy fleapits as arthouse cinemas to the redevelopment of redundant industrial areas – by processes (now on a grand scale) described by Walter Benjamin as: "the mark of a perception whose 'sense of the universal equality of things' has increased to such a degree that it extracts it even from a unique object by means of reproduction".[11] Popularisation and democratisation had not led automatically to multiplicity, but often stumbled into a commodification of space. Digitisation made all data potentially phantasmagoric; occult narratives around Nicholas Hawksmoor or the "Jack the Ripper" crimes were increasingly hard to distinguish from an expanding jumble of online conspiracy theory and "fake news".

The inviting metropolitan spaces of Asgar Jorn and Guy Debord's *Naked City* maps, designed in 1957 to identify urban oases free of the invasive media and image-based Spectacle's most intense activity, were, just as much as the soft places of occult psychogeography where the ancients lie just below the pavement, invaded by hand-held devices, recording, distributing and de-sacralising their everyday treasures. Little has been able to resist such representations; "secret" in relation to space has become a marketing term. The situationists' vision of a "New Babylon", a city of endless mobility, was realised, but only in relation to the movement of representation and information, while the human on the street had become an instrument: "the sexual organs of money, the genitalia of capital . . . the sexual apparatus of machines".[12]

Within the narrow parameters of radical walking, the male-privileged "ancient" and anti-spectacular space of literary and occult psychogeography has been increasingly democratised by a more activist and feminist wave of psychogeographers who were often critical of the "priestly class" of psychogeography's male literary elite. Where the walking arts of the 1960s through to the 1990s had been predominantly male, often solo and epic, there is now an explosion of women's participation in psychogeographical space (which mainstream media have continued to ignore, though Jo Norcup's *'Er Outdoors* programmes on Resonance FM [2017] have gone a little way to redress this). So Lucy Furlong's *Amniotic City* (2011) might map an area similar to that of the "Jack the Ripper" tours in London (a narrative of abiding interest to older psychogeographers; see Alan Moore and Eddie Campbell's *From Hell* [1999]), but shuns the misogynist characterisation in a 1954 issue of the SI's magazine *Potlach* of the murders as "probably psychogeographical in love" (the "magic geography" of London carved in female flesh). Instead, Furlong's work offers choices to the walker around emotion, desire, body and female agency in multi-layered discourses, liberating into action, rather than cryptic revelations. Her poem-map is open to re-enactment and recital.

Furlong and others pose an analogue challenge to psychogeography's paranoid reading of space – a default critical state that has been lambasted by Eve Kosofsky Sedgwick as "less diagnosis than a prescription"[13] – just as psychogeography is being destabilised by digitisation and its dialectic is diverted into repetitive syntheses. Psychogeography's key tactics of montage and *détournement* have been thoroughly commodified; commercial video mash-ups, sonic sampling and online memes – represented in *Hidden City* as disco wallpaper and porn video remixes for cocaine parties – that were once the preserve of a cultural avant-garde, are now standard currencies of exchange via small hand-held devices for most of the younger population. At the same time, there is no compensatory growth in a reparatory popular culture; instead, neo-liberal "shock" capitalism morphs towards a digitally fuelled authoritarianism.

Walking's new movement and its sites

The new ambulant artists organise differently to their predecessors; rather than in small groups committed to political-psychogeographical ends, the newer walkers more often participate in informal meshworks such as the Walking Artists Network or events like the annual *Fourth World Congress of Psychogeography*. Together these constitute a participation of (at least) hundreds of walkers in the UK and, on a global scale, probably thousands, most of whom have at least heard of psychogeography and many of whom are deeply influenced by it. More importantly, though, they have also heard of each other, connecting through a growing number of actions, workshops, projects, seminars and festivals.

From discrete products like novels and films, and punk-ish publications, there is now a much greater diversity of forms: painting, mapping, installations, sound walks, led, guided and mis-guided walks, blogs, relational arts, photography, community and spatial-political interventions, performances, live streaming and therapeutic or contemplative walking. The places have also changed. Whereas psychogeography was once almost exclusively urban – the situationists mocking the Surrealists' rural *dérive*: "open country is naturally depressing and the interventions of chance are poorer than anywhere else"[14] – psychogeographical wandering is now likely to include rural or edgeland spaces; practices range from Alison Lloyd's solo contouring of hills (occasionally transferring skills she has learned on mountains to cities) to Louise Wilson's ambulatory theatrical constructs that span valleys and hillsides and for which audiences walk many miles; from walks like those of Still Walking's beneath Birmingham to Richard White's retracing and memorialising of death marches in displaced rural settings.

The plethora of aesthetic methods now deployed represent a considerable resource for psychogeographical practice, which was hamstrung in the past by the flip-flopping of the Situationist International and its successors between modernist experiment and anti-art iconoclasm. There has been a rediscovery of psychogeography's inherent resistant qualities, partly by a super-connective, multiplicitous, fluidly-gendered, "drift-for-drift's-sake" or "situational-*dérive*"[15] that seeks to transform space through the very act of walking itself; less an instrumental part of the situationist strategy, more a political act in itself.

Sustaining this multiplicity is the influence of general, rarely methodically articulated, ideas around ecological reparation. These included Thierry Bardini's proposal for "junk", "not waste [but] . . . all kinds of stuff that grows in stacks and patiently waits for renewed use",[16] and Evan Calder Williams's "salvagepunk", which opposed the morbid nostalgia of "steampunk" and offered an anti-technocratic alternative: "a kicking back against those visions of the rational management of life and death, of the industrial subcurrents hidden behind state care and humanitarian interventions".[17]

Crucial for entangling these ideas in psychogeography is the idea of "edgelands" introduced by Marion Shoard (2002) as "the only theatre in which the real desires of real people can be expressed".[18] This space between central urban and deep open country, comprised of what Robert Macfarlane called "jittery, jumbled, broken ground: brownfield sites and utilities infrastructure, crackling substations and pallet depots, transit hubs and sewage farms, scrub forests and sluggish canals" and popularised by Paul Farley and Michael Symmons Roberts in *Edgelands* (2011), has opened up a hinterland or portal, a segue between rural and urban, breaking down their separation and encouraging an ecological thinking that is not simply about the wild or the rural.[19] The term's valorising of wasted and abject spaces has helped to dispel any remaining elements of that "Merrie England" nostalgia which, even in apparently radical forms "organised around themes of communism, occultism and preservationism",[20] infected some earlier psychogeography with conservative tendencies. Now, Lucy Furlong can produce a work like *Over the Fields* (2015) for the greenbelt on the border of Surrey with Greater London without compromising the principles of her urban *Amniotic City*.

With the passing of modernism, the insistence on the city as site is less urgent. Urban psychogeography has been transformed through phenomenology and performativity – key themes in postmodernist and post-structuralist thinking. Though some psychogeographers continue to cite Fortean anomalies or an archaeology of the intuited past (despite the rearguard hyper-materialist efforts of Steve Hanson and Mark Rainey's Materialist Psychogeographical Affiliation), where such occult features appear – as in work by Lucy Furlong, Nick Papadimitriou (2012) or Gareth Rees (2013) – they are strands entangled with sexual politics, poetic-autobiography and the resilience of a returning organic world. Where the non-human is important, say in the practice of a walking artist like Helen Billinghurst, whose work as a painter is informed by her repeated walking of mostly rural routes between Devon and Cambridgeshire, collecting and using materials like chalk and red sandstone, it is more likely to be influenced by Jane Bennett's vibrant materialism or Donna Haraway's Cthulucene than Arthur Machen's neo-romanticism.

Embracing the flooding of land as a revival of old oceans, the beginnings of re-wilding and the transformation of the planet by climate change as the beginnings of a new ecology, many new psychogeographers are acknowledging how ecology and mobility are inter-linked – that in the same way as the empire has "come home" to Western cities, with the arrival of refugees from both its past and its margins, industrial capitalism's ecology is also coming home. Unexpected fauna appear: from ring-necked parakeets in London parks to herring gulls driven inland by the depletion of herring in the seas, organic life is finding new places for itself in the ruin and underfunding of public urban space. The progress of invasive flora, the eroding of infrastructure, agentive materials poisoning rivers, surfaces collapsing under the feet of pedestrians and the sun's reflections in signature buildings melting expensive sports cars are all entangled with the idea of the city as "a state of mind . . . organized attitudes and sentiments".[21] That connectivity enables radical walkers to first celebrate and then strategically redeploy such invasions, erosions and hybridisations in a "multiplicity of patterns and histories, locating, through a symbolist language, those tipping points and zones of satellite capture, where small cultural interventions can still destabilise existing orbits of meaning, creating fluid stages ('situations') for re-making living".[22] So, for example, Helen Billinghurst's paintings for her *Crossing England* exhibition (Ariel Centre, Totnes, 2016) reflect on her observing of the incursions of quarrying and hypermodernity onto greenbelt land, the resilience of stories in the landscape and the replacement of animals by their representations. Billinghurst then takes the lessons she has learned in her studio practice, both walking in her studio and working with found materials and objects, back onto the paths and lanes as part of a renewed walking practice.

The shifting of species across space has resonance both for ambulation and for the nomadic travel of meanings across categories. The geographer Steve Pile has argued that "the city – in its very use of natural elements, in its wondrous physicality – creates a magical environment". Alert to such enchantment and more alive now to the "alien" agency of materials and organisms – how "stuff at a distance, at a remove, beyond us, not even human, can exert such powerful effects and *affects* on our bodies, souls, and world"[23] – contemporary walkers are less sympathetic to conservation or the defence of "indigenous" species. In a post-colonialist context, they are prepared to champion invasions of buddleia, Himalayan balsam and Spanish bluebells as no different to the arrival of oak trees in what was to become Southern England after the last ice age (after the arrivals of hazel and lime).

Unlike earlier psychogeographers with absolute referents (supernatural or political), contemporary walkers are more hyper-empirical and more opportunistic; the most influential line of thinking in psychogeography is the rhizomatic philosophy of Gilles Deleuze and Felix Guattari. Generating assemblages from the "AND . . . AND . . . AND"[24] of its free-ranging scholarship, their nomadic thinking cuts across the striations of categorising and "passes between things, between points . . . the multiplicity it constitutes is no longer subordinated to the One, but takes on a consistency of its own".[25] In tune with this, contemporary psychogeographical outputs are often assemblages that arrive by eccentricities, then develop across their own plane of consistency, "enabl[ing] the formation of heterogeneity-preserving emergent structures".[26] So, for example, in the recording contexts and musical ambiences of the work of composer Drew Mullholland (Mount Vernon Arts Lab), ancient sites, nuclear bunkers and eerie movies are woven together without hierarchical ordering, the listeners left to make their own emotional judgements about the relative importance of the music's various atmospheres.

The principles of psychogeography's "study of the precise laws and specific effects of the geographical environment, whether consciously organized or not, on the emotions and behaviour of individuals"[27] are modest and subjective. By its exploration of what is familiar but not known, it favours by-passing appropriation and "using 'fragments' as starting points . . . tracking 'things' through time and space".[28] Given these traits, psychogeographers unsurprisingly seem to favour a more empirical, "chaotic" but constructive and reparative ecologism – so, for example, Vanessa Daws's "psychoswimography" draws upon Steve Mentz's "shipwreck modernity" which refutes ideas of historical ruptures in favour of composture[29] – rather than more global, holistic or apocalyptic forms. Where a first wave of urban psychogeographers often entertained a contra-natural Ballardian attraction to concrete-based modernist melancholy, the new wave looks for more layers in the city and beyond. So, for example, by ambulatory exploration rather than assumptions drawn from rushed media narratives, a city like Milton Keynes, a byword for gridded concrete homogeneity, turns out to be a "forest city" (with more trees per acre than in the surrounding countryside) in which wanderers are always likely to drop upon a brick obelisk, a grassy Saxon meeting mound or a Triceratops in Spider-Man colours.[30]

The determination of radical walkers to be immersed, embodied and phenomenological has led them to voids in the remains of modernism, to places where green is returning. While there are the beginnings of a re-wilding movement in the UK in pockets like those on the Knepp Estate or on the Knoydart peninsula, contemporary walkers are more likely to identify with micro-rewilding sites – in the spirit of guerrilla gardening – at the edges of industrial estates or on the fringes of car parks, taking literally Walter Benjamin's description of "the *flâneur* who goes botanizing on the asphalt".[31]

New affects, new challenges

The default dominance of the solo white male literary walker has been challenged by numerous female, ecological and other anti-normative walking presences, like that of Nando Messias's *The Sissy's Progress* (2015–2016), a processional exorcism of a homophobic attack, reclaiming the effeminacy that was cause for assault in the eyes of his attackers, or Rosana Cade's *Walking: Holding* (2011–2016) in which an "audience member" walks and holds hands with people of different ages, races, genders, sexualities and social backgrounds. The activities of walking groups, like Dee Heddon and Misha Meyer's *Walking Library* (2012 and ongoing), in which groups of walkers take books on walks with readings and borrowings, or the Loiterers Resistance Movement in Manchester convened by Morag Rose (2006 and ongoing), promote conviviality without the oppressive trappings of identifiable milieus.

These developments have changed the subjective plane of radical walking. Once the site of confident literary production, it is now a more contested ground, across which some in walking's new movement are deploying ultraromantic "fusion" – out-Romanticking the nature walkers – in a kind of neo-pilgrimage, seeking for (and cultivating the protection of) an embodied inner life, free from the invasive attentions of digital algorithms seeking personal information via hand-held devices to sell to marketing organisations, and using the weakening of the urban/rural divide to that end. Rather than with a commanding presence, contemporary psychogeographers walk less confidently and more questioningly about their purpose, wondering how future psychogeographers will walk around rising waters or on terrain where humans are no longer top predators.

Responding to ecological change is not restricted to observation. For her *Crossed Paths* project (2017), Miranda Whall has been dressing in wetsuit, cameras and sheep's fleece to crawl over five and a half miles of

Welsh uplands, "attempting to go deeply into a place, by briefly being in it like something else".[32] She draws on other performances by live artists and experimentalists like Sacha Dench, who became human/swan, Thomas Thwaites, who deployed an artificial stomach to live as a goat, and Charles Foster, who experimented with being badger, fox, red deer, otter and swift.[33]

Vanessa Daws, who has pioneered the idea of psychoswimography as an open-water version of radical walking, addresses the increasing presence of jellyfish in the seas around Britain and Ireland as part of "jellyfish supera-bundances [that] are a symptom that something is seriously wrong with the oceans".[34] Stacy Alaimo, participating in a group swim in 2014 organised for the *BABEL* conference at Santa Barbara (California) by Daws, remarked that "I won't say the event 'elevated' swimming to an art . . . [but it] allows us to hover in other ways of being that are, perhaps, less separate from the substances of the world".[35] This situates the body in psychogeography, land or sea-based, as paradoxically hovering and immersed, a contradictory presence that is both everyday and anomalous.

These expansions and diversifications of radical walking can, paradoxically, throw up unexpected normalisations. In a *Huck* article entitled "How Walking Became a Radical Act of Defiance", Dawn Foster criticises a "tendency to over-romanticise walking", a mistake "usually the preserve of a certain kind of middle-aged man, who valorises while only vaguely understanding Psychogeography". She cites Hannah Rose Woods's plea: "Bros of academia: sometimes it's not psychogeography. You are simply going out for a walk."[36] Even well-founded bubble-popping requires some care and contextualisation. For many walkers, misogyny, racism and other discriminations *do* mean that "simply going out for a walk" is an act of defiance. Garnette Cadogan has written of how "walking while black restricts the experience of walking" and of how he was "unable to join the New York *flâneurs* I had read about".[37]

At the same time, not every walk is resistant. The effort of making a *dérive* retains its strategic validity for resisting the policing (both subtle and aggressive) of the pedestrian passage by the *dérive*'s sensitisation to atmospheres, taking pleasure in details, combating the Spectacle's malevolent gazes and holding off the dissolution of thing-power and invasions by algorithms. If there is always a hint of resistance in the anachronism of walking, then, equally, there are also individuals and organisations ready to monetise alternative walking practices. More importantly, the dominance of health recreational walking (often bookended by car rides) almost entirely swamps resistant walking practices in the more general discourses around walking.

Econclusion

In a recent blog, the chronicler of "folk horror" Adam Scovell recounts a solo "drift" around the resort of New Brighton on Merseyside (2016), describing how it has been cleaned up, anonymised and emptied of people, in distinct contrast to the heaving resort he remembers visiting as a child: a place where working-class people – to the disgust of sections of the media – sat among piles of rubbish and thoroughly enjoyed themselves. Today, the workers have been hygienically liberated from their pleasure . . ..

Scovell's blog is an invitation to return to the earlier disturbance, to what can be salvaged, to a human re-wilding of sanitised spaces, to pleasures still available in what society throws off. His account of the seaside resort today dovetails with the 1980s metropolis as told by Poliakoff in *Hidden City*; in the first, the agents have disappeared; in the second, the agents discover that it is the place that is disappearing. The new walking movement's acknowledgement of non-human agents (its retreat from supernatural agency has partly been an embrace of natural agency) rescues the materiality of the terrain for itself, but it has yet to find an accessible and popular form to connect itself and such sites with those missing human agents described by Scovell. The democratisation of radical walking has been marginal. Aware of many of its shortcomings, it still performs its own exclusions. Meanwhile, the model for mass ambulatory participation in the UK remains rambling and leisure walking, with its jumbling of conservative and radical, appropriative and ecological elements, often antagonistically aligned even within its own organisations;[38] despite the potential audience for radical ideas about ambulation among leisure walking's mass participation, the new walking movement has done almost nothing to engage with it.

The dominant discourse within much UK rural or wilderness walking is about a direct connection to the landscape, ancestry and nature, a version of Romantic and even "mystical fusion"[39] that results in a therapeutic cleansing and renewal. It assumes a benevolent open country long stripped of its top predators. But what if radical walkers were to propose to leisure walkers a less passive and more psycho-active coming to terms with the darker phenomenology of entanglement with a suffering and wounded environment? That, just as the "fusion" with a natural landscape of leisure walking may have met a gap left at least in part by the decline of organised religion, so the threatening of that fusion by catastrophic climate change creates a new opportunity for different kinds of ambulatory relationship with the ambient landscape. That "as we move away from the idea of a spiritual existence – however slowly – and come to accept a material or realist existence, the world-for-us will only continue to descend into the horrific, the uncaring and barren . . ... Soon enough, a need develops – a return."[40]

Of all the many products of the new walking movement, the Fife Psychogeographical Collective's *From Hill to Sea* (2015) probably comes closest to a popular work that at least begins to address this possibility, with its combination of documentations of walks and their soundtracks and its implied handbook for how readers might make their own walking. On one of the Collective's journeys, they find a long-ruined agricultural petrol pump almost enveloped by a thorn bush. The book sets this abject object in the context of a "decline of the tenant farmer", and then asks of the thorn: "Is it a crown of thorns awaiting the petrochemical plants, power stations, cars, aeroplanes . . .?"[41]

Coming to terms with the effects of climate change will not be an easy realignment with nature. Whatever the intensity of their fusion with natural terrain, it is unlikely to prepare the leisure walker for what is to come. The embrace of accelerating invasion and extremity is sure to involve some rougher face-to-face encounters with our own marginality and frailty. It is this confrontation that the radical walking movement, with its deep engagement with the uneven site-specifics of climate change, is better prepared for than nature walking, ironically; and it should now be ready to offer its tactics to popular walking.

Of course, individual walking artists are already directly addressing ecological issues. Jess Allen practises "tracktivism"; walking footpaths, engaging those she meets in dialogues about climate change.[42] In a wholly different register (but in tune with the harsh cosmology above), Dominique Baron-Bonarjee carries an enigmatic black flag on her "Black Walks", not only challenging political assumptions provoked by its loaded space, but as a mark of a creative existential precarity, of a beginning again from the void, a physical paraphrasing of the artist Malevich's axiom that "upheavals of society, identity, history, require[d] darkness/blackness".[43] The times, however, challenge the new walking movement to make a more collective, if necessarily variegated, response.

The Fife Psychogeographical Collective have already articulated the basic principles for how nature walking, like sea urchin larvae giving birth to their adult form, might transform itself by turning itself inside out:

> yes, this is a beautiful landscape . . . this is also a landscape inextricably linked into the ebb and flow of the global capitalist economy . . . is there any more perfect spot to catalogue and observe the agents and consequences of . . . the Age of Entropy . . .. At the very least, the psychogeographer can reverse the panoptical gaze of the modern political machine. Standing here *we* can use landscape as a mirror to reflect back . . .. We can see what you are up to and imagine and enact alternative possibilities".[44]

To this mutability, radical walkers bring the details and tactics of their phenomenological close-to-hand engagement with the changing ecology through direct immersion in the terrain, ready to invert the default mode of leisure walking in favour of new and quite different kinds of fusion.

Notes

1 Sam Cooper, *The Situationist International in Britain: Modernism, Surrealism and the Avant-garde* (London: Taylor & Francis, 2016), 149.
2 Francesco Careri, *Walkscapes* (Barcelona, Spain: Editorial Gustavo Gili, 2002), 176, 181, 183.
3 Gilles Deleuze & Félix Guattari, *A Thousand Plateaus* Translated by Brian Massumi (London: Continuum, 1987), 79–80.

4 Cooper, *The Situationist International in Britain*, 145.
5 Ian Sinclair, "The Last London". *The Idler*, 8 November 2017. https://idler.co.uk/article/the-last-london/.
6 Peter Bradshaw, "Swandown – Review". *The Guardian*, 19 July 2012. www.theguardian.com/film/2012/july/19/swandown-review.
7 Will Self, "On Location: My Students' *Dérives*". *Will Self: Writer*, 4 February 2016. https://willself.com/2016/02/04/4631/.
8 Tina Richardson, "Conclusion: The New Psychogeography", in Tina Richardson (ed.), *Walking Inside Out* (London: Rowman & Littlefield, 2015), 250.
9 Lucy R. Lippard, *Six Years: The Dematerialisation of the Art Object from 1966 to 1972* (New York: Praeger, 1973), vii–xxii.
10 Bradley L. Garrett, *Explore Everything* (London: Verso, 2013), 4–8.
11 Walter Benjamin, *Illuminations: Essays and Reflections*. Edited by Hannah Arendt. Translated by Harry Zhon (New York: Schocken Books, 1969), 223.
12 Thierry Bardini, *Junkware* (Minneapolis, MN: University of Minnesota Press, 2011), 10.
13 Eve Kosovsky Sedgwick, *Touching, Feeling: Affect, Pedagogy, Performativity* (Durham, NC: Duke University Press, 2003), 125.
14 Guy Debord, "Theory of the Dérive" (1958), in Ken Knabb (ed.), *Situationist International Anthology* (Berkeley, CA: Bureau of Public Secrets, 1981), 63.
15 Phil Smith, *Walking's New Movement* (Axminster, UK: Triarchy Press, 2015), 24–25.
16 Bardini, *Junkware*, 7.
17 Evan Calder Williams, *Combined and Uneven Apocalypse* (Ropley, UK: Zero Books, 2011), 67.
18 Marion Shoard, "Edgelands", in Jennifer Jenkins (ed.), *Remaking The Landscape* (London: Profile Books, 2002), 140.
19 Robert Macfarlane, "Edgelands by Paul Farley and Michael Symmons Roberts – Review". *The Guardian*, 19 February 2011. www.theguardian.com/books/2011/feb/19/edgelands-farley-symmons-roberts-review.
20 Alastair Bonnett, "The Dilemmas of Radical Nostalgia in British Psychogeography", *Theory, Culture and Society*, 26(1), 2009: 64.
21 Robert Park, "The City: Suggestions for Investigation of Human Behaviour in the Urban Environment", in Robert Park, Ernest Burgess, Roderick McKenzie & Louis Wirth (eds), *The City: Suggestions for Investigation of Human Behaviour in the Urban Environment* (Chicago, IL: University of Chicago Press, 1925), 1.
22 Phil Smith, *Mythogeography: A Guide to Walking Sideways* (Axminster, UK: Triarchy Press, 2010), 23.
23 Chris Salter, *Alien Agency: Experimental Encounters with Art in the Making* (Cambridge, MA: MIT Press, 2015), 4.
24 Deleuze & Guattari, *A Thousand Plateaus*, 109.
25 Ibid., 557.
26 Mark Bonta & John Protevi, *Deleuze and Geophilosophy: A Guide and Glossary* (Edinburgh, UK: Edinburgh University Press, 2004), 124.
27 Guy Debord, "Introduction to a Critique of Urban Geography" (1955), in Ken Knabb (ed.), *Situationist International Anthology* (Berkeley, CA: Bureau of Public Secrets, 1981), 8.
28 Steve Pile, *Real Cities: Modernity, Space and Phantasmagorias of City Life* (London: SAGE Publications, 2005), 12.
29 Steve Mentz, *Shipwreck Modernity* (Minneapolis, MN: University of Minnesota Press, 2015), ix–x.
30 Phil Smith, *Storylines*. Northampton, UK: Threshold Studios, 2018.
31 Walter Benjamin, *Charles Baudelaire: A Lyric Poet in the Era of High Capitalism* (London: Verso, 1983), 36.

32 Miranda Whall, "Crossed Paths – a Trilogy", *Miranda Whall: Interdisciplinary Contemporary Artist*, 2017. www.mirandawhall.space/?page_id=2363.
33 Charles Foster, *Being a Beast*. London: Profile Books, 2016.
34 Lisa-Ann Gershwin, *Stung!* (Chicago, IL: University of Chicago Press, 2013), 332.
35 Vanessa Daws, *Psychoswimography: Santa Barbara* (self-published, no date, unpaginated).
36 Dawn Foster, "How Walking Became a Radical Act of Defiance". *Huck Magazine*, 9 November 2017. www.huckmagazine.com/perspectives/dawn-foster-radical-walking/.
37 Garnette Cadogan, "Black and Blue" in John Freeman (ed.), *Freeman's: Arrival* (New York: Grove Press, 2015), 140.
38 Phil Smith, "Radical Twenty-first Century Walkers and the Romantic Qualities of Leisure Walking", in Michael Hall, Yael Ram & Noam Shoval (eds), *The Routledge International Handbook of Walking* (Abingdon, UK: Routledge, 2018), pp. 37–45.
39 Frédéric Gros, *A Philosophy of Walking* (London: Verso, 2014), 181.
40 David Peak, *The Spectacle of the Void* (San Bernardino, CA: Schism Press, 2014), 37.
41 Fife Psychogeographical Collective, *From Hill to Sea* (London: Bread and Circuses, 2015),
42 Jess Allen, "Tracktivism", *All in a Day's Walk*, https://allinadayswalk.org.uk/tracktivism/.
43 Dominique Baron-Bonarjee, "Malevick to Mavo, and Walking", *Dominique Baron-Bonarjee*. https://dominiquebb.com/writings/malevich-to-mavo-and-walking/.
44 Fife Psychogeographical Collective, *From Hill to Sea*, 180.

Works cited

Allen, Jess. "Tracktivism". *All in a Day's Walk*, https://allinadayswalk.org.uk/tracktivism/.
Baron-Bonarjee, Dominique. "Malevick to Mavo, and Walking". *Dominique Baron-Bonarjee*, https://dominiquebb.com/writings/malevich-to-mavo-and-walking/.
Bardini, Thierry. *Junkware*. Minneapolis, MN: University of Minnesota Press, 2011.
Benjamin, Walter. *Illuminations: Essays and Reflections*. Edited by Hannah Arendt. Translated by Harry Zhon. New York: Schocken Books, 1969.
Benjamin, Walter. *Charles Baudelaire: A Lyric Poet in the Era of High Capitalism*. London: Verso, 1983.
Bonnett, Alastair. "The Dilemmas of Radical Nostalgia in British Psychogeography". *Theory, Culture and Society*, 26(1), 2009, pp. 45–70.
Bonta, Mark & John Protevi. *Deleuze and Geophilosophy: A Guide and Glossary*. Edinburgh, UK: Edinburgh University Press, 2004.
Bradshaw, Peter. "Swandown – Review". *The Guardian*, 19 July 2012, www.theguardian.com/film/2012/jul/19/swandown-review.
Cadogan, Garnette. "Black and Blue". In John Freeman (ed.), *Freeman's: Arrival*. New York: Grove Press, 2015.
Careri, Francesco. *Walkscapes*. Barcelona, Spain: Editorial Gustavo Gili, 2002.
Cooper, Sam. *The Situationist International in Britain: Modernism, Surrealism and the Avant-garde*. London: Taylor & Francis, 2016.
Coverley, Merlin. *Psychogeography*. Harpenden, UK: Pocket Essentials, 2006.
Daws, Vanessa. *Psychoswimography: Santa Barbara*. Self-published, no date.

Debord, Guy. "Introduction to a Critique of Urban Geography" (1955). In Ken Knabb (ed.), *Situationist International Anthology*. Berkeley, CA: Bureau of Public Secrets, 1981, pp. 8–11.

Debord, Guy. "Theory of the Dérive" (1958). In Ken Knabb (ed.), *Situationist International Anthology*. Berkeley, CA: Bureau of Public Secrets, 1981, pp. 62–66.

Deleuze, Gilles & Félix Guattari. *A Thousand Plateaus*. Translated by Brian Massumi. London: Continuum, 1987.

Farley, Paul & Michael Symmons Roberts. *Edgelands: Journeys into England's True Wilderness*. New York: Vintage Books, 2011.

Fife Psychogeographical Collective. *From Hill to Sea*. London: Bread and Circuses, 2015.

Foster, Charles. *Being a Beast*. London: Profile Books, 2016.

Foster, Dawn. "How Walking Became a Radical Act of Defiance". *Huck Magazine*, 9 November 2017, www.huckmagazine.com/perspectives/dawn-foster-radical-walking/.

Garrett, Bradley L. *Explore Everything*. London: Verso, 2013.

Gershwin, Lisa-Ann. *Stung!* Chicago, IL: University of Chicago Press, 2013.

Gros, Frédéric. *A Philosophy of Walking*. London: Verso, 2014.

Lippard, Lucy R. *Six Years: The Dematerialisation of the Art Object from 1966 to 1972*. New York: Praeger, 1973.

Macfarlane, Robert. "Edgelands by Paul Farley and Michael Symmons Roberts – Review". *The Guardian*, 19 February 2011, www.theguardian.com/books/2011/feb/19/edgelands-farley-symmons-roberts-review.

Mension, Jean-Michel. *The Tribe*. London: Verso, 2002.

Mentz, Steve. *Shipwreck Modernity*. Minneapolis, MN: University of Minnesota Press, 2015.

Michell, John. *The View Over Atlantis*. London: Abacus, 1973.

Moore, Alan & Eddie Campbell. *From Hell*. Marietta, GA: Topshelf Productions, 1999.

Papadimitriou, Nick. *Scarp*. London: Sceptre, 2012.

Park, Robert. "The City: Suggestions for Investigation of Human Behaviour in the Urban Environment". In Robert Park, Ernest Burgess, Roderick McKenzie & Louis Wirth (eds), *The City: Suggestions for Investigation of Human Behaviour in the Urban Environment*. Chicago, IL: University of Chicago Press, 1925, pp. 1–46.

Peak, David. *The Spectacle of the Void*. San Bernardino, CA: Schism Press, 2014.

Pile, Steve. *Real Cities: Modernity, Space and Phantasmagorias of City Life*. London: SAGE Publications, 2005.

Rasmussen, Mikel Bolt & Jakob Jakobsen. *Expect Anything, Fear Nothing*. Copenhagen, Denmark: Nebula, 2011.

Rees, Gareth E. *Marshland*. London: Influx, 2013.

Richardson, Tina. "Conclusion: The New Psychogeography". In Tina Richardson (ed.), *Walking Inside Out*. London: Rowman & Littlefield, 2015, pp. 241–254.

Salter, Chris. *Alien Agency: Experimental Encounters with Art in the Making*. Cambridge, MA: MIT Press, 2015.

Scovell, Adam. "Wanders: The Magnet and the Last Resort (New Brighton)". *Celluloid Wicker Man*, 19 August 2016, https://celluloidwickerman.com/2016/08/19/derives-the-magnet-and-the-last-resort-new-brighton/.

Sedgwick, Eve Kosovsky. *Touching, Feeling: Affect, Pedagogy, Performativity*. Durham, NC: Duke University Press, 2003.

Self, Will. "On Location: My Students' *Dérives*". *Will Self: Writer*, 4 February 2016, https://will-self.com/2016/02/04/4631/.

Shoard, Marion. "Edgelands". In Jennifer Jenkins (ed.), *Remaking the Landscape*. London: Profile Books, 2002, pp. 117–146.

Sinclair, Iain. "The Last London". *The Idler*, 8 November 2017. https://idler.co.uk/article/the-last-london/.

Smith, Phil. *Mythogeography: A Guide to Walking Sideways*. Axminster, UK: Triarchy Press, 2010.

Smith, Phil. *Walking's New Movement*. Axminster, UK: Triarchy Press, 2015.

Smith, Phil. "Radical Twenty-first Century Walkers and the Romantic Qualities of Leisure Walking". In Michael Hall, Yael Ram & Noam Shoval (eds), *The Routledge International Handbook of Walking*. Abingdon, UK: Routledge, 2018, pp. 37–45.

Smith, Phil. *Storylines*. Northampton, UK: Threshold Studios, 2018.

Wark, McKenzie. *50 Years of Recuperation of the Situationist International*. New York: Princeton Architectural Press, 2008.

Wark, McKenzie. *The Beach Beneath the Street*. London: Verso, 2011.

Wark, McKenzie. *The Spectacle of Disintegration*. London: Verso, 2013.

Watkins, Alfred. *The Old Straight Track: Its Mounds, Beacons, Moats, Sites and Mark Stones*. London: Abacus, 1925/1978.

Whall, Miranda. "Crossed Paths – a Trilogy". *Miranda Whall: Interdisciplinary Contemporary Artist*, 2017, www.mirandawhall.space/?page_id=2363.

Williams, Evan Calder. Combined and Uneven Apocalypse. Ropley, UK: Zero Books, 2011.

14 Mountaineering literature as dark pastoral

Terry Gifford

'Tidemark', 75m, Severe, Cíoch na h-Oighe, Isle of Arran, Scotland,
1 May 2017.

Is it dry?

> *The grey rock is dry.*

But we have to cross those two
wet patches of weeping moss.

> *Wet feet onto dry rock.*

Is the wind a problem round the arête?

> *We'll not hear each other.*

Is that mist rising or falling?

> *Hard to tell in this wind.*

Well, we've pushed it to get here
traversing those wet rock moves in big boots.

> *I took a different line*
> *but it was still dodgy.*

Are these twa corbies
telling us something?

> *Perhaps they have.*

Shall we wait awhile?

> *We are.*

Have we made a decision?

> *I think we have.*

Do you see that shaft of light on the sea?

> *It's changing by the second.*

What a place to be.

> *Two hours from the car*
> *and up that wet heather ramp.*

Shall we go to the summit?

> *Let's wait a bit longer.*

We are.

> *Look at that sea*
> *Shining back the sunlight.*

Now there's the ferry.

                                          What a place to be.

Let's wait a bit longer.

We were a seventy-year-old father and a forty-year-old son on our annual May Day climbing trip to Scotland from Somerset and Lincolnshire respectively. We had just avoided a rock-climb in these inauspicious conditions and turned our climbing trip into a walk. We had turned away from the darkness of a dangerous uncertainty and could now enjoy the pastoral view with a mixture of relief and relaxed delight. Not that our unroped 'walk' to reach this point had been without its dark moments as we had negotiated the undercut diagonal ramp of heather, loose rock and wet woodrush grass below the mountain's summit rock wall. Even the rock-climbing guide advised that 'great care should be exercised when ascending Ledge 3 as it involves exposed moves on dubious combinations of heather and crumbling rock'.[1] But now, as we leaned back on our heavy rucksacks of unused climbing gear in the sodden heather, we could zip up tight against the wind and watch the lightshow of sea and mist and sun in contention below.

There will be some readers who will already be regarding this poem and first paragraph as an apparently innocent pastoral indulgence, including the token 'machine in the garden' of the ferry,[2] that ignores the unsustainability of the practice of mountaineering in the Anthropocene and takes for granted the social, political, ableist, gendered and economic structures that sustain it. Even the act of writing this poem may be seen as an aesthetic escape from the urgent effects of climate change upon the weather, land, birds, sea level and people. Indeed, the ferry and its cars are contributory causes of the Anthropocene itself, a phenomenon that renders all travel writing unsustainable by definition. But maybe a poem that concerns two human animals attempting to read weather and rock in a specific situation – a material biosemiotics by which we try to intuit each other's signs[3] – might offer a starting point for a consideration of the wider issues that reverberate from their being there. Perhaps it would be helpful to make an early declaration that my son was a student of geology and that I had organised an International Festival of Mountaineering Literature for twenty-one years. However, all this should not deflect attention away from the crucial element of the risk – in a worst case, that of death – at the heart of this moment of biosemiotic reading of material conditions which is the focus of the poem and which language is barely adequate to evoke.

Our walk had begun with the familiar narrative of following a burn up over a boulder-strewn lip into a high corrie. Sheffield Hallam University lecturer and mountaineer Paul Nunn described in his book *At the Sharp End* (1988) this experience of walking into a mountain valley for a mountaineer as one of warm recognition: 'one feels that one is coming home'.[4] He probably knew that he was echoing John Muir, who wrote of late nineteenth-century Americans discovering their first National Parks that 'going to the mountains is going home'.[5] But Nunn was also aware that these were dangerous environments, referring enigmatically to an 'inescapable foreboding in Llanberis or Glencoe'.[6] Writing about walking on the approach to climbs in the Himalaya under ice blocks called 'seracs' hanging above the glacier, he knew that, even at this early stage of the mountaineering narrative, death was not far away: 'One day soon some must fall. Oh, that we will not be there!'[7] On 6 August 1995, walking down from the summit of Haromosh II (6,666 metres) in the Karakoram range, close to his base camp Paul Nunn was killed by a falling serac. An experienced and respected leading figure in the Sheffield climbing community, whose caution had resulted in a succession of expeditions on which he had turned back before the summit, Paul is still greatly missed by those of us who benefited from his generous and lively friendship.

In *Reconnecting with John Muir* (2006), I argued that the literature of mountaineering, at its best, could be read as post-pastoral[8] – enacting the classic pastoral movement of retreat and return, but all too aware of the dangers of idealisation in an unforgiving and unstable environment, one rendered all the more so by the various effects of climate change.[9] Discussing the amazing variety, quantity and quality of mountaineering literature, I wrote that 'the earliest British alpinists were scholars of English literature who wrote about their new sport as an escape from their professional business of writing about other people's writing'.[10] This tradition has continued from Leslie Stephen, who was a Victorian literary critic and author of *The Playground of Europe* (1871),[11] to the journalist, poet and writer Geoffrey Winthrop Young,[12] to the adult education university lecturer in English Literature George Mallory, to the languages teacher Wilfrid Noyce, author of *Scholar Mountaineers* (1950),[13] to Al Alvarez, kingmaker of poets in the 1950s and 1960s as Literary Editor of the *Observer*, to the current *Guardian* mountaineering correspondent Ed Douglas, Editor of the *Alpine Journal*. Women mountaineers, although fewer in number, have been equally talented writers, from the prolific American Himalayan explorer Fanny Bullock Workman, author of seven books published around the opening of the twentieth century, to Dorothy Pilley, wife of the critic I. A. Richards and author of *Climbing Days* (1935),[14] to Janet Adam Smith, Literary Editor of the *New Statesman* (1952–1960), to Katie Ives, current Editor of the leading American literary journal *Alpinist*. Anthologies of the best of this literary tradition abound, including *The Winding Trail: A Selection of Articles and Essays for Walkers and Backpackers* (1981), which retains a definitive status.[15] An anthology for walkers titled *The Open Road: A Little Book for Wayfarers* (1899)[16] was a set text for D. H. Lawrence at Nottingham University College when he took his Teacher's Certificate examinations.[17] Of course, Lawrence was a keen walker, having heard of the outbreak of the First World War only when he descended from a walking tour in the Lake District, and famously crossing the Alps with Frieda in what served as a rather trying honeymoon on which they occasionally lost their way on mountain passes.

Having already applied the notion of the post-pastoral to this body of literature, I'm led by the experience of the introductory poem to consider reading a sample of mountaineering literature through the frame of 'dark pastoral'. When Heather I. Sullivan coined the term 'dark pastoral' in 2016, she did not have in mind the mountaineering experience or its vast and varied literature. Her conception was a larger one that could characterise literature in a pastoral mode that engaged with the paradoxes of the Anthropocene in a strategic 'doubled movement closer towards and away from green fantasies'.[18] By 'refusing to separate our green dreams from the material manifestations of the new toxic nature', dark pastoral 'enacts the Anthropocene's vivid extremes'.[19] In order to propose a movement both towards potentially positive 'green fantasies' and away from illusory or escapist 'green fantasies', Sullivan conflates what she recognises as the apparently 'necessary fantasy' of 'deeply green ecological ideals' that underpin ecocriticism itself with 'our apparent need for greenscapes and non-human life' in idealised landscapes.[20] Could mountain walkers be accused of illusory 'green fantasies' if their need for 'greenscapes' such as the uplands actually fed their 'ecological ideals' by being attuned to nature in their reading of landscape? Indeed, does the personal renewal derived from the mountains translate into social concern for sea-level cities threatened by rising seas, for example? Might the 'green dreams' of a mountain walker's apparently feeling 'at home' in an environment that is not untouched by the consequences of the Anthropocene be read in the frame of dark pastoral? Can the 'darkness' of taking personal risks in reading the 'pastoral' mountain environment be 'doubled', in Sullivan's sense, by a movement towards, and engagement with, a wider awareness of environmental risk created by human culture?

I am myself in danger of conflating the unstable environment of mountains with a sense of their being a theatre of the Anthropocene. But wherever the mountaineer looks, there is evidence of the Anthropocene and a growing sense of culpability from the micro level of plant disturbance by the 'gardening' of cracks by rock-climbers documented by Paula Wright in *Alpinist*[21] to the macro level of the problems presented to the mountaineer by glacial retreat in the Anthropocene reported in the Alpine Club's annual publication for its members, the *Alpine Journal*.[22] What mountain walkers refer to as the daily 'conditions' are, of course, the micro-evidence of the Anthropocene. A walker on Ben Nevis on 21 August 2017 would find no snow patches anywhere on the mountain that day. She might not know that this is the first day for eleven years that this has been the case, but she is observing climate change at work.[23] Walkers in mountains, who by definition must have 'green dreams' of a certain kind, are also only too aware of the agency of their environment, and judging that agency is, of course, what is happening when mountaineers and hill-walkers 'assess the conditions', as my son and I were doing, to avoid dangerous choices. So there is clearly a relationship between a literal sense of dark pastoral as an experience of personal danger in a beautiful and often idealised mountain environment, and the human culpability in contributing to the larger forces of climate as weather, or climate change as rockfall, or global warming as glacial retreat. As Sullivan puts it, 'additionally dark pastoral is a means of thinking in terms of material ecocriticism's emphasis on flows and non-human agency together with human agency'.[24]

So might Sullivan's notion of dark pastoral offer a sharper, more nuanced way of reading mountaineering literature? What might be highlighted and what might be overlooked in applying this frame to reading this body of work? Indeed, what might be considered to be lacking in the literature if it is read as 'dark pastoral' in Sullivan's sense of 'green fantasies' shadowed by the Anthropocene? In order to provide a current sample of the genre, one might consider the five very different books shortlisted for the Boardman Tasker Award for Mountain Literature in 2016, for which I was one of the three judges. Established in memory of two mountaineering writers, Peter Boardman and Joe Tasker, who disappeared on the unclimbed North-East Ridge of Everest in 1982, this award currently attracts more than thirty new books each year, adding to a substantial tradition.

Alex Honnold's book *Alone on the Wall*, written with David Roberts, describes the life of an un-roped solo climber as its sensational subject. Its cover shows Honnold walking across the 'Thank God Ledge' high on the Northwest Face of Half Dome at the head of Yosemite Valley. Honnold has his back to the wall, and below his toes there is a vast drop as he edges sideways along the exposed ledge that is going to get narrower than his foot before he reaches a vertical crack. This is mountain climbing at most simple and most committing. But it is the quality of Honnold's articulation of his approach to this purest of pursuits – the simple reading of rock by a body unencumbered by ropes and safety gear – that engages the reader, together with his honesty about the personal costs of his lifestyle and amazing achievements. On the other hand, Honnold's climbing lifestyle choices led to his creation of the Honnold Foundation. After five years of living out of a van, the twenty-six-year-old was earning enough to have surplus income to donate to projects that make environmentally low impact, sustainable, alleviations of poverty worldwide:

> I'm deeply worried about the future of the world in the face of climate change, the unbridled use of fossil fuels, and so on. It's this passion, as much as anything, that led to the idea of the Honnold Foundation.[25]

At the end of making a film of his climbing, Honnold and his filmmaker climbed rooftops on the Navajo Reservation to install solar panels. At the end of the book, Honnold, still in his twenties, writes:

> With my Honnold Foundation, what I really hope to do in the coming years is to improve the lives of the most vulnerable people in the world

in a way that helps the environment. To support projects that both help the earth and lift people out of poverty.[26]

Honnold's ability to control his fear and have complete faith in the techniques of his body to read rock in situations that define the sublime might provide one sense of dark pastoral. But his choosing to use the rewards from his skill of the bodily attunement of fingers and feet to material nature – the forms and textures of the rock in front of him – to alleviate the consequences of the Anthropocene for some vulnerable groups of people completes a 'double movement' in Sullivan's terms of both horrific personal risk and environmental generosity. Honnold does not mention the Anthropocene, but perhaps his choosing to offer solar panels is a recognition of the need to engage with it.

Also without mention of the Anthropocene is Mark Vallance's memoir *Wild Country: The Man Who Made Friends* (2016). Vallance was a climber who became both an innovative entrepreneur and a participant in the policies and politics of outdoors activities. His crucial life-changing decision followed his meeting, while climbing in America, with Ray Jardine, who had invented a trigger-activated protection device of expanding parts that would fit into cracks, secretly coded between his trusted climbing partners as 'the Friends'. They could be removed by the second climber and thus leave the rock unscarred. They had too many parts to be judged commercially viable by all manufacturers, but Vallance came home to Derbyshire to take the financial risk and make them himself on his kitchen table for mail order sales, with the help of a TV appearance on *Tomorrow's World*. Thus was his business Wild Country formed, and as it prospered, Vallance established the Wild Country Foundation, writing:

> I wanted to make a forceful statement to the climbing world that a company was willing to take a stand in favour of certain values to do with sustainability and strong ethics, much as Patagonia does now in the United States.[27]

Although these innovations benefited the climbing and walking community, their purpose was, of course, to produce profits to provide Vallance's family with a comfortable lifestyle; Vallance was a capitalist entrepreneur. In addition, these profits were, in turn, used to support outdoor access and 'sustainable use' of the pastoral environment through the Wild Country Foundation. For the non-business reader of his book, part of its impact is the account of business dilemmas in which the family home is more than once on the line. On the other hand, there is the sheer hard work and bold direct action in protection of patents in business, for example, that is somehow balanced by his voluntary work for the national park authority driven by an ethical concern for the right policy decisions – balancing access with conservation needs – to be taken on behalf of those using the upland landscapes.

Five years of working for the Peak District National Park on return from the Antarctic informed six years on the board of the National Park as a nominee of the British Mountaineering Council (BMC), where Vallance had been founding Secretary of the Access and Conservation Committee, organising a mountain conservation symposium in 1977. So it was no surprise when he became president of the BMC in 2002, although there was a darker reason for his decision. Like the vulnerability of upland landscapes, Vallance had a human vulnerability. He had been diagnosed with Parkinson's disease, but wanted to keep 'involved in the mountaineering world': 'I like to think of my loss as the BMC's gain, but not everyone would agree with that.'[28] At the heart of his book is an appreciation of upland pastoral landscapes and their vulnerability, especially for walkers and climbers in Britain – Vallance's version of Sullivan's 'double movement'. His view that 'it gives me no pleasure to conclude that there are no national parks (in the American sense) in Britain' is based upon his reflections on quarrying in the Peak District National Park, in contrast to which, he says, 'little has been done to provide for the enjoyment of the landscape'.[29] Typically, he provides a strategy towards a statutory plan of landscape assessment and long-term purchase that would provide some forms of outdoor activity for the spiritual and bio-semiotic survival of urban populations in the Anthropocene.[30]

One mode of such mountain activity is illustrated by Simon McCartney's book, *The Bond* (2016), although the reader might be left feeling that his survival is most in doubt in McCartney's account of two climbs in Alaska. The title is the theme of his book – the bond between climbers upon which he increasingly comes to rely in his accounts of two epic new routes in Alaska in 1978 and 1980 that demonstrate a remarkable self-awareness verging upon hubris, as he readily admits. It would be easy to say of this book that it is mostly dark with very little pastoral, in that McCartney survives these two climbs only through a combination of luck and the generosity of other climbers. The beautiful mountains that he chose to climb happen to be the most dangerous, and the realisation after the second of these epics that both his skills and his psyche could not and must not be tested to such a degree ever again leads to his giving up mountaineering altogether. Only thirty years later could he reflect upon his experiences to write his book. Nevertheless it is a gripping example of a certain kind of narrative in the mountaineering genre, told with the maturity of age and hindsight that ultimately celebrates mutual human support in the harshest of environments. For a mountaineering audience, such qualities resulted in the book winning the Boardman Tasker Award for 2016. From an ecocritical perspective, perhaps the most telling image in the book is captioned 'The lighting of Studio City Macau is typical of our company's design build activity in Asia – calculated risks all'.[31] Now living in Australia and Hong Kong, McCartney makes his living from designing architectural lighting projects. In the Anthropocene, such light offers an image of a very dark urban pastoral dependent upon energy generated, doubtless, from such unsustainable sources that have created the Anthropocene.

Also shortlisted in 2016 was the biography of an Australian who travelled in the opposite direction and made his life in Britain. Robert Wainwright's biography of the Australian rebel George Finch, *The Maverick Mountaineer: The Remarkable Life of George Ingle Finch: Climber, Scientist, Inventor*, reveals an eccentric scientist and inventor with a complicated personal life. It was an experience, which Finch later described in pastoral terms, that motivated him as a thirteen-year-old boy to become a mountaineer – a view from a hill over the New South Wales bush in the spring of 1901: 'The picture was beautiful; precise and accurate as the work of a draughtsman's pen, but fuller of meaning than any map.'[32] Although conceived as an artifice, this view was embedded with 'meaning' as well as 'accuracy':

> I had made up my mind to see the world; to see it from above, from the tops of mountains whence I could get that wide and comprehensive view which is denied to those who observe things from their own plane.[33]

Such a privileged position from which to engage with the features of nature in an altered mode of contemplation is at the heart of hillwalking and mountaineering writing, including, perhaps, the poem with which this chapter began. George and his brother Max found themselves living in Paris with their bohemian mother, and they began a traditional alpine education by employing guides. Eventually one of the best climbers in Europe, George Finch also excelled academically, and devoted himself initially to researching the development of chemical technology at Imperial College, London.

Finch's research and personal experiments led him to controversially advocate the use of oxygen in early Everest expeditions, much against the views of the establishment and the cynicism of fellow climbers. With its help, he achieved the altitude record on the 1922 Everest expedition, going not only higher, but more easily and with better eventual recovery, than George Mallory had days before without it. But Finch's research back at Imperial College on his return came to earn him an international scientific reputation as he became a Fellow of the Royal Society and a member of the panel awarding the Nobel Prize for physics. His research ranged widely in exploring various modes of fuel efficiency that had industrial applications which were taken up in a variety of worldwide industries. Finch turned down an invitation to become the British government's scientific advisor, but accepted an invitation from Nehru to lead India's scientific research establishment for the first five years of its independence. In retirement, he experimented with hydroponics ahead of his time, and Wainwright notes that 'he called for lead-free petrol decades before its introduction'.[34] It is by no means clear that Finch's motivation for benefiting society was driven by anything other than industrial efficiency, and the frame of dark pastoral would therefore either find his book wanting or, indeed, contributing to what came to be known as the Anthropocene.

Finally, and by way of complete contrast, the shortlist of the Boardman Tasker Award included American science writer Steve Olson's book about a mountain event, *Eruption: The Untold Story of Mount St. Helens* (2016). When a smoking Mount St Helens actually erupted at 8.30 on a spring Sunday morning – 18 May 1980 – fifty-seven people were killed. Olson not only tells their personal stories, but turns the tension between the science and the cultural assumptions at play on that day into a tragic thriller. This is also a book that locates those lost lives within the new 'heightened environmental activism' of the 1970s and 1980s:

> In the midst of this upwelling of environmentalism, the eruption of Mount St. Helens added a note of uncertainty, of peril, to how people thought about the future [. . .]. The people who experienced the eruption could never again think of the ground on which they stood as beneficent and forgiving.[35]

In making this point, Olson recognises the double movement between the personal risk involved in the mountain climbing experience and the wider sense of the earth's vulnerability and indifference to the environmental risks taken by the human race. This is also a movement between the pastoral retreat into the social 'consumption' of the mountain experience and the material reality of their unpredictability that exposes human hubris. So Olson intends his book as a kind of allegory about our attitudes towards our planet in the Anthropocene, 'thinking the risk was small': 'We ignore the risks we face so we are not paralyzed by dread. Only in retrospect does the extent of our wilful ignorance become clear.'[36] When that retrospect condemns as illegal 'daredevils' many of the dead, Olson is concerned to discover the truth about exactly why they were on the mountain that day, which turns out to be closer to a pastoral awe than personal indulgence in adrenaline addiction. The weather forecast offered a perfect spring weekend for camping and hiking under clear skies. The mountain had been smoking for almost two months, and the Forest Service had not closed off the areas where those camping out chose to pitch their tents and tarps.

Olson carefully untangles the conflicting positions of the scientists, commercial logging interests, the Forest Service, the politicians of different levels, the conservationists, the forest cabin owners and the recreational users of the mountain in their responses to the first earthquake that rocked Mount St Helens on 20 March 1980 and subsequent events. It is a case study in the mismanagement of a natural event in which economic interests guided policy making that put hikers and others at risk. Early on, the scientists specialising in the history of this particular mountain were consulted, recounting a 'dire history for the assembled officials' of far-reaching mudflows and even further-reaching pyroclastic blasts.[37] But the Forest Service had come to serve the loggers by putting in roads, the loggers sought to continue work, and the politicians supported the major local employer.

That more people did not die was a matter of luck. If it had been a weekday, hundreds of loggers would have been killed. On the Saturday or the Sunday afternoons, there would have been day hikers. Only the weekend before, the Mount St. Helens Protective Association had led a group of twenty local people on a hike up the Green River to show supporters the old growth trees that they wanted to save from the loggers. The Forest Service gave them the all clear, but an elderly mountaineer in the party, who had climbed Mount St Helens twenty times, became increasingly uncomfortable and returned to his car. Actually, ash fell three feet thick up to twenty miles north of the mountain. Downwind to the east, two inches of ash fell from a black cloud a hundred and fifty miles away: 'Students at Washington State University in Pullman, on the border with Idaho, made emergency runs to convenience store to stock up on beer.'[38] And, of course, the landscape of the aftermath presented a unique opportunity for academic studies if it could be preserved. When the hearings took place for a proposed Mount St Helens Volcanic Monument, the voices of the Mount St. Helens Hiking Club were raised against further logging, including that of the mother in the Moore family who spoke eloquently of three generations of local recreational use of the mountain.[39] In 1982, the bill was passed designating the National Monument. Olson, in his Epilogue, points out the allegorical significance of this story as:

> everyone on earth faces the certainty of higher temperatures, more intense storms, degraded ecosystems, and higher sea levels as we continue to pump more carbon dioxide into the atmosphere. In many ways we are all like the people camping northwest of Mount St. Helens in the weeks and days before the volcano's eruption, blissfully unaware of the risks we face.[40]

Eruption represents the epitome of the dark pastoral: walkers drawn by the direct experience of pastoral awe, many of them having an intimate knowledge of this land, had underestimated its dark potential for life-threatening instability, having been left exposed by the compromises and complacency of the politicians and land managers. Actually, a Forest Service proposal for a new extension of the zones was lying unsigned on the desk of the governor that weekend.

When John Muir had written that 'going to the mountains is going home', he did not intend to invite a pastoral complacency. He had discovered by experience that the screes at the bottom of the walls of Yosemite were the result not of gradual erosion, but of seismic activity such as the earthquake that destroyed the pinnacle named Eagle Rock while he watched, crying, he claimed, as he ran from his cabin, 'A noble earthquake! A noble earthquake!'[41] This was a home about which many things were still to be understood. It still is. One evening, from our camp below the mountains on the Isle of Arran at Lochranza, Tom and I took a walk back into the history of geological knowledge. From our sea-level campsite, we walked along the raised beach to round Newton Point under increasingly high former sea cliffs to search for Hutton's Unconformity. Tom took a degree in geology, and hopping across rocks on the shoreline, he found it first, explaining that at this point the grey Precambrian schists sloping one way were overlaid by the sedimentary red sandstone sloping the other way. It was at this very point that in 1787 James Hutton first began his deductions that undermined the biblical view of the single-moment creation of the earth by showing that its formation was brought about by processes that are still continuously at work, as indeed, the raised beach on which we camped also demonstrated. Hutton's paper of 1788 concluded: 'The result, therefore, of our present enquiry is, that we find no vestige of a beginning, no prospect of an end.'[42] It was at this very spot on Arran that the modern science of geology began, and it is due to be changed again by the continuing, indeed accelerated, processes of the Anthropocene, as the sea will cover our campsite. Both short- and long-term 'darknesses' are at work on this pastoral mountainous island. Awareness of this lends a certain frisson to the psychogeography[43] of walking on Arran, just as it does to reading contemporary mountaineering literature.

Yet since we walkers and wanders are also wonderers, I could not help feeling that there was something missing from this notion of dark pastoral, something prompted by walking beside my son and wondering about his daughters, strong walkers and wonderers already: Elsbeth aged five, and Islay aged eight, named for the Scottish island her father visited for his first ten springs and returns to still with his own family in alternate years.[44] What exactly is this need to walk where we do not live and work, and to walk on mountains in sight of a sea that will eventually submerge our homes in Somerset and Lincolnshire? What do we take back from this archipelagic pastoral momentum of retreat and return between periphery and centre, between island and home, between outer and inner nature?[45] Is it something gained by the very process of negotiating between them with as much self-critical awareness as is currently possible? Perhaps it is a higher hope that we can engage with the darknesses, for all the unsatisfactory and paradoxically unsustainable costs of the retreat. Perhaps it is a belief that the fundamental power of awe will inform our anxieties, that awe and anxiety will heighten each other as, back in our home places, we negotiate our daily dilemmas carrying these precious memories as core values, which, in turn, are why we need to critique a notion like the dark pastoral itself. Perhaps, too, this is a negotiation at work in the minds of two climbers, caught between anxiety and hope as they say to each other, 'Let's wait a bit longer' up there, with the descent towards home still to come.

Where is the place for such a hope in Sullivan's dark pastoral? It seems to have been either relegated to the idealisation of 'green dreams' or projected into an equally idealised posthuman world of hybridity and harmony in a postapocalyptic 'rejuvenating Earth' such as represented at the end of Margaret Atwood's novel *MaddAddam*.[46] Sullivan seems to endorse Attwood's vision of a pastoral harmony dependent upon the elimination from the planet of most of the human race that is a not uncommon fatalism in current environmental discourse. So what does such fatalism offer the grandchildren of its advocates? If the 'dark' overwhelms the 'pastoral' in Sullivan's theory, it becomes just another critique of idealised pastoral. At least the notion of the post-pastoral is based upon an attempt to recognise and retain the fundamental quality of humbling awe and respect in confronting the complexities and necessity of the pastoral tradition. In one sense, to be environmentally concerned in the face of the Anthropocene is surely motivated by a presumption of deep grief for what might be lost. On the other hand, despite the apparent hubris of its name, the Anthropocene represents a challenge to translate personal uplift from journeys into mountains into social activity of amelioration such as displayed by some of the authors discussed above. The books considered here struggle to achieve this satisfactorily, but the notion of dark pastoral has at least drawn out their combinations of both elements.

Notes

1 Colin Moody and Graham Little, *Inner Hebrides and Arran: Scottish Mountaineering Club Climbers' Guide* (Glasgow, UK: Scottish Mountaineering Trust, 2014), 257.
2 See Leo Marx, *The Machine in the Garden: Technology and the Pastoral Ideal in America* (New York: Oxford University Press, 1964).
3 For more on biosemiotics, see Wendy Wheeler, *Expecting the Earth: Life, Culture, Biosemiotics* (London: Lawrence & Wishart, 2016).
4 Paul Nunn, *At the Sharp End* (London: Unwin Hyman, 1988), 197.
5 John Muir, *John Muir: The Eight Wilderness-discovery Books*, ed. Terry Gifford (London: Diadem, 1992 [1901]), 459.
6 Nunn, *At the Sharp End*, 176.
7 Ibid., 178.
8 See Terry Gifford, *Pastoral* (2nd edn., London: Routledge, 2020), 167–200.
9 Terry Gifford, *Reconnecting with John Muir: Essays in Post-pastoral Practice* (Athens, GA: University of Georgia Press, 2006), 155–168.
10 Ibid., 164. I emphasise the literary here in order to account for the quality and quantity of this particular sport's literature. This is not to discount often unrecorded earlier ascents in the Alps by local shepherds and crystal hunters. In the UK, the elitism traditionally associated with Raymond Williams' critique of pastoral literature was not breached until the biographies of post-Second World War working-class rock-climbers such as Joe Brown and Don Whillans.
11 Leslie Stephen, *The Playground of Europe* (London: Longman, Green & Co., 1871).
12 On an ableist note, Winthrop Young made an ascent of the Matterhorn after losing a leg in the First World War, his writing about which has led to a sub-genre that is typified by Norman Croucher's *Legless but Smiling: An Autobiography* (St Ives, UK: St Ives Printing and Publishing Co., 2000).
13 Wilfrid Noyce, *Scholar Mountaineers* (London: Dennis Dobson, 1950).
14 Dorothy Pilley, *Climbing Days* (London: Bell & Sons, 1935).
15 Roger Smith, *The Winding Trail: A Selection of Articles and Essays for Walkers and Backpackers* (London: Diadem, 1981).

16 E. V. Lucas (ed.), *The Open Road* (London: Grant Richards, 1899).
17 See editor's note in D. H. Lawrence, *Study of Thomas Hardy*, ed. Bruce Steele (Cambridge, UK: Cambridge University Press, 1985), 279.
18 Heather I. Sullivan, 'The Dark Pastoral: Goethe and Atwood', *Green Letters* 20(1) (2016): 48.
19 Ibid.
20 Ibid.
21 Paula Wright, 'Refuge', *Alpinist* 58 (2017): 105–110.
22 Wilfried Haeberli, 'The Alps without Ice?', *Alpine Journal* (2008): 201–202; Jonathan Bamber, Richard Alley and Dan Lunt, 'The Response of Glaciers to Climate Change', *Alpine Journal* (2017): 143–154.
23 See www.bbc.co.uk/news/uk-scotland-highlands-islands-41001234.
24 Sullivan, 'The Dark Pastoral', 49.
25 Alex Honnold, *Alone on the Wall* (London: Macmillan, 2015), 146.
26 Ibid., 229–230.
27 Mark Vallance, *Wild Country: The Man Who Made Friends* (Sheffield, UK: Vertebrate Publishing, 2016), 143–144.
28 Ibid., 201.
29 Ibid., 206.
30 Sadly, Mark Vallance died in Switzerland, according to his wishes, on 19 April 2018.
31 Simon McCartney, *The Bond* (Sheffield, UK: Vertebrate Publishing, 2016), plate 60.
32 Robert Wainwright, *The Maverick Mountaineer: The Remarkable Life of George Ingle Finch: Climber, Scientist, Inventor* (London: Allen & Unwin, 2016), 5.
33 Ibid., 6.
34 Ibid., 396.
35 Steve Olson, *Eruption: The Untold Story of Mount St. Helens* (London: W. W. Norton, 2016), xvii.
36 Ibid.
37 Ibid., 53.
38 Ibid., 186.
39 Ibid., 212.
40 Ibid., 244.
41 Muir, *John Muir: The Eight Wilderness-discovery Books*, 643.
42 James Hutton, 'Theory of the Earth', *Transactions of the Royal Society of Edinburgh* 1 (1788): 304.
43 See Merlin Coverley, *Psychogeography* (Harpenden, UK: Pocket Essentials, 2010). What is being suggested here is really ecopsychogeography – one that maps the emotional affects of the landscape (and also now of the Anthropocene) that come through its geological and environmental hauntings and premonitions considered over time running both backwards and forwards.
44 Rebecca Solnit characterises walking as 'a state in which the mind, the body, and the world are aligned' in conversation: *Wanderlust: A History of Walking* (London: Verso, 2000), 5. The conversation with which this chapter began exemplified this as a crux decision, but the conversation now needs to be widened to include the future as well as the past.
45 For the archipelagic dimensions hinted at here, see Jos Smith, *The New Nature Writing: Rethinking the Literature of Place* (London: Bloomsbury, 2017), 157–178.
46 Sullivan, 'The Dark Pastoral', 56–57.

Works cited

Bamber, Jonathan, Richard Alley and Dan Lunt. 'The Response of Glaciers to Climate Change'. *Alpine Journal* (2017): 143–154.
Coverley, Merlin. *Psychogeography*. Harpenden, UK: Pocket Essentials, 2010.

Croucher, Norman. *Legless but Smiling: An Autobiography*. St Ives, UK: St Ives Printing and Publishing Co., 2000.

Gifford, Terry. *Reconnecting with John Muir: Essays in Post-pastoral Practice*. Athens, GA: University of Georgia Press, 2006.

Gifford, Terry. *Pastoral* 2nd edn. London: Routledge, 2020.

Haeberli, Wilfried. 'The Alps without Ice?'. *Alpine Journal* (2008): 201–202.

Honnold, Alex. *Alone on the Wall*. London: Macmillan, 2015.

Hutton, James. 'Theory of the Earth'. *Transactions of the Royal Society of Edinburgh* 1 (1788): 209–304.

Lawrence, D. H. *Study of Thomas Hardy*, edited by Bruce Steele. Cambridge, UK: Cambridge University Press, 1981.

Lucas, E. V. (ed.). *The Open Road*. London: Grant Richards, 1899.

Marx, Leo. *The Machine in the Garden: Technology and the Pastoral Ideal in America*. New York: Oxford University Press, 1964.

McCartney, Simon. *The Bond*. Sheffield, UK: Vertebrate Publishing, 2016.

Moody, Colin and Graham Little. *Inner Hebrides and Arran: Scottish Mountaineering Club Climbers' Guide*. Glasgow, UK: Scottish Mountaineering Trust, 2014.

Muir, John. *John Muir: The Eight Wilderness-discovery Books*, edited by Terry Gifford. London: Diadem, 1992 [1901].

Noyce, Wilfrid. *Scholar Mountaineers*. London: Dennis Dobson, 1950.

Nunn, Paul. *At the Sharp End*. London: Unwin Hyman, 1988.

Olson, Steve. *Eruption: The Untold Story of Mount St. Helens*. London: W. W. Norton, 2016.

Pilley, Dorothy. *Climbing Days*. London: Bell & Sons, 1935.

Smith, Roger. *The Winding Trail: A Selection of Articles and Essays for Walkers and Backpackers*. London: Diadem, 1981.

Smith, Jos. *The New Nature Writing: Rethinking the Literature of Place*. London: Bloomsbury, 2017.

Solnit, Rebecca. *Wanderlust: A History of Walking*. London: Verso, 2000.

Stephen, Leslie. *The Playground of Europe*. London: Longman, Green & Co., 1871.

Sullivan, Heather I. 'The Dark Pastoral: Goethe and Atwood'. *Green Letters* 20(1) (2016): 47–59.

Vallance, Mark. *Wild Country: The Man Who Made Friends*. Sheffield, UK: Vertebrate Publishing, 2016.

Wainwright, Robert. *The Maverick Mountaineer: The Remarkable Life of George Ingle Finch: Climber, Scientist, Inventor*. London: Allen & Unwin, 2016.

Wheeler, Wendy. *Expecting the Earth: Life, Culture, Biosemiotics*. London: Lawrence & Wishart, 2016.

Wright, Paula. 'Refuge'. *Alpinist* 58 (2017): 105–110.

15 Walking on

Gerry Loose

My mother always told me I walked at 9 months, so counting on my fingers, I've been walking for several decades to date. Those of us who can walk are all experts.

Once, as a child, maybe 8 years old, I was left behind on the strand where my father had a nut-sweet clinker-built dinghy with another man. I was completely forgotten by the men, who concentrated on the catch. It was dusk and I thought it was time to set off for the hut. The way was through a wood, inland: this was my first solo walk of some miles and the wood was dark. Because no-one had taught me to be fearful, I was not.

Every walk is a step in the dark.

I lived in Glasgow and worked at the Botanic Gardens there. Every day I walked to work, thinking of plants, of poems. Along the kerbs were masons' marks. The granite of the kerb stones, the limestone paviours, the buildings with their Old Red Devonian ripples of embedded water were my markers and the masons' lettering became my flowers. In this way I walk where no-one has been.

I went to Tibet and walked everywhere at 4,500 metres or higher in thin air. Walking at this height, for me, was unsettling, hallucinogenic. I visited, as a pilgrim, Tsurphu Monastery, then the home of the 14-year-old Gyalwang Karmapa. While waiting for him to receive us all, Tibetans and me, I made a scrambling circumambulation of the monastery, climbing higher than I have ever been, on foot, in my life. Dizzy with fatigue and oxygen shortage, this walk lodged in my feet, my mind and body and remains there still, twenty years later. Sometimes a walk has a purpose that is uncertain, even while we think we know what we are walking on, why we are walking. Sometimes the outcome of a walk is very far from what is anticipated. Back in Lhasa, I joined the day-long *kora* of the Potala palace, walking round, round the exterior walls; one of a crowd of women, men and small Lhasa apso terriers, whose merit on this circumambulation grew with each step – those whose prayers, it's said, are also rooted in their feet, being attached to their minds, driven by their minds.

Back in Scotland, I led a walk for poets round Holy Island, once the dwelling place of St Molaise, whose name, from the 6th century, gives us Lamlash, in which bay of Arran the Holy Island shelters. A day-long circumambulation was a time of communal silence. Halfway round, though, at the north end of the island, looking up from our feet, began the exclamations of astonishment: an eagle; some seals; the psilocybe mushrooms growing in the dung pats left by the small, wild Eriskay ponies. We walked the paths Vikings would have made through furze and bracken. Our eyes led by our feet, there was no stumbling. Silence. The cries of shearwater and curlew. I carry those silent sounds with me today. It was here I scattered my mother's ashes, here I made *kora* for a lost love, here I celebrated the drawing near of new love, walking on.

Another monastery: Eihei-ji in Fukui Prefecture in Japan, founded by the philosopher Dogen who established sitting meditation in Japan after his visit to China in the 13th century. I had been following the long-gone trail of the poet Matsuo Bashō who passed this way in 1689. Along my route, also Bashō's, I had been greeted by an old friend: shepherd's purse, that small and low-growing white-flowered plant with heart-shaped seed heads as small as the purse of a poor person. No coins ever change hands for these wee tokens of imperishability. Two new friends (for minutes each) had granted me gifts. The first was a man, walking at low water mark (I was at high water mark) near Kanazawa. We both walked slowly northwards, aware of each other, curious. When we came together, he gave me a single stone, one of a few he had collected, though language difficulties stopped his explanation. The only stone I carried on that walk. I enjoyed his wayfaring, at home here, his dwelling among the stones thrown by the sea, dice of immanence, shared, walking. Like me, he blew his nose into the sea water one nostril at a time. The body ever with us. At the top of a steep hill the orange seller, no-one around for miles – I had encountered only one man, a potter, on my walk the other side of Kanazawa – refused my few coins for one of his fruits; placed two oranges and some strawberries into my hands, with no words. Humbled, I passed along the hillside where a raccoon ambled across my path as I sucked an orange, refreshed: my left foot now a sea stone, surfing, surfing, my right foot a sandal of shepherd's purse. At long last near Eihei-ji, wandering the byway, I could not find the monastery, nor understand the directions asked from an old woman selling pestles with stone mortars. Wordlessly, she took my hand as one does a child and led me for half an hour to the monastery gates, bowed and left. My herbs are ground in one of her mortars now. Her kindness balm. How stories create our paths. That sea stone gatherer reminded me of an anecdote in Nyogen Senzaki's collection of anecdotes from the 13th century *Sasekishu* ("Sand and Pebbles") retold by Paul Reps: a monk is reproved for using paper to blow his nose: so wasteful of resources. Eihei-ji is the monastery, of Dogen's mind puzzle: that the bluegreen hills are constantly walking and that in order to live this, not to understand, we must first know our own walking. Which is always someone else's walking as well.

It was halfway through this walk that I sat down on a boulder by the sea for my lunch. A single peanut butter sandwich was all that was to be had in a little wayside store. It was torn from my hand by a small and fast-flying kite, stooping on prey like any other raptor, leaving only a bloodied thumb and palm. The walking of a bird. So we bring our own bodies and awareness and memory to bear; that memory which is faulty: was it that walk or another where the kite tore my hand?

On a two-month walk through south western US deserts, visiting atomic and nuclear weapons test sites, another stone, or rather atomic-bomb-fused desert sand, was my pocket touch piece: Trinitite, named after the site of the first weapon test site at Trinity New Mexico. Here J. Robert Oppenheimer, the conductor of atomic warfare scientists, told another story, from the *Bhagavad Gita*: "Now I am become Death, destroyer of Worlds." In his walk Oppenheimer has become multi-armed Vishnu. Trinity itself, in the Jornada del Muerto desert (which might be translated as "the day-walk of the dead") is named after John Donne's Holy Sonnet XIV: "Batter my heart, three-person'd God . . .". Time in loops, feet in circles, minds in confusion, our gods ever with us. I came eventually to Death Valley, 80 metres below sea level, passing down, then up, on day walks of dissolution.

Walking is repetitive. Sometimes we do forget our own walking but we come to remember it through precisely that repetition. Upwards of thirty years I've walked round here: Cumbrae, Faslane, Carbeth, Glendaruel, a few square miles of woodland, glen and mountain. I step into the names and languages of each place. I note the other inhabitants of my territory, the shepherd's purse, the eagles, mud and the sandy strands. And the stories and the strange occurrences of white harts, of mountains walking alongside me: Dumgoyne, Dumgoyach, Beinn Bhuide, Auchengaich, Maol an Fheidh, and the razor-fenced nuclear capability of Faslane below Glen Fruin, scene of ancient slaughter; where I walk to protest. *Fas lann*, meaning an enclosure of wasteland, with its ruined 13th-century chapel dedicated to St Michael the Archangel who will "arise at the end time".

I walk my island daily, through inhibiting estate land then along the long strand to where headland becomes rocks slick with weed, first one way, left foot lower on the camber, then back, right foot lower, and know through my feet I am the true inheritor of this land; me and those like me and before me, who possess land, who, through virtue of walking it, with purpose, dwell here. The gift of a book as a young child had me believe in tracking done on foot, by indigenous north Americans who walked with their toes in line with their heels. White folk, the book informed me, walked with toes pointed out, splay footed. A story I carry on my walks, especially those hirples of two years' standing after my broken Achilles tendon, my walking vulnerability exposed, spirit willing, but flesh weakened.

The philosophy of walks eludes me. There are only individual walks in places made unique each day with each new cloud pattern, each new flowering of season, each washing tide shifting stones, but also literal flowerings, coltsfoot, wood sorrel, broom, and from the dark mycelium underfoot, chanterelles: for me there is just the walking, the process.

To engage with a story, our own stories, is to step into the world as it is. There is no dichotomy between where we walk and how and on what we walk. No culture, no nature. From this place springs all cultures, all of our natures. Bashō, at the start of his 1689 walk, heard the singing voices of farmers planting rice: "culture's beginning / from the heart of the country / rice-planting songs". Rice planting is a walk through paddies, a step at a time, while placing seedlings in the wet earth. What Bashō heard was humans as part of nature, which is always local, creating a specific of culture. The word translated here as culture is *fūryū*, literally "flowing wind", which in Japanese can mean both culture and nature. Little differentiation. Culture in English may mean the ideas and customs of a society as well as to nurture cells for growth. Here we might have the Gaelic *dualchas*, meaning "culture passed across generations", which would include plant and animal knowledge.

So we carry our bodies with us, daily laden with memory, a mental backpack of which the mind-memory is only part: it's all body memory. I once walked across Scotland planting tree seeds as I went. Another time, again across the country, I walked coast to coast for Sense, the charity for deaf-blind and complex communication needs people – 33 miles the first day in rain so unremittingly heavy that towards the end of that day I looked longingly at the cemetery toward the end of the route: how sweet to lie down; but those of us who walk, who cannot but walk, already have a home.

I'm writing this in order to find out what walking is; the names of plants, rocks, birds in the local tongues. I walked round the small island of Cumbrae in a day and wrote a poem: "the island in September", which a friend translated into old Scots. My knowledge of the island was broadened by language strata. Does it matter which island if it is a circumambulation – *kora* – an embodiment of the littoral, a literal rounding of headlands: all *muthos* become text of my re-marking of territory as in my identity dissolving loss of lover, loss of mother, gaining of blue mountain walking, gaining of love itself: a mild and irreverent humility born of the knowledge and cherishing of evanescence. As ever then, how to know the island is knowing the stories, the Gaelic of here; but also my own hard-won physical knowledge of agriculture, of horticulture's old ways, old footpaths of being.

Each walk is a new story, or a new chapter in a long story; we may limit the walking to one place or include many; these are variations on a theme, these are the narratives we live by, that we jump into, feet first.

A pilgrimage is a walk with a spiritual purpose. *Kinhin* is a walk with no purpose. A shepherd walks for protective purposes. A boundary walk is a walk with proprietorial purposes. None of these is mutually exclusive.

And the miles I racked up on the farm walking the cows home to the milking parlour, observing the cut-willow fence-stakes root, leaf and grow over the seasons. As a poet it is not purposeful that each instance becomes a poem, if poetry comes from reverie, of bovine rumination; a meditation where the mind is as empty as the habituated walking body is alert.

Walking is dwelling: in common with every species, every living being, we are hefted here on this luminous sphere, since there can be no dwelling without a dwelling place. It is our only dwelling we are walking on.

"And when you change the landscape" (not land skip, midden of plastic) "is it with bare hands or with gloves?" asked Pablo Neruda. Is it with cars or our feet? With our feet we activate the verbs of the earth.

Index

Figures are indicated by *italic* text; endnotes are indicated by "n" after the page number e.g., 164n5 refers to endnote number 5 on page 164.